P9-CKS-768

Current
CONTROVERSIES

Returning Soldiers and PTSD

Other Books in the Current Controversies Series

The Border Wall with Mexico
Drones, Surveillance, and Targeted Killings
Fracking
Genetic Engineering
Homelessness and Street Crime
LGBTQ Rights
Political Correctness
The Political Elite and Special Interests
Privacy and Security in the Digital Age

Current
CONTROVERSIES

Returning Soldiers and PTSD

Barbara Krasner, Book Editor

GREENHAVEN
PUBLISHING

Published in 2018 by Greenhaven Publishing, LLC
353 3rd Avenue, Suite 255, New York, NY 10010

Cover image: John Gomez/Shutterstock.com

Library of Congress Cataloging-in-Publication Data

Names: Krasner, Barbara, editor.
Title: Returning soldiers and PTSD / Barbara Krasner, book editor.
Other titles: Returning soldiers and post-traumatic stress disorder
Description: New York : Greenhaven Publishing, 2018. | Series: Current
  controversies | Audience: Grade 9 to 12. | Includes bibliographical
  references and index.
Identifiers: LCCN 2017013599| ISBN 9781534500914 (library bound) | ISBN
  9781534500877 (pbk.)
Subjects: LCSH: Post-traumatic stress disorder--Juvenile literature. |
  Soldiers--Mental health--Juvenile literature.
Classification: LCC RC552.P67 R4845 2017 | DDC 616.85/21--dc23
LC record available at https://lccn.loc.gov/2017013599

Manufactured in the United States of America

Website: http://greenhavenpublishing.com

Contents

Foreword   **11**

Introduction   **14**

Chapter 1: Is PTSD Among Returning Soldiers Widespread?

Overview: Post-Traumatic Stress Disorder Affects   **19**
Soldiers Returning Home

Celia Simon

War veteran anecdotes and scientific study results provide a broad context for combat-induced post-traumatic stress disorder (PTSD) and its causes.

Yes: PTSD Is Very Common

PTSD Threatens Lives and Challenges Public Health   **40**

Mohammad S. Jalali

It is estimated that eight million people in the United States suffer from PTSD. Those who served in Iraq and Afghanistan are reportedly at greater risk of this disease, which if left untreated can lead to drug and alcohol addiction and suicide.

Mental Health Professionals Take Veterans' PTSD   **44**
Seriously

Elizabeth Roberts-Pedersen

Inclusion of PTSD in the third edition of the *Diagnostic and Statistical Manual of Mental Disorders* (*DSM-III*) helped to legitimize the illness as more than just shell-shock and raise awareness of the need for medical treatment of the disease.

No: PTSD Is Over-Diagnosed

PTSD Has Taken Over America   **48**

Alice Karekezi

A professor of psychology in the United Kingdom warns that PTSD as a diagnosis has become too prevalent and is frequently used to address normal, everyday experiences instead of trauma-induced mental illness.

PTSD Claims Inspire Skepticism Among Active   **56**
Military Members

Scott Faith
An army veteran explains how, from his perspective, many returning
soldiers wear PTSD as a badge of honor. To that end, he claims,
if everyone has PTSD then it's likely no one has it—and these
unnecessary claims clog the Veterans Affairs system.

Chapter 2: Can a PTSD Diagnosis Be Exploited?

Overview: Exposure to Combat and Physical Assault   **61**
Leads to PTSD

Mayo Clinic Staff
People exposed to horrific events, such as those that occur in
wartime, may suffer from PTSD, affecting their everyday lives,
relationships, and jobs. But they may also be suffering from other
illnesses entirely.

Yes: Diagnosing PTSD Is Fraught with Complications

PTSD Needs Better and Consistent Diagnosis   **69**

Peter Barglow
Despite its acceptance as a condition by the U.S. Department of
Veterans Affairs, PTSD diagnoses vary widely, and the condition is
not clearly distinguishable from other major psychiatric disorders.

There's No Wrong Way to Respond to Post-Traumatic   **82**
Stress

National Depressive and Manic-Depressive Association
A person's response to traumatic events is individualized and
there is no right or wrong way to react. All responses need to be
acknowledged, valued, and afforded the proper medical treatment.

Returning Soldiers View PTSD Diagnoses as   **91**
Self-Fulfilling Doom

David Dobbs
Today's medical professionals often cannot separate those with PTSD
from those with depression, anxiety, and reintegration issues. Slapped
with the PTSD label, patients who may not really have the condition
see little hope for their future and grow worse over time.

No: Diagnosing PTSD in Soldiers Is Standard Operating Procedure

Extensive Research Results in New, Effective Diagnosis   **102**
Guidelines

> *Tori DeAngelis*
> Studies of the recent wars in Afghanistan and Iraq have given
> researchers new evidence pertaining to the causes of stress and
> trauma. This knowledge has resulted in more effective processes for
> diagnosis and treatment of PTSD.

Iraq and Afghan War Vets Reap the Benefits of   **109**
Technological Advances

> *Wayne Kinney*
> Advances in medicine and technology have enabled soldiers
> returning from conflicts in Iraq and Afghanistan to get easily
> diagnosed and treated for PTSD—a boon that was unavailable to
> veterans of previous wars.

Be Aware of the New Standard for PTSD Diagnosis   **115**

> *Matthew J. Friedman*
> PTSD is not some haphazard collection of symptoms named on a
> whim. Based on new evidence, the 2013 revision of the *Diagnostic
> and Statistical Manual of Mental Disorders* (*DSM-5*) has improved
> diagnosis of PTSD and clinical practice.

Chapter 3: Is PTSD a Valid Mental Health Disorder?

Overview: Literature, History, and the DSM All   **129**
Document PTSD

> *Marc-Antoine Crocq and Louis Crocq*
> Over time and throughout history, the meaning and diagnosis of
> PTSD has evolved—starting with references in the Bible and ancient
> epics, all the way to its inclusion in the *DSM-IV*, where the condition
> is made clearly distinct from acute stress disorder.

Yes: PTSD Is a Real Mental Illness

In Some Cultures, PTSD Is Understood as a Part of War   **146**

> *Sebastian Junger*
> In some Native American and Israeli communities, returning soldiers
> with PTSD automatically get the support they need because war and

its fallout are subject to deeper cultural exploration and considered a huge part of their history.

Many Different Factors Can Cause PTSD   **166**

Sally Satel

War veterans are now able to file claims with the Department of Veterans Affairs for PTSD benefits for events they did not actually experience, thus broadening the definition of what constitutes post-traumatic stress.

Identifying Psychological Injury Helps Diagnosis and   **172**
Treatment

David Forbes

The Australian Defense Force has gained expertise in identifying psychological injuries and posits that the frequency and severity of a soldier's exposure to traumatic events puts that individual at risk for PTSD.

No: PTSD Is a Misdiagnosis and a Misnomer

PTSD Is Not a Mental Illness   **176**

Denise Williams

Although the best treatment for PTSD is mental health counseling, it is not itself a mental illness. Its symptoms are frequently misinterpreted and are actually the result of the various drugs used for treatment.

Pre-Wartime Experiences Contribute to PTSD   **179**

Morena Lauth-Lebens and Gerhard W. Lauth

Emotional and environmental conditions prior to a soldier's wartime experiences are what make them vulnerable to PTSD. Traumatic events experienced in a warzone are not, by themselves, sufficient to cause post-traumatic stress.

PTSD Is Really Just a Political Ploy   **196**

John Grant

Civilian research provides substantial evidence that PTSD is a result of traumatic brain injury (TBI) and not a psychological condition born of war. Politicians use the classification of it as a mental illness as a means of furthering their agendas.

Chapter 4: Do Returning Soldiers with PTSD Get the Treatment They Need?

Overview: The VA Faces Challenges with Returning   **209**
Soldiers' Mental Health Claims

> *Leighton Walter Kille*
> Extensive research details the slew of issues that the VA deals with
> in fulfilling veterans' claims for PTSD treatment, including long wait
> times and excessive red tape.

Yes: Returning Soldiers Are Given the Proper Amount of Help

A Carolina Community Provides Resources for   **219**
Treatment

> *Charlotte Bridge Home, Foundation for the Carolinas*
> Organizations like Charlotte Bridge Home connect veterans and their
> families to both national and community resources to help them deal
> with PTSD and reintegration into regular society.

Creative Expression Is Effective in Treating PTSD   **228**

> *Joshua Smyth and Jeremy Nobel*
> Successful treatment of PTSD is difficult and complex, but certain
> behavioral methods have been found to work wonders, including
> nontraditional creative expression through writing, art, music, and
> drama.

Talking It Out Helps Veterans Deal with PTSD   **248**

> *Goodtherapy.org*
> Along with commonly prescribed mood-regulating drugs used
> to treat PTSD, talk therapy can also be effective. However, many
> veterans refuse treatment for their mental health issues and crucial
> counseling services go unused.

No: Returning Soldiers With PTSD Are Left in the Lurch

PTSD Treatment Is Barely Adequate   **257**

> *Terri Tanielian*
> About half of returning soldiers with PTSD actively seek treatment
> for their illness. Those who do seek help often encounter a system
> ill-equipped to handle their needs because of fundamental gaps in a
> large-scale understanding of PTSD and treatment methods.

VA Health Program Falls Short in Providing Care   **267**

Shefali Luthra

Only about one in three veterans diagnosed with PTSD receive appropriate follow-up care via Veterans Affairs after their initial treatment. Soldiers may not return because of dissatisfaction with service, lack of access to medical professionals, and the stigma of mental illness.

Suicide Is a Tragic Outcome of Inadequate PTSD Care   **271**

Robert Wilbur and James L. Knoll, IV

Without easy access to experienced mental health professionals and treatment with drugs and/or psychotherapy, veterans of multiple deployments feel failed by the VA and isolated from their family and peers, and often turn to suicide to ease their pain.

Organizations to Contact   **278**

Bibliography   **283**

Index   **287**

Foreword

Controversy is a word that has an undeniably unpleasant connotation. It carries a definite negative charge. Controversy can spoil family gatherings, spread a chill around classroom and campus discussion, inflame public discourse, open raw civic wounds, and lead to the ouster of public officials. We often feel that controversy is almost akin to bad manners, a rude and shocking eruption of that which must not be spoken or thought of in polite, tightly guarded society. To avoid controversy, to quell controversy, is often seen as a public good, a victory for etiquette, perhaps even a moral or ethical imperative.

Yet the studious, deliberate avoidance of controversy is also a whitewashing, a denial, a death threat to democracy. It is a false sterilizing and sanitizing and superficial ordering of the messy, ragged, chaotic, at times ugly processes by which a healthy democracy identifies and confronts challenges, engages in passionate debate about appropriate approaches and solutions, and arrives at something like a consensus and a broadly accepted and supported way forward. Controversy is the megaphone, the speaker's corner, the public square through which the citizenry finds and uses its voice. Controversy is the life's blood of our democracy and absolutely essential to the vibrant health of our society.

Our present age is certainly no stranger to controversy. We are consumed by fierce debates about technology, privacy, political correctness, poverty, violence, crime and policing, guns, immigration, civil and human rights, terrorism, militarism, environmental protection, and gender and racial equality. Loudly competing voices are raised every day, shouting opposing opinions, putting forth competing agendas, and summoning starkly different visions of a utopian or dystopian future. Often these voices attempt to shout the others down; there is precious little listening and considering among the cacophonous din. Yet listening and considering, too, are essential to the health of a democracy. If controversy is democracy's lusty lifeblood, respectful listening and careful thought are its higher faculties, its brain, its conscience.

Current Controversies does not shy away from or attempt to hush the loudly competing voices. It seeks to provide readers with as wide and representative as possible a range of articulate voices on any given controversy of the day, separates each one out to allow it to be heard clearly and fairly, and encourages careful listening to each of these well-crafted, thoughtfully expressed opinions, supplied by some of today's leading academics, thinkers, analysts, politicians, policy makers, economists, activists, change agents, and advocates. Only after listening to a wide range of opinions on an issue, evaluating the strengths and weaknesses of each argument, assessing how well the facts and available evidence mesh with the stated opinions and conclusions, and thoughtfully and critically examining one's own beliefs and conscience can the reader begin to arrive at his or her own conclusions and articulate his or her own stance on the spotlighted controversy.

This process is facilitated and supported in each Current Controversies volume by an introduction and chapter overviews that provide readers with the essential context they need to begin engaging with the spotlighted controversies, with the debates surrounding them, and with their own perhaps shifting or nascent opinions on them. Chapters are organized around several key questions that are answered with diverse opinions representing all points on the political spectrum. In its content, organization, and methodology, readers are encouraged to determine the authors' point of view and purpose, interrogate and analyze the various arguments and their rhetoric and structure, evaluate the arguments' strengths and weaknesses, test their claims against available facts and evidence, judge the validity of the reasoning, and bring into clearer, sharper focus the reader's own beliefs and conclusions and how they may differ from or align with those in the collection or those of classmates.

Research has shown that reading comprehension skills improve dramatically when students are provided with compelling, intriguing, and relevant "discussable" texts. The subject matter of these collections could not be more compelling, intriguing, or urgently relevant to today's students and the world they are poised to inherit. The anthologized articles also provide the basis for stimulating, lively, and passionate classroom debates. Students who are compelled to anticipate objections to their own argument and identify the flaws in those of an opponent read more carefully, think more critically, and steep themselves in relevant context, facts, and information more thoroughly. In short, using discussable text of the kind provided by every single volume in the Current Controversies series encourages close reading, facilitates reading comprehension, fosters research, strengthens critical thinking, and greatly enlivens and energizes classroom discussion and participation. The entire learning process is deepened, extended, and strengthened.

If we are to foster a knowledgeable, responsible, active, and engaged citizenry, we must provide readers with the intellectual, interpretive, and critical-thinking tools and experience necessary to make sense of the world around them and of the all-important debates and arguments that inform it. We must encourage them not to run away from or attempt to quell controversy but to embrace it in a responsible, conscientious, and thoughtful way, to sharpen and strengthen their own informed opinions by listening to and critically analyzing those of others. This series encourages respectful engagement with and analysis of current controversies and competing opinions and fosters a resulting increase in the strength and rigor of one's own opinions and stances. As such, it helps readers assume their rightful place in the public square and provides them with the skills necessary to uphold their awesome responsibility—guaranteeing the continued and future health of a vital, vibrant, and free democracy.

Introduction

> *"In World War One, they called it*
> *shell shock. Second time around, they*
> *called it battle fatigue. After 'Nam, it*
> *was post-traumatic stress disorder."*
>
> —*Jan Karon, Home*
> *to Holly Springs*

According to the Mayo Clinic, post-traumatic stress disorder (PTSD) is a mental health illness caused by experiencing or witnessing a traumatic event. Among soldiers, such an event could include watching a buddy get blown up, having to kill an enemy combatant or seeing civilians caught in the crossfire. However, survival skills that protect the soldier in combat often do not work when that soldier comes home. Symptoms can flare up within months or years later. The condition can lead to difficulties reintegrating into civilian life. It can also hamper a returning soldier's relationships and potentially threaten their lives, creating suicidal thoughts. Flashbacks of the traumatic event and nightmares may occur on a consistent basis.

Since before the American Civil War, soldiers have returned home with severe disorders brought about by combat. During World War I, this was called shell shock. In 1952, the American Psychiatric Association introduced a guide to disorders, *Diagnostic and Statistical Manual of Mental Disorders* (*DSM*). Nearly 30 years later, based on research involving returning veterans from the Vietnam War and others, the third edition of this guide, DSM-III, included PTSD for the first time. This inclusion verified the link between wartime trauma and civilian life after military service.

Because symptoms of PTSD may appear decades after exposure, researchers have found it necessary to interview veterans well after they complete military service, as accurate counts may not happen directly after a war. For example, while statistics vary, figures for the Vietnam War period show that 25 percent of returning veterans were suffering from PTSD. Figures for Afghanistan and Iraq range from 20 to 75 percent. Researchers must also take into account how pre-existing conditions—such as exposure to traumatic events as children or the way a person's brain releases hormones to deal with stress—and multiple deployments impact the risk of PTSD.

Now, the umbrella classification of PTSD encompasses many of the mental health problems returning veterans face. It can be diagnosed and treated by qualified medical professionals. Medical and other service professionals, such as military clergymen, require special training to help identify, diagnose, and counsel returning soldiers with PTSD.

The prevalence of PTSD in returning soldiers raises many issues that are both cause for concern and cause for debate. One debate centers around whether PTSD among veterans is a serious problem or whether it is diagnosed too frequently or cavalierly. Studies have shown that returning soldiers with PTSD are more likely to become addicted to drugs and alcohol, or to become depressed or suicidal. According to the PTSD Foundation of America, more veterans died as a result of PTSD-related suicide than they did in combat in 2008.

On the other hand, some experts insist PTSD has become a "buzz word" for psychological problems among veterans, especially those who fought in Afghanistan and Iraq. Misdiagnosis and over-diagnosis of PTSD have led to the perception that PTSD is rampant when it's really quite rare, according to some experts.

Diagnosis is indeed a controversial subject. Although the most well-known and respected guide to disorders, *Diagnostic and Statistical Manual of Mental Disorders,* now in its fifth edition (DSM-V) lays out clear criteria for PTSD and helps medical professionals appropriately identify and treat this serious disorder, accurate diagnosis is complicated. PTSD symptoms can be confused with those of acute stress. Returning vets may also show signs of depression, suicidal thoughts, anger, substance abuse, concussions (brought on by traumatic brain injury or TBI), and abusive behavior; these are not necessarily linked to PTSD. Some critics view PTSD diagnosis as a home-grown disorder created by politics and society. Others believe PTSD is a physical problem related to TBI and not a mental illness at all.

Soldiers' experiences in Iraq and Afghanistan have allowed researchers to delve more deeply into PTSD, its root causes, and effects. This research, especially a RAND Corporation study commissioned by the U.S. Department of Veterans Affairs (VA), helps medical professionals determine effective treatments. For some patients, creative expression has been helpful. For others, group therapy or a therapeutic approach that involves talking it out is effective. Yet for many, mood-altering drugs prove to be the most helpful, although there are potentially harmful side effects. But the research also shows where clinical care for the returning soldier who thinks he or she may have PTSD often falls short of expectations and need.

Resources for working with returning soldiers are limited, and while specialists are available to treat returning soldiers, treatment only succeeds if the veterans return after an initial consultation. Many soldiers resist the label of PTSD because it signals they are mentally ill. Furthermore, many find that successive treatments are not with a physician or psychiatrist but with a physician's assistant. The VA has also been criticized for its long bureaucratic process and its long wait times for processing claims.

The Veterans Affairs PTSD Center offers returning veterans and families the support they need for treating PTSD, including counseling, healthcare services, and support groups. Resources also exist at the state level, and in some cases, local communities play a role in helping veterans re-enter society and deal with PTSD.

Some studies show that returning soldiers may not seek a medical diagnosis but are comfortable telling a researcher they suffer from PTSD. Complaints among vets include that therapists "just don't get it," because they don't understand the context of the historical, social, and cultural situations of the trauma. However, without a medical diagnosis, these soldiers may not get access to necessary treatments; a few months of rest and counseling won't cut it.

Medical professionals, veterans and their loved ones, researchers, and journalists debate the complex facets of post-traumatic stress syndrome in *Current Controversies: Returning Soldiers with PTSD*, shedding light on medical, psychological, social, and political issues.

CHAPTER 1

Is PTSD Among Returning Soldiers Widespread?

Overview: Post-Traumatic Stress Disorder Affects Soldiers Returning Home

Celia Simon

Celia Simon writes and edits articles about psychology, education, and media. She is the former contributing editor to Psychotherapy Networker *magazine. Her writing has appeared in leading newspapers and magazines. She has an advanced degree in journalism and teaches writing at American University's School of Communication in Washington, DC.*

Sometimes it's a loud bang, like a car's backfire. Sometimes it's the sound of children screaming or crying. Sometimes it's the benign drone of a classroom lecture, or a stranger's ill-informed comments about the war in Iraq, or the drive over a bridge in the dark of night. All are triggers that send Jesus Bocanegra's mind straight back to the hot, dusty streets of Tikrit, where he and his unit of cavalry scouts tore down Iraqi flags and monuments and raided homes searching for weapons caches, civilian soldiers, and Saddam Hussein himself.

It was a tour of duty that Bocanegra, now 24, unemployed and suffering a 100-percent disability from post-traumatic stress disorder, signed on for willingly, but wishes he hadn't. When he joined the Army in 2000, it was a way out of his small Mexican border town of McAllen, Texas, he says, and a future of flipping burgers. After a year in Ft. Hood and another in Korea, Bocanegra liked military life well enough to reenlist. But his plan "backfired," he notes. Within a month, he was shipped out to Iraq.

As a scout, Bocanegra says, you're trained to be the eyes and ears of the mission commander--"You look for the enemy, spot them, and report back." But in Iraq, his job was different. "My initial thought was that we'd be fighting people in uniform." What

"Bringing The War Home: The Challenge of Helping Iraq War Vets," Cecilia Capuzzi Simon, PESI, Inc.Septembet 7, 2014. Reprinted by permission.

he found instead was a lack of mission, little planning, and an elusive, often invisible, enemy. All of which left him questioning the war's meaning, sowed the seeds of self-doubt, and wore him down emotionally.

"It was patrol, patrol, patrol," he observes. "Break down murals. Look for WMDs. Pull people over and search their cars. When we went on raids, we'd knock doors down, pull the family out of their homes, scare the living shit out of them, and then find out we had the wrong house."

What Bocanegra witnessed in Iraq, he says, was "the worst that a human can see." Murdered women and children, dismembered and incinerated bodies. Utter fear. Debilitating guilt.

"I don't want to go into detail," Bocanegra says of an incident that to this day makes him avoid children. But when he discovered crates of enemy ammunition being moved into a house along the Tigris River, he called for an Apache helicopter strike. He discovered there were children inside only after the gunfire stopped and he heard their screams. "That," he says, "is my nightmare. My flashback. It was nothing we did intentionally."

One night, driving patrol in the city, an improvised explosive device (IED) detonated on the side of the road, rocking, but not damaging, his truck. For Bocanegra, it was "the last straw," he says. "You feel the concussion. Your heart skips. You don't know what to do. I grabbed my arms, legs, checked my body. I kept on driving." But emotionally, he shut down.

"There was no time for emotion," he says. "I told myself, 'I'll deal with it when I get home. I just want to make it out alive.'"

A Very Special War

All wars are hell. Iraq, however, is a unique brand of horror--a confluence of environmental, political, and cultural factors that make it "the perfect festering pot for psychological damage," says former Iraq sniper and Veterans for America outreach coordinator Garett Reppenhagen, who finished a yearlong tour in Iraq in May 2005.

Some 17 percent of Iraq soldiers suffer from major depression, generalized anxiety, or post-traumatic stress disorder (PTSD), according to a 2004 Department of Defense (DOD) study published in the New England Journal of Medicine and conducted three to four months after the troops' return from combat. But it's PTSD that's emerging as this war's signature disability. In this study, its prevalence ranged from 10 percent to 20 percent, depending on the number of firefights a soldier was involved in. And while its toll isn't as visible as that of a missing leg or arm, or multiple amputations--the injuries we've come to most associate with the guerilla warfare of Iraq--it's the most pervasive and, perhaps, pernicious. It's "the number one issue facing soldiers of Iraq and Afghanistan," says Paul Rieckhoff, the founder of advocacy group Iraq and Afghanistan Veterans of America.

There are signs that the incidence of mental health problems among the troops may be even larger than the 2004 study suggests. Conducted early in the war and soon after those surveyed concluded six- to eight-month deployments, that study doesn't take into account that PTSD, characterized by flashbacks, nightmares, intrusive thoughts, anxiety, and social withdrawal, often manifests months or years after the trauma. Furthermore, much has changed in the two years since the research. Now many of the troops are on second and third tours of duty, and the war itself has dragged on much longer than expected, while its objectives are becoming increasingly muddy and support for the war is rapidly waning.

A newer DOD study offers more detailed information on the scope of the mental health difficulties encountered by veterans, and is now being cited more frequently than the earlier one. Published in March 2006 in the Journal of the American Medical Association, it reports that 35 percent of Iraq war veterans sought treatment for mental health issues within a year of coming home--a startling percentage given the military's well-known resistance to therapy, and these were only the soldiers who admitted needing help. Some 12 percent of those who sought help received a psychiatric diagnosis. Veterans who served in Iraq, where there's more combat, were twice as likely to seek help as those returning from Afghanistan, and 19 percent of the Iraq veterans met criteria for a "mental health concern." The DOD now estimates that between 15 percent and 29 percent of veterans from the wars in Iraq and Afghanistan will suffer from PTSD.

Those numbers echo what the Veterans Administration is reporting in its caseload, which is six times higher than anticipated and has caught it off guard. With 1.3 million troops deployed so far, more than 400,000 could need mental health treatment by 2008, if the trend continues. There has been no large-scale study on the war's emotional toll on Iraqis, but pieces of data are beginning to paint a grim picture. For example, children are suffering depression and behavioral problems at a rate three times greater than that before the war, according to a BBC report.

A "tsunami" of mental health problems resulting from the war in Iraq is "headed our way," concludes Charles Figley, director of the Traumatology Institute at Florida State University, and a Vietnam veteran. Neither the government, nor the mental health community, nor society, he adds, is prepared to handle it. He testified as much before Congress. "No one disagreed," he says of his testimony before the country's lawmakers. "But they shrugged their shoulders." The subject of Iraq and troop mental health is so politically polarizing, he says, that no one wants to speak out for fear of "giving the impression that the war is bad."

Unfortunately, avoiding the subject won't change the rightness or wrongness of the war, nor will it make PTSD go away. As Steve Robinson, director of government relations for Veterans for America says, post-traumatic stress disorder is "the elephant in the room. It's leaning on everybody. You can pretend it isn't there, but it's coming home."

Dirt, Fear, and Misery: Daily Life Outside the "Green Zone"

Many questions dog our engagement in Iraq--the biggest and deepest surrounding the purpose of the conflict and what America stands to gain, or lose, from it. But there are also the microcosmic questions, those that relate to individual human sacrifice and suffering--the inevitable cost of any war--and are the more painful to consider. More than 2,800 American troops have died in the wars in Iraq and Afghanistan as of the end of 2006. In addition, a huge number of Iraqis have lost their lives. A controversial study published in Lancet by researchers at Johns Hopkins University, who compared mortality rates in 47 different areas of the country, puts that figure at 655,000. Another group, The Iraq Body Count, which compiles civilian deaths based on credible media reports, says up to 53,000 have died as a result of the war.

But body counts don't quantify the war's emotional toll. The media has reported in detail the guerilla tactics that characterize combat in Iraq: roadside IEDs, suicide bombers, sniper fire, an undistinguishable insurgency. There's no front line, no safe zone. Nearly 90 percent of troops are involved in some kind of firefight. Many have seen buddies blown to pieces, and more than half of the soldiers there have handled human remains. All of this increases the risk for PTSD. As one veteran put it: "Dealing with exploded vehicles and body parts and roadways blanketed with shrapnel all day, every day, is incomprehensible." Less well known is the harsh relentlessness of daily life in this kind of war zone, which slowly chips away at one's sense of safety, emotional resiliency and character. Soldiers live in combat 24/7. Some call it a "360-degree war."

"You're in a war where you are isolated at base. There's no rear," says Reppenhagen, who was stationed in Baquba, about 35 miles northeast of Baghdad, and was part of a sniper team whose main mission was to kill Abu Masab Al-Zarqawi, known to be hiding out in the nearby town of Hibhib. (He was killed there about a year after Reppenhagen's tour ended). "You can't put your rifle down to go off base and get a drink at the local bar like you could in Saigon. You're trapped, isolated. You can't leave your hooch without your helmet on, because there are falling mortars and RPGs [rocket propelled grenades] coming over the wire all the time.

There's no rest or relaxation for these soldiers--they're sleeping, eating, living in war. When they roll out of the wire, the common form of weapons the insurgents use is indirect--roadside bombs, car bombs, suicide bombs, RPGs, mortar attack. They have an ability to damage you without an enemy to retaliate against, and they come out of nowhere. No matter how skilled you are, no matter how alert you are as a soldier, it's indiscriminate. It doesn't matter how good you are at low-crawling or moving, shooting or communicating: if your number's up, your number's up."

Add to such combat strain a series of lesser but continuous assaults to one's personal dignity--what Colonel Kathy Platoni calls "the hardship of living in a place like Iraq." A clinical psychologist in civilian life in Beavercreek, Ohio, Platoni has been in the Army for 27 years, 23 as a Reservist. She spent the last year in Iraq as part of a combat stress team--military mental health professionals who work in the battlefields. During her time in Iraq, Platoni made eight stops in various combat theaters--"godawful places," she calls them in an interview. The last was at a base in Ramadi, an insurgent stronghold she described in an article in the Columbus Federal Register as "what the devil envisioned when he created hell." With an average temperature of 126 degrees ("130 in the steaming latrines") the summer she helicoptered in, even her glasses were affected by the "blistering heat and blowing grit," she wrote. Lack of privacy, bad food, difficulty sleeping because of the heat and noise, limited ability to shower ("You just make up your mind that no one smells better than you do, and live with it"), and often limited access to latrines ("You use a bag and carry it to the poo-burning pile") are all typical of a soldier's daily life in Iraq, says Platoni--all of it lived with "the constant threat of your own demise, as well as those that you slept with or ate with the day before."

In addition, says Figley, soldiers suffer persistent physical discomfort. They're often dehydrated, but drenched in sweat. Because of the nature of the fighting, they're usually carrying their own weight in protective clothing and gear. And then there's the Sinai sand: fine as talcum powder, it floats in the air, soldiers breathe it all day long, and it settles onto everything--clothing, skin, hair, food, equipment. "You feel like a wreck," says Figley.

The day-to-day monotony of base life can also be wearing. With no clear rules of engagement, soldiers spend time waiting on orders and thinking about home. If Vietnam was the first "television war," Iraq is the first "Internet war." In many areas of Iraq, the availability of computers makes e-mailing and blogging commonplace; cell phone service gives many soldiers a regular connection to friends and family--and dramas they can do little about from the Middle East. It seems counterintuitive, but trouble on the home front is one of the leading stressors at base camp, says Platoni. Financial worries, marital problems, kid troubles: "If you're worried about family issues all of the time," she says, "it's hard to concentrate. Too much of that information can be bone crushing." For soldiers on second and third tours of duty--half of whom are Reservists or National Guard who leave jobs or businesses for wartime service--repeated and unpredictable separations from home are often devastating to family and career.

The availability of news sites and a 24-hour news cycle can add to a sense of agitation and helplessness, keeping soldiers who are in the thick of war briefed on its developments. Living with a foot in both the wartime and civilian worlds, says Figley, "is a surreal experience for these men and women."

Coming Home

Just as surreal for many is coming home. Specialist Abbie Picket was 20 years old when she was deployed to Baquba. In the field, she'd been prescribed Ambien and antidepressants after a mortar attack hit her chow hall one night and she attended to the bleeding and injured in the chaos and the dark, an experience that left her panicked, depressed, and "spazzing out." "It's stuff you can't talk about in the civilian world," says Pickett, who wasn't diagnosed with PTSD until three months after her return stateside. "I came back and my friends wanted to talk about American Idol. I had no idea what that was."

She remembers seeing Fahrenheit 911 and crying throughout the movie. "It was way too much, too soon," she says. But the reaction she got from the friend who accompanied her was the coarsely flippant question: "Why would you ever go over there with that attitude?"

As Rieckhoff puts it, "You're in Baghdad one day, Brooklyn the next." Though not suffering from PTSD, he says even he had problems reentering a society he called detached from the war and "almost entirely deaf to the issues" because only one percent of the population is directly touched by service, and life for most Americans has gone on normally. "It's like a reality TV show that people think they can turn off," he says. "I was out with my girlfriend last night, everyone was hanging out and enjoying themselves, and I thought, 'Okay, but don't you realize people are being blown up in Ramadi right now?' You feel like you don't fit in."

That outsider status may be showing up in the employment numbers for the youngest veterans--15 percent can't find work, about three times the national average, according to the Bureau of Labor Statistics. Some veterans expressed concern that employers are biased against them; 11 percent wouldn't identify themselves as such.

In a veterans' blog, former army specialist scout Matt Frank starkly sums up what it feels like to come home from Iraq having been psychologically changed by warfare: "For the soldier, war is his drug," he writes. "Life [back home] becomes dull and frustrating. Normal situations make one feel a sense of anxiety, of desperation, as if constantly hoping for a sudden, horrible rage to sweep across and take normal right down to hell, where things are violent and gruesome and stimulating and the adrenaline flows. Where veins bulge and the mind sweats and purpose is abundantly clear. . . . I am alienated from these people who buy me drinks and praise me for service to their country. Who thank me for all those dirty Arab bastards I ghosted in the name of freedom, democracy, basic cable and free trips to the salad bar."

Legacy of Vietnam: What's Wrong with the PTSD Diagnosis?

More than 25 years ago, Vietnam veterans forced the military and mental health communities to pay attention to the psychological costs of war and give a name to the mental injuries afflicting as many as 31 percent of those returning soldiers. "Post traumatic stress disorder" was added to the DSM-III in 1980 after heavy lobbying by veterans' advocates and prominent mental health professionals who made no secret of their anti-war stance. The PTSD diagnosis medicalized the Vietnam veterans' symptoms, providing an opportunity for treatment and a kind of redemption by forcing a cultural and scientific recognition of the mental, physical, and social impact of traumatic stress, especially in warfare.

But today, some of the loudest voices who led the PTSD charge are rethinking the parameters and implications of the diagnosis drafted a quarter-century ago. "We took a lot of angry, dysfunctional vets and got them labeled PTSD," says Bobby Muller, who heads Veterans for America, founded Vietnam Veterans of America, and is the winner of the 1997 Nobel Peace Prize for another of his organizations, the International Campaign to Ban Landmines. "Now, 26 years later, this stuff has become institutionalized, and a medical industry has grown around PTSD. But there was something wrong about what we did back then, and something wrong with what we're doing today."

What's wrong, says Muller, is that nowhere in the diagnosis, which describes the results of traumatic stress stemming from a variety of incidents--rape, car accident, witnessing street-gang violence--are the specific ramifications of wartime trauma acknowledged. Muller, now silver-haired and 60, should know. Paralyzed from the waist down after being shot in battle at the age of 23, he animatedly talks about his near-death Vietnam experiences--in the battlefield and at home--from a wheelchair in his bright office in downtown Washington, alternating between hearty laughter and ongoing anger.

For Muller and others, the most important missing piece in our understanding and treatment of combat PTSD has to do with the meaning attached to the sacrifices we ask soldiers to make. That Vietnam was "the wrong war," as Muller puts it--a futile, failed effort that the American public would just as soon forget, along with those who fought it--contributed mightily to the mental problems those vets developed, and continue to have, he says. Finding social vindication and an overriding sense of purpose for wartime trauma is critical to recovery. It likely accounts for the lower number of traumatized vets of other wars, especially World War II, which had a clear and indisputable purpose for both soldiers and civilians. When a sense of purpose that gives meaning to wartime sacrifice is missing, the soldiers who actually made the sacrifice can experience an overriding and destructive feeling of betrayal.

War changes a person, says Muller. "You go down a path of darkness. You warp." Back from war, he adds, a person will experience predictable emotions: "Guilt, in part because you've come back--survivor guilt; shame, because, trust me, shameful things happen all over the place in war; and trauma, because when you're dealing with killing and the degradation of human beings that happens when fighting a war, there's a lot of trauma. When you come back, you need society's absolution to help you heal, knowing that what you did had to be done."

Among Vietnam vets, he says, "most came to terms with the horror piece." But once home and "out of that bubble of war," they grew in political awareness, determining that the war was a scam and that the government had lied to them. "You shake your head and start asking questions," he notes. "And you get angry because you realize you've been fucked politically." He calls this the "What the Fuck" syndrome, and he and others predict that soldiers from this war will experience the same reaction, if they haven't already, particularly since more than 60 percent of the American public now oppose the war in Iraq, 55 percent think we made a mistake sending troops there to begin with, and nearly 60 percent believe we were purposely misled in the reasons given for going to war.

"These people are clinging desperately to a sense of purpose to this mission," Muller says, motioning to the staff beyond his office working on Iraq veterans' issues, "just like I saw guys in the hospital with me clinging desperately to the belief that they were heroes. It took them time, but as the inevitability of the outcome of Vietnam registered, and the public verdict that it was not only unnecessary but in fact wrong registered, they really paid a price." He pauses, and speaks slowly: "So. Will. They," he says of Iraq vets. "It hasn't even begun."

The Endless Politics of PTSD

Despite our deep and growing understanding of post-traumatic stress disorder, it remains a controversial diagnosis that can't overcome its politicized genesis. As cost and criticism for this war escalate, there's a growing movement to knock the diagnosis.

Psychiatrists treating this new generation of veterans are "urged to learn the lessons of Vietnam," according to Simon Wessely, a prominent British combat-trauma researcher, who speaks frequently on the disorder while questioning its prevalence. "But no one is sure what those lessons are," he's quoted as saying. "Do the explanations for allegedly high rates [among Vietnam vets] lie in the jungles of Vietnam, in America's struggle to come to terms with the war, or with symptoms manufactured to fit a cultural narrative and expectation of what kinds of mental stress these veterans would experience?"

In September, Science published a report by Columbia University researchers, who reexamined the widely accepted results of a 1988 government study and downsized the number of Vietnam veterans suffering from PTSD from 31 percent to 19 percent, with about 9 percent still showing PTSD symptoms today. Researchers said they cross-referenced military records unavailable at the time of the original study and corroborated veterans' exposure to combat stress, with the result that some were found to have psychological problems that predated service and others had symptoms that didn't impair daily functioning, which wasn't a criterion for diagnosis then, but is now.

The authors explain that the point of the new study is to offer a clearer picture of what to expect from soldiers returning from Iraq. But in some ways, it does just the opposite, casting doubt on the whole diagnosis of PTSD. One can't help wonder if that wasn't, perhaps, the intention.

It's easy to understand why the federal government and others are concerned about the attention focused on PTSD: for Vietnam veterans alone, PTSD disability payments rose 150 percent between 1999 and 2005--that's about 100,000 new cases among veterans of a 30-year-old war. Some are being diagnosed three decades after service; some are being treated again because the events in Iraq have caused flashbacks of their own experiences, in effect retraumatizing them. Compensation for full disability is about $2,300 a month, and between 1999 and 2004, PTSD benefit payments rose from $1.7 billion to $4.3 billion. As of August 2006, 63,767 discharged soldiers from Iraq and Afghanistan were diagnosed by the Department of Veterans Affairs (VA) with a mental disorder, 34,380 of them with PTSD. Richard Lynch, a retired brigadier general who founded the annual National Tri-Service Combat Stress conference 14 years ago with colleague Bart Billings, a psychologist and now retired colonel, predicts the mental wounds from PTSD and traumatic brain injury will cost the country "a couple hundred billion dollars a year in care" for many years.

Given these potentially huge costs, it's perhaps inevitable that the apparently escalating presence of PTSD is getting close scrutiny. Even with "total buy-in" among top military leadership this time around that PTSD issues are indeed a "clear consequence of war," as Col. Charles Engel, director of the DOD's Deployment Health Clinical Center at Walter Reed Army Medical Center, maintains, many in and out of the military still wonder if the diagnosis is overblown. They worry that every mental health issue coming out of Iraq is being viewed through the PTSD lens.

"It's a diagnosis that invites people to speculate on what has traumatized them," said Sally Satel, a psychiatrist and resident scholar at the conservative think tank American Enterprise Institute, speaking last February at an Institute of Medicine hearing sponsored by the Department of Veterans of Affairs (VA) to review the PTSD diagnosis. Satel, who once worked with the VA, has become the voice of skepticism for the disorder, and many share her views. Two years earlier, testifying before Congress, she speculated that PTSD could provide a "medicalized explanation" for "unhappy but not necessarily traumatized veterans who'd been trying to make sense of their experience."

Veterans, by contrast, contend that it's common to have their mental problems diagnosed as preexisting conditions, such as bipolar disorder and personality disorder, that aren't covered by VA benefits.

The Danger of Overdiagnosis

It's easy to dismiss such comments as political shots, but beneath what may be partisan positioning are some difficult truths: combat PTSD is hard to define; those who have it or are susceptible to it are hard to identify; and not everyone agrees on who should be treated, when they should be treated, or which interventions are most effective for veterans. Another question is whether we should make a distinction between the normal reactions to a highly abnormal and gruesome situation--the emotional and psychological problems we'd expect anyone to have after seeing his buddy ripped apart by an IED--and the pathological symptoms described in the PTSD diagnosis? Figley thinks we should. Most returning soldiers, he says have severe transitional problems, suffering not from PTSD but what he calls "Post Combat Freakout."

For soldiers on constant high alert in Iraq, for example, it isn't easy to turn off the habits of wartime survival, but this may not amount to pathology. Hypervigilance has its place in a world where you're being mortared all day long, but it can interfere with life back home. Likewise, driving fast and aggressively, all the while scanning the landscape for roadside bombs, can keep you from getting blown up in Baghdad, but it'll probably get you ticketed or arrested in your hometown. Even interpersonal relationships must be relearned. During war, soldiers are trained to parse information, but if you can't communicate with your spouse or boss, you become withdrawn and alienated--and probably divorced and unemployed.

"We have to take a careful look at those we're diagnosing with a major medical disorder based on the symptoms they display and wonder if the symptoms wouldn't be there if not for the war," says Figley. "Maybe we need to call it a different name. We may be overpathologizing the combat stress reaction, too quickly perceiving it as PTSD instead of a natural, normal adjustment to recovery." Rushing to pathologize these behaviors as PTSD, he says, keeps veterans from getting the help they need to readjust after service--which can cause the behaviors to fester and, paradoxically, turn into full blown PTSD.

Others suggest that, as it stands, the PTSD diagnosis is too limited to encompass the many manifestations of postwar reactions. Perhaps, says Garett Reppenhagen, a military expert and Iraq War veteran, the PTSD diagnosis needs to "evolve" to include symptoms, emotions, and behaviors not now associated with it. "Some are addicted to war and want to go back [to Iraq], but feel guilty about it," he says. "Some have severe PTSD from actual incidents. Some have general stress and tension just from the pressures of war. A lot feel alienated from society--not only do they hate the administration, but they hate America for sending them there and allowing them to do the things they've had to do. The emotional experience of war is so intense that it creates a rainbow of mental illnesses. It's hard to classify them in a DSM. And it's hard to treat them."

Trauma Treatment Vacuum

It's impossible to truly gauge what kind of psychotherapeutic services or interventions a soldier with PTSD will receive in military medical centers, because there are no standard treatment protocols. The DOD and VA have jointly published clinical guidelines for treating PTSD, which recommend four evidence-based therapies: cognitive therapy, exposure therapy, Eye Movement Desensitization Reprocessing (EMDR), and Stress Inoculation Therapy. A fifth therapy, Cognitive Processing Therapy, is expected to be rolled out in a training program for clinicians in 2007.

But therapy providers working the armed forces aren't required to use these therapies, and their use isn't tracked. Therapist training also varies widely. A survey of mental health providers from the VA and DOD conducted by Steven Silver, director of the PTSD program at the VA Medical Center in Coatesville, Pennsylvania, found that 90 percent of the 137 surveyed had no training in any of the four recommended therapies. Of those who were trained, most got it prior to working in the military, and few had experience using the therapy to treat PTSD. Many respondents said they didn't treat PTSD at all because they didn't know how. A study in the Federal Practitioner echoes these findings, citing "a paucity of research regarding treatment outcomes and a lack of evidence-based psychotherapies in use within VA PTSD treatment programs."

It's a frustrating situation for many military mental health providers, who want and need the expertise to respond better to an obvious need. Patricia Resick, who developed Cognitive Processing Therapy and now works at the VA's National Center for PTSD (NCPTSD), says VA therapists have been "flooded" and many are playing "catch-up." The central office, she says, is making a concerted effort at training, but it takes time. "You can't possibly teach enough in a two-day workshop," she says. Collaborative learning, online resources, and e-mail groups are all being developed to help speed up the training process.

The obstacles aren't only institutional, says Lee Bridgewater, a clinical psychologist at the Daytona Beach VA Outpatient Clinic who's writing a PTSD treatment manual. While cognitive behavioral and exposure therapies are widely recognized as the "standard of care" for PTSD, within the VA, "there's a lot getting in the way of therapists doing [these therapies]." A person with combat PTSD typically doesn't come for treatment until 10 years after a war. They try everything to distract themselves from the symptoms: marriages, jobs, alcohol, sex. Meanwhile, the condition becomes chronic and resistant to treatment, and usually remains that way throughout the lifespan. The newest veterans, at 18 to 24 years old, believe they're invincible and they, too, often don't seek the treatment the VA offers, adds Bridgewater. Many, he says, see it as "Vietnam veterans disease" and don't want any part of it. They also stay away because of negative perceptions about the efficacy of psychotherapy, distrust of providers, and difficulty in scheduling appointments, according to DOD research. In addition, service members in an all-volunteer, professional military worry greatly about the stigma associated with mental illness, and are concerned, with good reason, that it will compromise their standing with unit leaders and their careers. Of the 13 percent of Iraq soldiers diagnosed with PTSD, 80 percent recognized they had a problem. But only 40 percent of those said they wanted help--and a little more than half of them actually got it.

The situation is somewhat ironic: never in the history of the military has so much energy and so many resources been expended to treat troop mental health, The Army now has 200 mental health workers deployed in Iraq and another 25 in Afghanistan who dispense meds and provide counseling. It's also instituted post-deployment health assessments (PDHAs) that screen for PTSD and that returning troops are required to fill out. But is it enough? Is the military doing the right things?

Psychotropic meds can get a troubled soldier through his deployment, but prescribing such drugs to troops in combat has become a point of huge controversy. Likewise, the PDHAs sound like a good idea, but the DOD doesn't put much faith in their results, nor is every positive screen a cause for concern. Of the

5 percent of returning troops who screened positive for PTSD, only 22 percent were referred for further mental health consultation, based on an evaluation made in the primary care system. Even the government's own oversight agency took the DOD to task for the lax follow-up, and questioned whether mental health professionals shouldn't conduct the evaluations.

The DOD says its intent is to draw more service members into mental health treatment by focusing efforts at the primary care level. A pilot program, called "RespectMil"--Re-engineering the System of Primary Care in the Military--is operating at Ft. Bragg, North Carolina, and will be expanded to 15 other sites in the Army medical system. It's designed to improve early recognition and management of PTSD and depression in returned troops, and to reduce stigma by folding the mental health assessments into primary health care visits. Nearly 95 percent of returned troops have at least one health care visit a year within either the DOD or VA systems, Engel points out. Educating primary care physicians to spot mental problems at the "front end" of the medical system seems the logical and least threatening way to flag servicemembers who need psychotherapy--"many of whom, quite honestly, might not want to see a specialist," he says--and direct them to the appropriate mental health provider. Another program, called De-Stress, is a therapist-assisted interactive web base being tested for use with veterans who either don't want to see a specialist in person or who live in areas where it's geographically difficult.

But many veterans see DOD's primary care focus as another attempt to stall and defer real mental health treatment, a strategy that suits the department's needs, says Robinson. "Honestly? They don't have the doctor-patient ratio, and this is a way to get rid of them and send them down the road to the VA."

Wayne's World

How to deal with these problems once home is the question, and a difficult one. For many soldiers, that's where the real battle begins --a battle that Gary Trudeau aptly titled "The War Within" in a much-discussed collection of cartoons depicting his character B.D.'s struggle with amputation and PTSD on his return from a tour in Iraq.

It's a war few who haven't seen combat can truly understand, and it poses a dilemma in treatment. The most effective therapies for PTSD have been developed and are most widely available in the civilian world, but veterans are least likely to go there for help, according to Charles Figley. Soldiers who've lived the horrors of war believe that unless you've been there, you just don't get it. Many feel shamed by their wartime acts and fear misunderstanding and harsh judgment--even from those who are psychologically trained. Civilian therapists must be extremely knowledgeable about the war experience if they're to help veterans. Says Figley: "There's a cultural gulf between those who've been socialized to survive in combat and those who haven't."

How to bridge that gulf is the challenge. It's an age-old artistic theme: ordinary people are trained and transformed into killers to go to battle, but how do we prepare war-weary soldiers to go to peace? It took Odysseus 10 years to figure out how to get home. By the end of the movie The Deer Hunter, we're still unsure whether Robert De Niro's character will ever fit in again. But Trudeau's B.D., who struggles to find someone who can relate to the residue of his Iraq experience and pull him out of the resulting emotional hell, discovers hope in a single counselor at his local Vet Center--a character named Elias. He's based on a former marine corporal named Wayne Miller, who's the team leader at the Vet Center in Silver Spring, Maryland. Vet Centers, part of the VA system, started as rap groups created by Vietnam vets for peer support at a time when there were no services for their problems. They're staffed by civilian and military therapists, with a strong emphasis on peer support and clinicians who are veterans.

Trudeau spent time with Miller, witnessing his methods, hearing about his past, and observing the veteran culture. Like Elias, Miller is a burly, gruff, and welcoming Vietnam vet with one leg and tired eyes. Elias lost his leg in a motorcycle accident, but Miller's was blown off in a mortar attack on July 4, 1969. His other leg was "mangled," and his hands and arms disfigured in combat, too. He spent six months paralyzed after coming home from Vietnam. He was 18 years old.

Miller modeled for Trudeau what Elias does for B.D. He seeks out hurting vets where they tend to gather. "Under bridges, inside bars and churches, at disaster areas. We go and pick them up," says Miller. He discreetly passes along his card if he overhears "buzzwords" or conversation that suggests a veteran needs help. Those who walk into the center from the street are greeted quickly and eased in. Once in counseling, he treads softly, reminding veterans that they aren't "crazy" (their greatest fear, he says), but merely experiencing what many returning from combat inevitably go through--and that they aren't alone. He tells them: "PTSD isn't a mental illness: it's an anxiety disorder. 'Crazy' is when you take your K-bar, cut your stomach open, and take your guts out!" He laughs at his own bluntness. But in his speech, one hears traces of Elias: "See, Bro, sometimes combat comes at you so hard, the memories don't get processed properly. They become free floating, like raw footage that hasn't been edited down to make sense."

Miller shares pieces of his past that "trigger" similar experiences and feelings in his patients, which they might then talk about. He lets them know clearly that he's been where they are--and that nothing can shock him. "I'm a Marine, I've seen combat, I'm a social worker, I'm an amputee," he says, sitting back in his chair. Glancing around his cluttered but precisely arranged office, one gets the message loud and clear. In fact, behind him, hovering like a doppelganger of his former self, is his neatly pressed Marine Corps uniform with his helmet propped above it. By the shoulder is a hand grenade. His shelves are lined with books on war and psychological healing. His desk, tables, and walls hold war photos and memorabilia, veterans' group mementos, and family pictures that illustrate how life can still go on when the war is over.

"Everything changes after war. That's the message I give to veterans," he says. "For me, I wake up every morning and put my leg on to walk. I'm constantly reminded--24/7, 365 days a year--of the war and my injuries. A lot of times, you don't think you can survive, especially with PTSD. But I'm living proof that change occurs--that you can still live and breathe and survive after war."

But to do that, says Miller, takes hard work, retraining of mind and spirit, and relearning everyday habits--even how to make small talk or be with your spouse--that were warped in the war zone. To change what have become maladaptive means of survival once back in the civilian world, Miller runs what he calls a "PTSD Boot Camp." Just like military boot camp, it lasts eight weeks, and Miller plays the badass drill instructor--at least initially.

"Okay you doggies, squids, jarheads," he barks at them at the first meeting. "You won't be called a civilian until you graduate from my boot camp!" On the floor in front of each veteran are two yellow footprints (in front of Miller there's just one), the same type that direct fresh Marine recruits off the bus and into the barracks. These footprints, Miller hopes, will redirect his recruits. "You have 10 seconds to get on the yellow footprints!" he yells at them.

Then he sits and waits before a quiet, stunned group of veterans. Finally he laughs: "Didn't any of you think I was crazy?"

Over the weeks, he leads the group through stages of understanding and recovery that Miller call's "neither the right way, nor the wrong way, but Wayne's Way." He borrows heavily from many schools of psychotherapy and the trauma research literature, while educating vets about PTSD and life post-combat. Those who "graduate" may simply go about their civilian lives, while others may go on to individual, specialized treatment, or get referred to a VA clinic.

Listening to Miller, I'm struck by the grittiness of the therapy. To heal a psychologically wounded vet requires more than developing the perfect screening methods, or prescribing the latest meds, or performing cutting-edge neurobiologically informed protocols. It requires an intimate understanding of what if feels like to have been to hell and not come back fully. It calls for the willingness and ability to re-experience that terror with a veteran, and to reach across the frightening chasm that separates war from peace, soldier from civilian.

Combat trauma is different from other kinds of trauma because the horror of war--the trauma-inducing murderousness of it--is inextricably linked with sacrifice, courage, honor, pride, and patriotism. And the trauma occurs in the context of profound personal loyalty. Some soldiers will never experience bonds as intense as those formed with buddies fighting or dying beside them in the desperation of battle or the confines of an exploding Humvee. No other trauma is so intermingled with our deepest values and strongest fears of overwhelming loss. Is it any wonder that soldiers have a hard time letting it go?

It isn't surprising that those who've been through war feel they possess a terrible, secret knowledge that no ordinary citizen, even a well-meaning therapist, can imagine or understand. But to help, we must imagine it. We must understand the oddly thrilling, adrenaline rush of combat--what Matt Frank called a kind of "drug" earlier in this story--as well as its corrupting horror. We must realize that coming back from such a brutal landscape makes the flatlands of civilian life seem, well, pretty flat--even for someone tortured with PTSD. And that makes recovery all the more difficult.

Of course, only those who've been to war can truly know its devastating effects. But it doesn't follow that only former soldiers can lead other soldiers back. The rest of the therapeutic world has much to offer, but also much to learn. Beyond the bells and whistles of the latest trauma treatments, one must also keep in mind a simple human truth that Wayne Miller models in his outreach and therapy: emotional healing comes in intimate form--the acknowledgment of another's suffering and the willingness and ability to get down and dirty with that person to the point that you can truthfully say, "I get it." To bring a veteran out of Hades requires not so much a collection of methods as a sure-footed personal guide like Miller, who can lead a psychologically wounded soldier back into the light, and all the way home.

PTSD Threatens Lives and Challenges Public Health

Mohammad S. Jalali is a research scientist at the MIT Sloan School of Management. A former consultant at the World Bank and former researcher for the U.S. Department of Energy, he is interested in complex health and social issues. His research is shaped by wanting his work to have impact in the real world.

Post-traumatic stress disorder is a serious public health challenge. It is estimated that about eight million people in the U.S. (2.5 percent of the total population) suffer from it. This rate jumps to about 11 to 20 percent among Iraq and Afghanistan veterans who suffer from diagnosed or undiagnosed PTSD.

Affected individuals might lose their career or family or even commit suicide due to the consequences of PTSD. The effects go beyond the individuals coping with it, extending to their family, friends, colleagues and communities.

Both military personnel and veterans can be affected by PTSD. However, the exact prevalence of PTSD among these two groups is unknown. This not only makes it hard to know how many people actually have PTSD but also makes it even harder to project how many will in the future. And if we don't know how many people actually have PTSD, it can be hard to find out what policies work best to mitigate it.

To address these concerns, my colleagues Navid Ghaffarzadegan and Alireza Ebrahimvandi at Virginia Tech and I decided to take a systems science approach which lets us study how parts of a large system, such as the Department of Veterans Affairs and the Department of Defense, interconnect.

"Fighting Another War: How Many Military Personnel and Veterans Will Have PTSD in 2025?" by Mohammad S. Jalali, The Conversation, October 8, 2016. https://theconversation.com/fighting-another-war-how-many-military-personnel-and-veterans-will-have-ptsd-in-2025-65542. Licensed Under CC BY-ND 4.0 International.

We developed a simulation model to project the prevalence of PTSD by 2025 among military personnel and veterans and to find out what policies actually reduce the burden. Our study presenting the model was recently published in PLOS ONE.

The Challenge of Estimating PTSD Prevalence

Because screening of PTSD is based on self-reported surveys, estimating its true prevalence among veterans and current military personnel is hard to do. Answers to surveys can suffer from patients' errors.

But more importantly, some PTSD patients may intentionally underplay their mental health condition to avoid being labeled as mentally ill. In a few cases, patients may exaggerate their problems for motives of secondary gain, such as disability compensation.

Our task was to put all of this information together to gain a true sense of the future prevalence of PTSD among military personnel and veterans.

PTSD is a Multi-organizational Challenge

Another challenge is that we are talking about two different populations: people currently in the military, and veterans.

The VA and the military are two systems within a larger system. They establish different policies, which may result in improvements in their own sectors, but are not so effective in the larger system. For instance, policies implemented in the early stages of a person's military career, when combat readiness is a major concern, can cause serious consequences years after separation from the military.

In systems science, this is called "shifting the burden." Unless the military and the VA come together to develop integrated policies, the big picture of the system will be missed by disjointed policies implemented in each organization.

Since PTSD is a multi-organizational challenge, estimates should take both populations into account simultaneously, which is what we did in our model.

Simulating the Burden of PTSD

Our model includes both military personnel and veterans affected by PTSD in a "system of systems." It uses historical data on PTSD prevalence among military personnel and veterans from the DOD, the Institute of Medicine, the VA and other sources, from 2000 to 2014. This let us validate our model and generate a more exact estimate of PTSD prevalence.

Our approach also allows us to ask "what-if" questions about the consequences of current policies – such as what if we focus solely on improving screening or improving screening and treatment.

Then we used the model to forecast PTSD prevalence over the next decade under several scenarios. These scenarios are based on common "what-ifs," including different levels of U.S. involvement in future wars and improvements in prevention, screening and treatment.

What Happens if We Fight Another War?

In an optimistic scenario where 1 percent of all military personnel are deployed to combat zones (which reflects deployment in 2014) that no war happens in the next decade, we estimate that 7 percent of military personnel and 10 percent of veterans will have PTSD by 2025.

But that could increase to 20 percent in the military and more than 11 percent among veterans in 2025 if the U.S. gets involved in a war requiring 5 percent deployment of all military personnel on battlefield. For perspective, from 2001 to 2014, on average, 6.6 percent were deployed annually. Larger wars with higher deployment rates will noticeably increase the prevalence of PTSD.

We also estimated the delay in mitigating the effects of a hypothetical war. Let's assume that the U.S. involves in a five-year war with 10 percent troop deployment (similar to the maximum deployment in Iraq in 2008).

After the end of this hypothetical war, it will take about 40 years for PTSD prevalence to go back to its initial rate. This estimation shows how long the effects of war can endure.

What Policies Work Best?

We also tried to get a sense of what policies work best at mitigating the problem of PTSD. Using the model, we examined the long-term effects of policies within the individual components of the system, the VA and the DOD, as well as across the entire system.

We found that, before and during wars, prevention interventions (focusing on resiliency-related training) are the most effective policy to decrease the prevalence of PTSD. Improving resiliency can work as a "vaccine" or early treatment before the onset of the cascading effects of PTSD.

However, social barriers such as the stigma of PTSD are still in place, affecting willingness to receive early treatment.

Overall, our results show that in a post-war period there is no easy solution for overcoming the problem of PTSD, and the current screening and treatment policies used by the VA and the DOD must be revolutionized to have any noticeable effect.

The VA and the DOD should work together and try to offer timely service to patients. However, we showed that they cannot do much to decrease health care costs. These are the consequences of wars.

Mental Health Professionals Take Veterans' PTSD Seriously

Elizabeth Roberts-Pedersen

Elizabeth Roberts-Pedersen, PhD, is a lecturer in history in the School of Humanities and Communication Arts at Western Sydney University in Australia. Her work examines the experience of "soldiers of conscience" in 19th- and 20th-century wars, regimes of discipline and punishment in the armed forces, and wartime psychiatry.

2015 marks several important First World War anniversaries: the centenary of the first use of poison gas in January; the centenary of the Gallipoli landings and the Armenian genocide in April. It is also 100 years since *The Lancet* published Charles S. Myers' article, "A Contribution to the Study of Shell Shock."

The Study of Shell Shock

Myers' article is generally regarded as the first use of the term "shell shock" in medical literature. It was used as a descriptor for "three cases of loss of memory, vision, smell and taste" in British soldiers admitted to a military hospital in France.

While Myers presented these cases as evidence of the spectacular concussive effects of artillery on the Western Front, British medical opinion soon came to regard these symptoms as psychological in origin. The men presenting to medical officers with tics, tremors and palpitations, as well as more serious symptoms of "functional" blindness, paralysis and loss of speech, were not concussed – but nor were they necessarily cowards or malingerers.

Instead, these were men simply worn down by the unprecedented stresses of trench warfare – in particular, the effort required to push out of one's mind the prospect of joining the ranks of the maimed or the corpses lying in no man's land. Myers later wrote:

> Even those who start with the strongest "nerves" are not immune from "shell shock", if exposed to sufficiently often repeated, or to incessant, strain, or if subjected to severe enough shock.

For contemporaries and later for historians, shell shock came to encapsulate all the horror of this new form of industrialised warfare. As historian Jay Winter suggests, it moved "from a diagnosis into a metaphor,"

The effects of shell shock could linger. In his celebrated "Good-Bye to All That," poet Robert Graves recounted returning to England trembling at strong smells (from fear of gas attacks) and loud noises. He judged that it took: "… some ten years for my blood to recover."

Developing a Diagnosis

It is tempting to view shell shock as the unambiguous turning point in psychiatry's history, popularising the idea that unconscious processes might produce symptoms that operate separately from moral qualities such as endurance and courage. However, scholarship over the last 15 years suggests that this position was far from widely accepted.

Shell-shocked soldiers were as likely to be subject to harsh "disciplinary" treatments, such as "faradism" – the application of alternating electric currents to stimulate paralysed limbs or target other physical symptoms – as they were to receive psychotherapy. The notion that many patients had some "predisposing" weakness – independent of their combat experiences – persisted throughout the interwar period and into the Second World War.

It wasn't until the Vietnam War that this formulation was reversed, which in turn bridged the gap between combatant syndromes and the civilian sphere.

This development is only comprehensible as part of a broader political context. The notion that the Vietnam War exacted a form of psychic damage on American soldiers was championed by the anti-war activists of Vietnam Veterans Against the War (VVAW) and psychiatrists Chaim Shatan and Robert Jay Lifton. "Post-Vietnam syndrome", Shatan wrote, was caused by the "unconsummated grief" of a brutal and brutalising war.

The VVAW's advocacy was instrumental in securing official recognition for this condition. It was included in 1980 in the third edition of the Diagnostic and Statistical Manual of Mental Disorders (DSM-III) as "Post-Traumatic Stress Disorder".

PTSD's inclusion in DMS-III legitimated the suffering of Vietnam veterans and held out the possibility of subsidised medical care and compensation. But the DSM-III definition of PTSD was significant in two additional ways.

First, it identified the disorder as a condition that could afflict soldiers and civilians alike – not a diagnosis exclusive to combat, like shell shock.

Second, it focused attention on the continuing effects of a traumatic experience, rather than on the personality and constitution of the patient.

The ramifications of these changes have been immense. PTSD and a broader field of "traumatology" are now entrenched in psychiatric and popular discourse. In Australia, we now assume that warfare is objectively traumatising, and that governments ought to provide medical and financial support for affected service personnel, even if a recent Four Corners program confirmed that this is not always the case.

How Is PTSD Viewed Today?

Though PTSD has its origins in opposition to the Vietnam War, the politics of the condition are now largely ambivalent, with its significance shifting according to circumstance.

This point is well illustrated by the film *American Sniper*, which demonstrates the possibility of two contrary positions. After his return to civilian life, SEAL sniper Chris Kyle (Bradley Cooper) is shown to be suffering from some characteristic after-effects of combat. He is startled at loud noises, sees scenes of combat on a blank TV and becomes enraged at a barking dog during a family barbecue. This leads his wife to call in assistance from a Veterans Administration psychiatrist.

On the one hand, we could view this evidence of psychological damage as an implicit critique of the Iraq war, serving the same function as the damaged Vietnam veteran in Hollywood cinema of the late 1970s and 1980s. But there is also a converse reaction that values this pain as a worthy sacrifice in the fight against the "savages" Kyle sees through his rifle scope. This reaction discounts entirely the damage done to civilian populations by years of occupation and mutually destructive fighting.

The potential for this second reading is perhaps greater in this particular film, which for the most part portrays Iraqis as marginal and malign figures.

Interestingly, the film also depicts Kyle as ambivalent in the face of his symptoms, with Kyle objecting to the psychiatrist's suggestion that he may be suffering from the repercussions of multiple tours of duty. Yet he is depicted as a sympathetic support figure for other veterans suffering from physical and psychological injuries.

The real Chris Kyle was shot dead by one of these men, Eddie Ray Routh, in 2013. At trial, the accused's lawyers pursued a defense of insanity, compounded by the inadequate care provided by veterans' mental health services. Routh was found guilty of Kyle's murder late last month.

In the 100 years since Myers' article on shell shock, the psychological consequences of war remain as relevant as ever.

PTSD Has Taken Over America

Alice Karekezi

Alice Karekezi is a New York-based freelance writer who was a graduate student at NYU at the time she authored this piece.

In the past 30 years, post-traumatic stress disorder has gone from exotic rarity to omnipresent. Once chiefly applied to wartime veterans returning from combat, it is now a much more common diagnosis, still linked to traumatic events but now including those occurring outside the battle zone: the death of a loved one on a hospital bed, a car crash on the highway, an assault in the neighborhood park. Many would argue that this is a good thing: greater recognition of psychologically distressing events will lead to more people seeking treatment and a decrease in the preponderance of PTSD – a win-win.

Stephen Joseph disagrees. In his new book, "What Doesn't Kill Us," the professor of psychology, health and social care at the University of Nottingham (in the U.K.) warns that our culture's acceptance of PTSD has become excessive and has led to an over-medicalization of experiences that should be considered part of ordinary, normal, human experience. This has kept us from proactively working through our grief and anxiety: We've become too quick to go to the shrink expecting him to fix us, rather than allowing ourselves the opportunity to grow and find new meaning in our lives as a result of painful, but common, events. Joseph advocates for a push toward post-traumatic growth as therapy to treat the stress of trauma, which he distinguishes as being different from the hokey, blue skies and rainbows, pop psychology that he claims has exploded in our culture in the past decade.

"How PTSD took over America," by Alice Karekezi, Salon Media Group, Inc, November 16, 2011. Reprinted by permission.

Joseph spoke to Salon over the phone to discuss our misunderstanding of the disorders, the meaning and usefulness of suffering, and if some cultures are more prone to PTSD than others.

How would you define a traumatic event? Is it subjective or are there some basic requirements that must be met?

I see trauma as a psychological rupturing. It's when something happens to us that ruptures our psychological skin. Or, something which shatters our assumptions about ourselves in the world. That's what I think of as traumatic, and in a way that can be many things. So, that can include a wider range of experience, and I can understand trauma in that broader way. There are lots of different experiences, such as being in a road traffic collision, or experiencing an illness – those sorts of things can be traumatic to people. It can be experienced as psychologically traumatic. But whether it's necessary to create a psychiatric diagnostic category to capture those experiences is perhaps not necessary.

Do you believe that PTSD is over-diagnosed?

Well, that's a really, really tricky question to answer because in a way it's diagnosed pretty much exactly as it's described in the Diagnostic and Statistical Manual (DSM). So whether the definition of PTSD is too broad is a different question, if you see what I mean. When PTSD was first introduced in 1980, it was defined much more tightly. The gatekeeper criterion to the diagnosis was: Have you experienced a traumatic event? In 1980, it was defined in such a way that only people who had experienced an event that was really outside the range of usual human experience, [like] Vietnam or the Holocaust, had experienced the sorts of experiences that were thought to elicit PTSD. So if you experienced something like a car accident or a traumatic birth, then you couldn't get a diagnosis of PTSD, because, by definition, you hadn't experienced a traumatic event.

In 1994, the definition changed in such a way as to include other, broader experiences. Equally persistent was the person's subjective experiences of what they thought was traumatic.

When that happened, people who had experienced car accidents, traumatic births, what we would have otherwise thought of as more ordinary life events, insofar as they are not statistically unusual, could then be diagnosed as a having PTSD. So now we are in a position where lots of people are able to receive the diagnosis of PTSD. So it's not that it's being over-diagnosed in that sense. The difficulty or problem, if there is one, is whether, generally speaking – PTSD would be part of this – the DSM over-medicalizes human experience. Things which are relatively common, relatively normal, are turned into psychiatric disorders.

Can you describe some of the typical symptoms of PTSD?

When people experience trauma, when their assumptions about themselves and the world come crashing down, there's often a period of avoidance. People just try to block out what happened. Switch off. Turn their attention to other things. That's quite understandable. Then, over time, that gives rise to memories and emotions that come flooding in as the person sort of begins to try to make sense of what happened, and that can become so powerful and distressing that they have to push that away again and go back into a period of avoidance. So sometimes people go through that, periods of avoidance and intrusion. That seems to me as a healthy and adaptive way of working through something painful, emotionally painful, that has happened to us. So those are the experiences. PTSD is when those experiences become so overwhelming that the person can't function anymore – at work, or school, or in their social life. It takes over so much. But otherwise the symptoms of PTSD are fairly normal, natural ways of dealing with adaptation.

It's important to see those experiences as quite normal and natural. They are not symptoms of a disorder by themselves. They're just the way that people deal with an upsetting event in order to be able to make sense of things and to move on. It's only when they become so overwhelmingly intense that they might be considered a disorder. I think that's where we get into the problem with what PTSD is: when people are going through that normal experience, but they see it as having a disorder rather than a normal process of adaptation.

That will diminish over time?

Exactly.

Is the emotional pain overblown in such cases?

The suffering is very real. We're not saying that people don't have difficult emotional experiences and aren't suffering. What we're saying is this is not necessarily a disorder that people are experiencing, and if people think like that, it can be very disempowering to them.

What is the detrimental effect of over-medicalizing these more common human experiences of grief and pain?

When we think of ourselves as suffering from a disorder in a medical sense, well we go to the doctor and we expect the doctor to prescribe whatever the medical treatment is. We're not in the driver's seat. We go along – we tell them [our] symptoms, they listen to us, they diagnose what the problem is, and then they work out what the appropriate treatment is. That's the mind-set when we're working within a medical framework and we think of ourselves as suffering from a disorder. We sit down in front of the therapist and we expect the therapist to be like a doctor – to be looking out for what the symptoms are so that they can make the correct diagnosis and prescribe us the right treatment. The language of PTSD invokes those ideas, and I think it's those ideas that can be quite unhelpful at times. For what we're talking about here, if it's a normal, natural process, what's really important is for the person to be in the driver's seat for themselves – to make their own choices, their own decisions, because we're dealing not with a disorder, but a battle within the person to find new meanings and new ways of understanding the world. That's what they have to do. Nobody else can do that for them.

What is "post-traumatic growth"?

Post-traumatic growth is when people come out of trauma having learned new things about themselves and about the world and about their relationship with the world. People develop new philosophies of life. They develop new priorities in life. People learn an awful lot about themselves: their strengths; what they're good at; having new respect for themselves. They sort of see their lives as divided into two halves: before the event happened and after the event happened. There is a clear demarcation. And they recognize that something happened to them that sliced their world in half in that way, and things for them are now completely different. How they lead their lives has been transformed – their priorities about life, their relationships.

I think one of the things that captures that the most [starts with] the idea that, sometimes, people lead their lives in a way that is dictated by external forces of status and wealth, which are very much big drivers in our capitalist society. We often, in our everyday lives, forget about the small things that are quite important – our relationships: remembering to nurture them, to look after the people around us, to be giving, to be compassionate. When traumatic events happen, people are often shaken back to reality, and remember what really matters to them. Often it is those other things – remembering somebody's birthday; nurturing our friendships; looking after our parents, the people around us; really embracing our relationships; and letting go of a more materialistic outlook. People often describe it as getting back to who they really are, or feeling more true to themselves, or being more genuine or more authentic. Somehow the idea of the false self that people create around them is shattered, like Humpty Dumpty falling off a wall. The essence of who they are emerges.

Yes, becoming truer to oneself captures the idea very well. Realizing that life is short and sometimes there isn't as much time left as we thought to put up facades.

This kind of makes trauma sound like a blessing (you even mention people describing it as a "gift"). Is finding meaning the same thing as condoning the traumatic event? And doesn't this talk of growth all sound very "kumbaya-ish" and unrealistic?

One of the reasons, sometimes, that post-traumatic growth can be seen unfavorably is that it seems like saying that trauma can lead to greater happiness; that for people who have been through trauma, it's a good for them – they're happier. That's just so not the message. It's not saying that trauma leads to happiness, in terms of smiling and feeling good and laughing and joy – not that type of happiness. What we're talking about is how trauma can lead to a deeper, more existentially meaningful and fulfilling life, and that in turn may lead to greater happiness further down the road. But, post-traumatic growth is not about happiness in the sort of yellow, smiley face sense.

In essence, post-traumatic growth is a very simple idea, but it has been overshadowed by this mass of psychiatric literature over the past 30 or 40 years about the overwhelming destructive side of trauma, and about how these lead to medical problems. It's a very simple idea, but [post-traumatic growth] sits, on the one hand, very uncomfortably within mainstream culture of the world of psychology and psychiatry, and on the other hand it seems to sit very comfortably with some other parts of Western culture, such as positive thinking, but it also clashes with some of that literature which is quite superficial, and not grounded in scientific research, and makes unsupported claims.

So, no, post-traumatic growth] doesn't mean that [people] value or cherish the bad thing that has happened to them. They just accept that it has happened to them. People will often say they wish it hadn't happened, or they wish they could go back, but there is a realism that they know they can't. So it's accepting that they can't go back; they can't change things. The only way forward is to go forward. It's when people can't accept that something has happened, and they [try] to go back to how they were before, is when they struggle. Acceptance is just being realistic – not seeing it as a good thing.

And someone not experiencing growth — or experiencing PTSD — is that person always trying to go back?

I think that often that's what gets people stuck – trying to go back, trying to rebuild their lives exactly as it was before. That can lead people to get very stuck because it just isn't possible when traumatic events happen and we're presented with new information about the world, or with losses. It just isn't possible to go back and make things as they were. We have to somehow accept what has happened to us and move on.

Is post-traumatic growth something completely in opposition to PTSD or post-traumatic stress? Either you have one or the other?

They can sit together. The way I see it, post-traumatic growth mostly arises out of post-traumatic stress. So it's how people deal with the post-traumatic stress; how they manage to deal with the intrusive thoughts that are plaguing them; and the new sense they make of their experiences. So it's through the post-traumatic stress, through the struggle of post-traumatic stress that post-traumatic growth arises. So often there's a period of time in which people will begin to talk about post-traumatic growth but they will still be suffering from post-traumatic stress. They're not in opposition. In a way, they are opposite sides of a coin.

You make a claim that true happiness is something that in and of itself cannot be pursued, and one is doomed to fail if one tries. How is that?

Well, that's an idea that some philosophers have put forward. Some of the research seems to suggest that what's really important to finding happiness is meaning and purpose in life. If we think our road to happiness is through seeking hedonistic pleasures night after night, then that's not likely to lead to a deep, fulfilling level of happiness. But, if we find ways of finding meaning and purpose, wherever that might be, then we're not setting out directly aiming for happiness but that's what we're going to get. We're going to find a more fulfilling life. Happiness is a byproduct, but in a sense it's more guaranteed.

When we think of psychological therapies, and the helping professions in general, they often have been about helping people feel better. [For] people with various problems of depression, anxiety or post-traumatic stress, therapy is about getting the person to have a more positive emotional state. That's been, really, what the therapy world has been about for 50 years, and yet that's only half the picture. The other half is about the meaning we put on things, our purpose in life, our sense of ourselves, our sense of autonomy, our relationships. Psychology can also be about those things. I'm not saying that therapists have ignored them altogether; for sure, they haven't, but those more existential ideas have been overshadowed by trying to feel good. This is the idea between what psychologists call subjective well-being, which is about feeling good, and psychological well-being, which is what you could call "meaning-good," and it's just about getting the balance between those two things right.

Are there some cultures that are more prone to post-traumatic growth?

That's a really good question. I don't think the research has really documented that yet as to whether it may be more common. What the research has shown, however, is that post-traumatic growth is something observed in pretty much all cultures that have been investigated, though differently defined in slight ways. "Post-traumatic growth" sounds like a very Western idea, but [it's one that] gets back into history and into all sorts of cultures. It's an idea that's very resonant with Buddhist and some Chinese philosophy ideas, as well as ideas in Western religion.

PTSD Claims Inspire Skepticism Among Active Military Members

Scott Faith

Havok Journal editor Scott Faith is a veteran of several combat deployments, having served in many Special Operations units during his Army career. Scott's writing focuses largely on veterans' issues, Constitutional rights and politics.

I know I'm going to catch hell from my brothers and sisters in the veteran community on this one, but it needs to be said: I'm becoming skeptical of some PTSD claims, and you should be too.

Post Traumatic Stress Disorder is to this generation of veterans what "back pain" was to mine; both are real conditions with real victims, but the symptoms are so common and so easily faked that anyone can claim they have the condition, and no one can prove that they don't.

PTSD has become a "get out of jail free" card, or at least a "feel sorry for me and excuse my behavior card," a very powerful one with no expiration date. This has become increasingly — and distressingly — true in the veteran community.

Don't believe me? Read any news story about a veteran who gets in trouble with the law, either military or civilian, and I guarantee that in at least ¾ cases (and nearly 100% of felony cases) either the individual charged or one of the lawyers involved will explicitly or implicitly claim "the PSTD made me do it." These days, in the veteran community no offense is too big, or too small, to use PTSD as an excuse. Examples:

Plagiarized your War College thesis? PTSD! Like to get drunk and pick fights with civilian women? PTSD! Murdered a police officer? PTSD! Drug smuggling, kidnapping, spousal abuse, sexual assault? PTSD! Made some really, really bad life choices? PTSD!

"Why I'm Skeptical Of PTSD Claims… And Why You Should Be Too," by Scott Faith, Havok Media, January 28, 2016. Reprinted by permission.

Want to get paid, get attention, or get sympathy? PTSD, PTSD, PTSD!!!

Additionally, PTSD has become sort of a "third rail" within the veteran community, to the point that few people are willing to write objectively about it. Even fewer major publications are willing to run articles the slightest bit critical of anyone who has, or who claims to have PTSD. Well, that's not how we roll here. Sometimes the truth hurts, but that doesn't make it any less true. So if you don't appreciate Real Talk, then do us both a favor and stop reading Havok Journal.

How easy is it to get a PTSD diagnosis? The short answer is, "too easy." Here's a personal anecdote: I was once referred to a civilian, off-post doctor to seek relief for my sleep apnea. The discussion was going well until he found out I'm a veteran, at which time he wanted to put me on all kinds of drugs for PTSD. I had to talk him out of it by categorically refusing to go on PTSD meds in the first place. As confirmed by 2nd and 3rd opinions as well as my objective self-evaluation, I don't have PTSD; I have sleep apnea.

Whether my sleep apnea is pre-existing, age-related, or service-related, I don't know. But I *do* know that if I went with the PTSD diagnosis, I would have joined a long line of people who were misdiagnosed with the condition. I would have been on a cocktail of behavior-modifying, mood-altering, and thought-inhibiting drugs. I felt that I also would have been at risk to lose access to my firearms or perhaps even my security clearance (although I later found out PTSD is not necessarily a disqualifier for a clearance). And most importantly, I never would have gotten help with my real, underlying health condition.

I respect doctors and almost always heed medical advice or believe professional diagnoses. If a doctor looks at an X-ray and tells me my leg is broken, I believe him. If a doctor does an MRI and says she thinks I have cancer, I take it seriously. But telling me I have PTSD simply because I'm a veteran is the kind of voodoo, kneejerk misdiagnosis that clogs the medical system and does a disservice to the veteran community.

Further complicating the situation is that many symptoms of PTSD are similar to those of other conditions. In my case, my sleep apnea was characterized by nightmares, sleep deprivation, headaches, dry mouth, mood swings, and anxiety. All of these things, it turned out, were my body's reaction to not sleeping. So if I would not have questioned the initial diagnosis, I would have been on a treatment regimen of questionable effectiveness AND my underlying condition, sleep apnea, would have remained untreated, leaving me drugged up AND still unable to sleep. But hey, at least I could tell people I have PTSD!

The evidence of over-diagnosis of PTSD in the veteran community is not just anecdotal, nor is it unique to the US military. In a January 2016 article posted by The Guardian, a leading newspaper in Great Britain, the former head of the UK's veterans' mental health program opined that 42% of PTSD claims were for issues unrelated to military service, and that at least 10% of claims were either grossly exaggerated or were based on total fabrications. If true, those are some pretty damning figures.

Of course, the "PTSD for profit" problem is not confined to the veteran community. The easily-offended, everyone-is-a-victim, "trigger-warning" culture of America has its share of sketchy PTSD claims as well. But within the veteran community, it has becoming increasingly acute. For a small, but growing segment of veterans, fueled by perverse incentives including VA payouts, sympathy, and attention, a PTSD claim is a badge of honor, whether earned or not. And for many outside of our community, PTSD is now not only accepted, but expected. The attitude almost seems to be, "if you went to war and didn't come back with PTSD, did you even deploy at all?" That's not a healthy perception for the American people, or for vets themselves, to have of the veteran community.

Before I wrap this article up, I want to make a couple of things clear. First of all, I whole-heartedly agree that PTSD is a real condition that genuinely affects many people, including several of my personal friends. People should continue to get help for their conditions, and if a diagnosis of PTSD is confirmed (by multiple doctors!), then they should follow the treatment regimen accordingly. But the problem of misdiagnosis and false PTSD claims has become so widespread that it is seeming more and more like "everyone" has it. And if everyone has it, then no one has it, and that's really, really bad for those few who genuinely suffer from the disorder. That pisses me off, and it should piss you off as well.

So yeah, I'm skeptical when I hear people, especially veterans, trot out claims of PTSD to explain away their criminal actions, boorish behavior, or poor life decisions. Bogus, weak, or misdiagnosed PTSD cases are overloading the system at a time that it should have been laser focused on those with real problems.

And that should concern all of us.

CHAPTER 2

Can a PTSD Diagnosis
Be Exploited?

Overview: Exposure to Combat and Physical Assault Leads to PTSD

Mayo Clinic Staff

The staff of the Mayo Clinic includes doctors, scientists, and other medical experts who dedicate some of their clinical time to producing informative content. In this way, they share their vast base of knowledge, and experiences at the Mayo Clinic with a broad audience.

Post-traumatic stress disorder (PTSD) is a mental health condition that's triggered by a terrifying event — either experiencing it or witnessing it. Symptoms may include flashbacks, nightmares and severe anxiety, as well as uncontrollable thoughts about the event.

Most people who go through traumatic events may have temporary difficulty adjusting and coping, but with time and good self-care, they usually get better. If the symptoms get worse, last for months or even years, and interfere with your day-to-day functioning, you may have PTSD.

Getting effective treatment after PTSD symptoms develop can be critical to reduce symptoms and improve function.

Symptoms

Post-traumatic stress disorder symptoms may start within one month of a traumatic event, but sometimes symptoms may not appear until years after the event. These symptoms cause significant problems in social or work situations and in relationships. They can also interfere with your ability to go about your normal daily tasks.

PTSD symptoms are generally grouped into four types: intrusive memories, avoidance, negative changes in thinking and mood, and changes in physical and emotional reactions. Symptoms can vary over time or vary from person to person.

Intrusive memories

- Recurrent, unwanted distressing memories of the traumatic event
- Reliving the traumatic event as if it were happening again (flashbacks)
- Upsetting dreams or nightmares about the traumatic event
- Severe emotional distress or physical reactions to something that reminds you of the traumatic event

Avoidance

- Trying to avoid thinking or talking about the traumatic event
- Avoiding places, activities or people that remind you of the traumatic event

Negative changes in thinking and mood

- Negative thoughts about yourself, other people or the world
- Hopelessness about the future
- Memory problems, including not remembering important aspects of the traumatic event
- Difficulty maintaining close relationships
- Feeling detached from family and friends
- Lack of interest in activities you once enjoyed
- Difficulty experiencing positive emotions
- Feeling emotionally numb

Changes in physical and emotional reactions

- Being easily startled or frightened
- Always being on guard for danger
- Self-destructive behavior, such as drinking too much or driving too fast
- Trouble sleeping

- Trouble concentrating
- Irritability, angry outbursts or aggressive behavior
- Overwhelming guilt or shame

For children 6 years old and younger, signs and symptoms may also include:

- Re-enacting the traumatic event or aspects of the traumatic event through play
- Frightening dreams that may or may not include aspects of the traumatic event

Intensity of symptoms

PTSD symptoms can vary in intensity over time. You may have more PTSD symptoms when you're stressed in general, or when you come across reminders of what you went through. For example, you may hear a car backfire and relive combat experiences. Or you may see a report on the news about a sexual assault and feel overcome by memories of your own assault.

When to see a doctor

If you have disturbing thoughts and feelings about a traumatic event for more than a month, if they're severe, or if you feel you're having trouble getting your life back under control, talk to your doctor or a mental health professional. Getting treatment as soon as possible can help prevent PTSD symptoms from getting worse.

If you have suicidal thoughts

If you or someone you know has suicidal thoughts, get help right away through one or more of these resources:

- Reach out to a close friend or loved one.
- Contact a minister, a spiritual leader or someone in your faith community.
- Call a suicide hotline number — in the United States, call the National Suicide Prevention Lifeline at 1-800-273-TALK (1-800-273-8255) to reach a trained counselor. Use that same number and press 1 to reach the Veterans Crisis Line.

- Make an appointment with your doctor or a mental health professional.

When to get emergency help

If you think you may hurt yourself or attempt suicide, call 911 or your local emergency number immediately.

If you know someone who's in danger of attempting suicide or has made a suicide attempt, make sure someone stays with that person to keep him or her safe. Call 911 or your local emergency number immediately. Or, if you can do so safely, take the person to the nearest hospital emergency room.

Causes

You can develop post-traumatic stress disorder when you go through, see or learn about an event involving actual or threatened death, serious injury or sexual violation.

Doctors aren't sure why some people get PTSD. As with most mental health problems, PTSD is probably caused by a complex mix of:

- Stressful experiences, including the amount and severity of trauma you've gone through in your life
- Inherited mental health risks, such as a family history of anxiety and depression
- Inherited features of your personality — often called your temperament
- The way your brain regulates the chemicals and hormones your body releases in response to stress

Risk factors

People of all ages can have post-traumatic stress disorder. However, some factors may make you more likely to develop PTSD after a traumatic event, such as:

- Experiencing intense or long-lasting trauma

- Having experienced other trauma earlier in life, such as childhood abuse
- Having a job that increases your risk of being exposed to traumatic events, such as military personnel and first responders
- Having other mental health problems, such as anxiety or depression
- Having problems with substance misuse, such as excess drinking or drug use
- Lacking a good support system of family and friends
- Having blood relatives with mental health problems, including anxiety or depression

Kinds of traumatic events

The most common events leading to the development of PTSD include:

- Combat exposure
- Childhood physical abuse
- Sexual violence
- Physical assault
- Being threatened with a weapon
- An accident

Many other traumatic events also can lead to PTSD, such as fire, natural disaster, mugging, robbery, plane crash, torture, kidnapping, life-threatening medical diagnosis, terrorist attack, and other extreme or life-threatening events.

Complications

Post-traumatic stress disorder can disrupt your whole life—your job, your relationships, your health and your enjoyment of everyday activities.

Having PTSD may also increase your risk of other mental health problems, such as:

- Depression and anxiety

- Issues with drugs or alcohol use
- Eating disorders
- Suicidal thoughts and actions

Diagnosis

To diagnose post-traumatic stress disorder, your doctor will likely:

- **Perform a physical exam** to check for medical problems that may be causing your symptoms
- **Do a psychological evaluation** that includes a discussion of your signs and symptoms and the event or events that led up to them
- **Use the criteria in the Diagnostic and Statistical Manual of Mental Disorders (DSM-5)**, published by the American Psychiatric Association

Diagnosis of PTSD requires exposure to an event that involved the actual or possible threat of death, violence or serious injury. Your exposure can happen in one or more of these ways:

- You directly experienced the traumatic event
- You witnessed, in person, the traumatic event occurring to others
- You learned someone close to you experienced or was threatened by the traumatic event
- You are repeatedly exposed to graphic details of traumatic events (for example, if you are a first responder to the scene of traumatic events)

You may have PTSD if the problems you experience after this exposure continue for more than a month and cause significant problems in your ability to function in social and work settings and negatively impact relationships.

Treatment

Post-traumatic stress disorder treatment can help you regain a sense of control over your life. The primary treatment is psychotherapy, but can also include medication. Combining these treatments can help improve your symptoms by:

- Teaching you skills to address your symptoms
- Helping you think better about yourself, others and the world
- Learning ways to cope if any symptoms arise again
- Treating other problems often related to traumatic experiences, such as depression, anxiety, or misuse of alcohol or drugs

You don't have to try to handle the burden of PTSD on your own.

Psychotherapy

Several types of psychotherapy, also called talk therapy, may be used to treat children and adults with PTSD. Some types of psychotherapy used in PTSD treatment include:

- **Cognitive therapy.** This type of talk therapy helps you recognize the ways of thinking (cognitive patterns) that are keeping you stuck — for example, negative beliefs about yourself and the risk of traumatic things happening again. For PTSD, cognitive therapy often is used along with exposure therapy.
- **Exposure therapy.** This behavioral therapy helps you safely face both situations and memories that you find frightening so that you can learn to cope with them effectively. Exposure therapy can be particularly helpful for flashbacks and nightmares. One approach uses virtual reality programs that allow you to re-enter the setting in which you experienced trauma.
- **Eye movement desensitization and reprocessing (EMDR).** EMDR combines exposure therapy with a series of guided eye movements that help you process traumatic memories and change how you react to them.

Your therapist can help you develop stress management skills to help you better handle stressful situations and cope with stress in your life.

All these approaches can help you gain control of lasting fear after a traumatic event. You and your mental health professional can discuss what type of therapy or combination of therapies may best meet your needs.

You may try individual therapy, group therapy or both. Group therapy can offer a way to connect with others going through similar experiences.

Medications

Several types of medications can help improve symptoms of PTSD:

- **Antidepressants.** These medications can help symptoms of depression and anxiety. They can also help improve sleep problems and concentration. The selective serotonin reuptake inhibitor (SSRI) medications sertraline (Zoloft) and paroxetine (Paxil) are approved by the Food and Drug Administration (FDA) for PTSD treatment.
- **Anti-anxiety medications.** These drugs can relieve severe anxiety and related problems. Some anti-anxiety medications have the potential for abuse, so they are generally used only for a short time.
- **Prazosin.** If symptoms include insomnia with recurrent nightmares, a drug called prazosin (Minipress) may help. Although not specifically FDA approved for PTSD treatment, prazosin may reduce or suppress nightmares in many people with PTSD.

You and your doctor can work together to figure out the best medication, with the fewest side effects, for your symptoms and situation. You may see an improvement in your mood and other symptoms within a few weeks.

Tell your doctor about any side effects or problems with medications. You may need to try more than one or a combination of medications, or your doctor may need to adjust your dosage or medication schedule before finding the right fit for you.

PTSD Needs Better and Consistent Diagnosis

Peter Barglow

Dr. Peter Barglow practices psychiatry in Berkeley, California. He received his medical degree from Northwestern University's Feinberg School of Medicine.

Post-Traumatic Stress Disorder is a diagnosis fully accepted by the U.S. Veterans Administration, psychiatrists, and the American public. But PTSD does not meet the criteria for a real psychiatric-medical disease.

Since 1980 Post-Traumatic Stress Disorder (PTSD) has been a major mental illness category of the American Psychiatric Association's (APA) *Diagnostic and Statistical Manual of Mental Disorders* (DSM). In this article I critically examine the use of this diagnosis to treat soldiers suffering from the aftermath of physical and emotional war trauma. The term *PTSD*, referring to a psychiatric disease or disorder, appeared in the *New York Times* 19,000 times in the ten years between August 14, 2000, and August 15, 2010, compared to only 450 times during the prior twenty years.

Today, 400,000 war veterans obtain financial assistance for this medical condition. Of two million Iraq and Afghanistan veterans, 10 percent are estimated to have PTSD. It is the topic of hundreds of psychiatric and psychology articles per year and absorbs large annual national expenditures for treatment and research. Out of $3.8 billion awarded as a result of U.S. Congressional funding bill HR2638 to the U.S. Veterans Administration (VA) in 2009 for mental illness, the single largest mental disease category funded was PTSD. Between 2004 and 2009, 20 percent of the estimated half a million Iraq-Afghanistan war veteran patients were treated for PTSD. The first year of this health care cost was 1.4 billion dollars (U.S. Congressional Budget Office 2012). How did it come

"We Can't Treat Soldiers' PTSD Without a Better Diagnosis," by Peter Barglow, The Committee for Skeptical Inquiry (CSI), May-June 2012. Reprinted by permission of Skeptical Inquiry.

about that the diagnosis of PTSD became so widely accepted by the Veterans Health System (VHA), the American Psychiatric Association, and the American public?

This question first was raised in my mind when two decades ago I did a psychiatric evaluation of a fifty-year-old Vietnam veteran, a Purple Heart recipient with a voluminous official history of treatment for PTSD. A few weeks earlier he had threatened to kill both himself and his therapist in her office at a VA outpatient psychiatric clinic. He was disabled by use of a Taser gun by police, who had stormed the building.

They seized him while he was unconscious, and transported him to a prison. The patient was an unemployed married Hispanic man, wounded during the war's Tet offensive. His record indicated that he had suffered for many years from PTSD symptoms such as hyper-arousal, insomnia with nightmares about Viet Cong snipers, and paranoid fears; these increased during binges of alcohol use. I had anticipated a confrontation with a huge, menacing figure but found the man to be a mild-mannered little guy who resembled Woody Allen. He said that he had noted none of the above PTSD symptoms for many months, but he was deeply concerned about retaining maximum VA compensation for this diagnosis.

My surprise at the apparent cure of this former soldier's mental disease prompted me to review several dozen medical-psychiatric records of Vietnam veterans diagnosed with PTSD by me or other VA and military psychiatrists. I also reinterviewed over a dozen patients. PTSD symptoms listed in DSM-IV are memory loss or distressing flashbacks referring to battle events, hyper-vigilance, poor sleep with recurrent nightmares, irritability, startles, and episodes of emotional numbness. (This last symptom appears to be the single most important one in verifying the PTSD diagnosis [Pietrzak 2009].) The current APA diagnosis requires appearance of characteristic symptoms after a latency period of time subsequent to a specific severe precipitating traumatic event—constituting "Criterion A," discussed below.

Several patients also shared with me considerable discomfort with the label of PTSD, which to them signified an emasculating weakness or dishonesty rather than a genuine illness. A search for financial benefits did appear to be one important factor in shaping the narratives of both patients and clinicians. This suggested the advantages for veterans ("secondary gain") of reporting typical PTSD symptoms, but it also reflected compassion of VA evaluating staff toward patients who clearly had suffered severely during and after warfare. The record review showed considerable co-morbidity (when a disease category overlaps with one or more other major psychiatric diagnoses, such as Major Depressive Disorder or Acute Stress Disorder), and many of the patients used addicting drugs (alcohol, marijuana, pain killers, or amphetamine stimulants). Substance dependence was almost impossible to disentangle from PTSD symptoms.

Unlike my patient whom I described earlier, few veterans with PTSD improved very much during the many years that had elapsed since their initial clinical assessment. Often DSM-IV clinical criteria for PTSD had been carelessly applied to veterans whose post-war lives had been dominated by poverty, unemployment, homelessness, and family disruptions because of violence, drugs, or divorce.

A Brief History of PTSD

The DSM classification system was created in 1952. Its first two editions (I [1952] and II [1968]) were based upon Freud's psychoanalytic formulations. The etiology of mental disorders was thought to originate in early-life traumatic experiences. However, a major change in thinking about the concept of a mental disorder and its etiology occurred in the 1970s, reflected in DSM-III (1980). There was a marked shift away from attention to early childhood histories. Valiant attempts were made to mimic mainstream medicine and surgery using their ancient etiological categories— trauma, cancer producing, infectious, toxic, degenerative, genetic, metabolic, and endocrine.

But psychiatric disorders proved difficult to classify with quantifiable chemical findings or specific identifying clinical signs. The revised DSM systems (in an effort to establish reliable guidelines for diagnosticians) still had to rely substantially upon self-reported descriptions of symptoms, not on measurable data. DSM I–III systems' categorical decisions reflected literature reviews, some data analysis, periodic field trials, and the outcome of verbal debates between experts. That complex decision-making process used patients' clinical information but had to rely upon fallible doctors' judgments. A better approach to diagnosis creation was clearly needed, and so psychiatric research in the early 1990s was increasingly devoted to the human brain.

PTSD was first listed in the 1980 edition of the APA's *Diagnostic and Statistical Manual of Mental Disorders* (DSM-III) and modified later in DSM-IV and DSM-IV-TR. Its appearance in the official APA nomenclature followed years of intense lobbying effort by Vietnam veterans' organizations, activist social workers, psychologists, and anti-war psychiatrists. Advocates for the PTSD diagnosis asserted that traumatic memories of war experiences were being revived in contemporary time, producing a new serious mental illness. Soldiers should be treated and compensated for a disorder attributable to events that took place many years earlier. This understanding necessitated a shift in attention away from the psychodynamics of individual veterans, and other risk variables, to a heavy emphasis upon a single major factor—the negative aftereffects of war trauma on later mental health.

The leaders of the American psychiatric profession who became midwives to the official birth of PTSD during the 1970s shared today's almost universal belief that large-scale suffering of others matters universally and that it demands to be recognized and ameliorated. This moral value probably accounted for the diagnostic inclusion of Criterion A, which has generated heated debate since its original inclusion in the 1980 DSM-III. Criterion A for PTSD states that a patient diagnosed with PTSD was confronted with "events that involved actual or threatened death or serious injury..."

and responded with "intense fear, helplessness, or horror." Criterion A made PTSD the only DSM mental disorder that required a subjective appraisal of an external environmental stressor as part of its diagnosis. Retention of the trauma criterion has been supported by the observation that studies of symptoms unconnected to a specific precipitant have failed to identify any "characteristic set of symptoms" (North et al. 2009). Also this position is consistent with the conclusion that treatment concentrating on specific trauma memories and their meaning is more effective than nontrauma-focused therapy (Ehlers et al. 2010).

But the criterion does have many problems. One statistical piece of evidence against inclusion of documentation of a quantitative trigger to facilitate making a diagnosis is that most soldiers do not develop an anxiety disorder or any major psychiatric disorder even when exposed to the most horrific trauma. The widespread application of Criterion A ignores vast individual variations in patients' resilience and capacity to adapt. Its reliance upon subjective reports rather than objective eyewitness evidence further weakens its scientific status. For the preceding reasons, Criterion A does not appear in the PTSD diagnosis category of the International Classification of Mental Diseases (ICD-10).

The importance of this diagnostic criterion in determining the size of disability benefits for veterans with PTSD has been diminished by new VA standards issued by the Obama administration in 2010. The VA policy now states that VA psychiatrists need not require proof of the quantitative impact of a traumatic precipitant. This VA policy change was inspired by a deep concern for the suffering of victims and largely ignored the APA's PTSD Criterion A, which may be deleted from DSM-V's definition.

Does PTSD Meet the Criteria for a Valid Psychiatric Diagnosis?

The diagnosis of PTSD has always had many critics, ranging from McHugh and Treisman (2007), who boldly consider PTSD to be a "faddish postulate" that "creates a medical condition out of normal distress," to the meticulous scholars Rosen and Lilienfeld (2007), who concluded that the disorder's "core assumptions and hypothesized mechanisms lack compelling or consistent empirical support." Robins and Guze (1970) proposed five research areas in which a psychiatric diagnosis might be validated: (1) clinical description including precipitants and diagnostic stability over time; (2) biological, hormonal, and radiological quantitative evidence; (3) distinct boundaries between the disorder's characteristics and other psychiatric conditions; (4) family or genetic statistical connections between patients in the diagnostic category; (5) treatment relevance and success related to precise diagnosis. Schizophrenia, major depression, and alcohol dependence are examples of mental disorders that have achieved considerable legitimacy through this process, but PTSD as a diagnosis for war veterans has not yet attained comparable validity.

The above five research domains constitute fertile ground for further re-examining PTSD's diagnostic weaknesses and generating potential remedies:

Clinical Description and Precipitants. The VA patient I described earlier is an example of diagnostic instability. The weakness of Criterion A suggests a problematic relation between PTSD and specific precipitants. These days it is obvious that patients suffering from the emotional aftermath of warfare have not demonstrated consistent symptom patterns. Perhaps, then, we can better comprehend the emotional toll of recent American wars by applying the sociological concept that throughout history powerful professional and political communities have constructed truth, established definitions, and generated rules for the interpretation of trauma's impact. This viewpoint provides insight into the history of emotional war trauma and explains its massively varying conceptualizations and manifestations. Like "Historical Critical Psychopathology" (Baldwin et al. 2004), it emphasizes "historically situated and contingent aspects of mental disorders."

Using such a framework of understanding, the earliest PTSD portrayal may be the fourth-century character Herakles, created

Iraq and Afghan war veterans

Since September 11, 2001, more than 2.2 million US service members have been deployed to war zones.

PATIENTS TREATED
1.4 million Afghan and Iraq war veterans eligible for VA health care

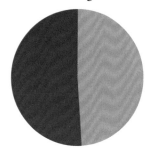

711,986
VA patients treated

MENTAL HEALTH
Treated patients who had mental health conditions

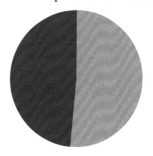

367,749
With mental health conditions

POST-TRAUMATIC STRESS
Treated patients with potential post-traumatic stress disorder

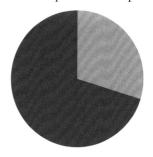

211,819
With potential PTSD

9,700 average number of new veteran patients each month
938,000 estimated new veteran claims by the end of 2013

SOURCE: Veterans for Common Sense

by the dramatist Euripides. Driven insane by a Greek goddess, he suffered a transitory murderous frenzy precipitated by the violence of his twelve labors. A messenger inquires of him, "Has the blood of the men you recently killed driven you out of your wits?" Over two millennia later, emotional victims of American Civil War trauma were said to be afflicted with "Soldier's Heart" (1864–1868), and those suffering from "Railway Spine" in America (circa 1886) showed psychological and physical characteristics quite different from those used currently to identify PTSD. Such patients in the latter half of the nineteenth century experienced bodily shaking and tremors of arms and legs, stuttering, and limping, but they did not report anger, numbing sensations, or flashback symptoms as contemporary PTSD victims often do.

Civil War victims' clinical presentations resembled those reported during the Russo-Japanese War (1904–1905), when emotional casualties began to be treated with considerable respect. Many Russian psychiatrists argued that afflicted soldiers had a "real illness." English and German "shell shock" victims and Russian "contusion" casualties during World War I (1914–1918) also demonstrated a quite different symptom constellation from that characteristic of PTSD in twenty-first-century America. European patients manifested multiple sensory-motor signs such as deafness, muteness, and blindness. Such striking historical dissimilarities in the psychological clinical phenomena of post-war emotional syndromes suggest they resemble cultural constructions more than disease categories. Cultural factors may also influence treatment outcome; PTSD victims in Kenya found help in their religious community, in contrast to Oklahoma City bombing survivors who received benefit from medical treatments (North 2009).

Brain Structure and Neurophysiologic Studies. Since DSM-IV appeared in 1994, there has been a massive increase in U.S. research efforts to demonstrate that an organic central nervous system disturbance causes PTSD. This campaign was named "embodiment" by skeptics who deplored the use of inappropriate comparison groups and the contaminating role of "cultural expectancy" in the studies mobilized to create a more precise and useful PTSD diagnostic category (Baldwin et al. 2004). The search for organic brain changes as the source of PTSD symptoms was fueled by the belief that war's emotional stress could affect brain physiology and chemistry negatively, producing permanent and characteristic post-trauma symptom patterns. The first major effort to argue this position originated during the 1905 Russo-Japanese war through studies of soldiers who suffered from "contusion," a puzzling nervous breakdown during or after combat. The psychology versus brain change etiological debate became even more active during World War I (1914–1918) in Europe with research about "shell shock."

Since the Korean War (1950–1953), multiple research efforts in English-speaking countries have sought distinct patterns of psycho-physiological arousal in PTSD. But measurements of neurotransmitter levels across most populations with the disease showed marked differences of quantity, including a complete failure to show heightened responses in a quarter of cases. Acute stress has been shown to activate the central nervous system to release catecholamines, norepinephrine and epinephrine, into the bloodstream. But patients with acute PTSD symptoms have normal plasma concentrations of these substances. Only those with chronic PTSD have increased cerebrospinal fluid norepinephrine levels that correlate with the severity of PTSD symptoms. But all situations that produce stress for human primates—not just emotional war trauma—are associated with catecholamine release.

Malfunction of the hypothalamus-pituitary-adrenal hormonal axis has been postulated in those PTSD victims who have lowered blood cortisol levels and who demonstrate enhanced cortisol suppression with dexamethasone and exaggerated cortisol secretion during stressful exposure. But findings have been inconsistent or subtle, and many hormonal studies lack hormone level data pre-exposure to stress. Recent prospective longitudinal studies have shown that low cortisol levels in PTSD patients may actually have preceded, not followed, a traumatic event. Finally, cortisol levels vary dramatically secondary to numerous biological, temporal, and psychological variables, making them an unreliable biological marker.

Another major effort to find a neurobiological correlate to PTSD has focused upon brain morphology studied through brain scanning. Extrapolating from animal stress models, it was suggested that elevated corticosteroids (adrenocorticotropic hormone, or cortisol) in patients with PTSD could produce toxic damage to the hippocampus. The function of memory is thought to reside there, and the structure's compromise might be related to flashbacks and nightmare symptoms. But there is only weak evidence for this link in humans. Also, most human studies have failed to control for other psychiatric disorders associated with hippocampal atrophy, including alcoholism. Smaller hippocampal volume is a relatively nonspecific finding that also has been reported to be associated with depression and even borderline personality disorder. Statistical associations between emotional war trauma, PTSD, and size of brain structures remain highly speculative and unproven.

PTSD Boundaries with Other Psychiatric Disorders. The diagnosis of PTSD today is made by the use of standardized tests, such as the self-report PTSD Symptoms Checklist, the Clinician Administered PTSD Scale, and a Clinical Interview for DSM Disorders. But still, PTSD is poorly separated from other major psychological disorders, and its diagnostic stability is low, as illustrated by my patient vignette in the introduction of this article. Using current diagnostic criteria, PTSD has consistently been found to overlap other major psychiatric disorders. Kessler et al. (1996) found that 88 percent of a large sample of U.S. patients with PTSD met DSM-III or IV clinical-case data criteria for at least one other major mental disorder, most often chemical dependence. PTSD does have convergent validity with major depressive disorder (95 percent lifetime and 50 percent co-occurring) in combat veterans. Further research on the centrality of "numbing" may help establish PTSD as an independent diagnostic entity (Pietrzak 2009).

The medical condition traumatic brain injury (TBI) is also difficult to distinguish from PTSD. TBI is a brain concussion caused by a blow to the head that changes a soldier's consciousness, resulting in amnesia and neurological abnormalities. TBI can result from damage sustained from bullets, bombs, falls, or vehicle accidents. TBIs may be conceptually related to the above historical concepts of English "shell shock" and Russian "contusion" traumata.

Genetic Studies Related to Emotional Consequences of Battle Trauma. Such research remains suggestive rather than convincing. Molecular genetics has yet to identify specific genes that confer a vulnerability to PTSD. Although genetic research does support a biological component of PTSD, it has failed to distinguish it from other related (co-morbid) psychiatric diagnoses. One study showed that shared genetics accounted for 30 percent of the variance in PTSD symptoms in Vietnam War veteran twins, even after taking into account different levels of combat exposure. Stein et al. (2002) proved in 1999 that genetics contributes to both the tendency for a subject to be exposed to traumas involving assault and a vulnerability to develop PTSD after exposure. Such results have led to the theory that a combination of genes and environment are necessary to develop PTSD symptoms, a proposal that contradicts the assumption that trauma is the core etiological agent. The preceding observations are consistent with the idea that PTSD may be distinguishable from other common disorders.

The PTSD Diagnosis Used to Guide Treatment of the Illness. Experts today do not yet know if the prolonged emotional suffering following physical or emotional war trauma can be ameliorated, let alone cured. The Institute of Medicine carefully evaluated fifty-three drug studies and thirty-seven psychotherapy studies (National Academy of Sciences 2008). Their team of academic specialists examined the evidence (or lack of evidence) for the success of anticonvulsants, benzodiazepines, MAOIs, SSRIs and other antidepressants, and other remedies such as Eye Movement Desensitization and Reprocessing (EMDR). Their summary concluded that there was insufficient scientific evidence to determine that any treatment (except possibly Prolonged Exposure Therapy) had beneficial long-term effects for PTSD. Their report noted that drug manufacturers had funded many studies, possibly biasing their outcomes, and that too many research patients had dropped out of experiments to allow robust conclusions about efficacy. Little is known about what kind of patients benefit from which treatments.

On April 26, 2010, the *New York Times* published an article that described the plight of veterans who were physical and emotional casualties, slated for discharge, temporarily hospitalized at Fort Carson's Warrior Transition Battalion unit. Inmates and their close family members depicted absent or poor psychiatric treatment, overmedication, bureaucratic delays, and prescription of drugs that fostered addiction to heroin. Poly-pharmacy treatment for PTSD (combining anti-anxiety, antidepressant, antipsychotic, and anti-insomnia agents) recently has been associated with accidental death in U.S. veterans with this condition (*New York Times*, February 14, 2011). Such reports are painful reminders that neither the U.S. military establishment nor the Veterans Administration has learned quite enough to treat victims of emotional war trauma effectively.

"Prolonged Exposure Therapy," originated and proven efficacious by Edna Foa, remains the most evidence-supported successful intervention. It helps traumatized soldiers to approach trauma-related thoughts, feelings, and situations previously avoided because they cause distress. The technique uses education, breathing exercises, safe re-exposure to painful avoided or unavoidable war experiences, and "talking through" a patient's individual history of trauma. A couple of my own PTSD patients who tried this method felt that it reawakened and reactivated traumatic memories that appeared to have been forgotten, making their emotional distress even worse. This possible disadvantage for a portion of the war-traumatized population may be comparable to the reaction that some alcoholic addicts have experienced during Alcoholics Anonymous meetings. The explicit sharing with others of vivid experiences associated with the ravages of the disease stimulates them to drink right after a seemingly successful meeting. Also evidence for effectiveness of exposure therapy is not as strong for veterans as it is for civilians.

Recent empirical research studies indicate that cognitive processing therapy (CPT) is also often effective in treating the emotional aftermath of warfare. The method tries to modify perceptions of a specific war trauma and its reproduction.

Conclusions

Currently there is little benefit in directing treatment interventions toward patients diagnosed with PTSD, an amorphous disease category with indistinct conceptual boundaries and without a firm biological foundation. Money might be more prudently spent on immediate post-trauma intervention addressing individual patients' symptoms. Treatment of concurrent depression, addiction, and other anxiety conditions may be far more valuable than targeting chronic symptoms and decades-later psychological aftermaths. All approaches must ameliorate veterans' social conditions— poverty, homelessness, and marital and familial friction. Acute post-traumatic symptoms must not be transformed into a chronic compensated disability, set in stone by its designation as an official major DSM disease syndrome.

The use of the PTSD diagnosis may contribute to treatment failures because it fabricates a spurious invalid category of illness, rather than seeing a unique sufferer. A humane society must compensate and reward all military victims with generosity, but strict application of Criterion A of the PTSD diagnosis does not accomplish this purpose. PTSD appears to be more of a social construction than a medical brain disease, and as of this date can best be considered "as encompassing a broad range of possible reactions to adverse events" (Rosen and Lilienfeld 2007, 858). Finally, the stigma associated with this diagnosis of a mental illness may keep some veterans from seeking care. The shortcomings of the current PTSD diagnosis jeopardize the treatment of the terrible aftermath of war's emotional trauma.

There's No Wrong Way to Respond to Post-Traumatic Stress

The National Depressive and Manic-Depressive Association

National Depressive and Manic-Depressive Association, now called Depressive and Bipolar Support Alliance, is a Chicago-based organization that offers online and print resources and sponsors close to 650 support groups and more than 250 chapters.

Responding to Traumatic Events

When we witness or experience a traumatic event, such as an act of violence or a natural disaster, we are affected mentally and emotionally. Whether we are personally involved in the incident, have family or friends who are injured or killed, are a rescue worker or health care provider, or even if we learn about the event through the news, we will experience some sort of emotional response. Each of us will react differently and there is no right or wrong way to feel. The emotional response each person has is a normal part of the healing process.

What you might feel
Though everyone is affected differently at different times, you may experience:

- Numbness, inability to experience feelings, feelings of disconnectedness
- Changing emotions such as shock, denial, guilt or self-blame
- Extreme sadness, crying
- Mood changes such as irritability, anxiousness, nervousness, pessimism or indifference
- Inability to concentrate
- Recurring memories or bad dreams about the event
- Social withdrawal, isolation, strained personal relationships

"Coping With Unexpected Events: Depression and Trauma," Depression and Bipolar Support Alliance (DBSA). Reprinted by permission .

- Physical symptoms such as unexplained aches and pains, nausea, fatigue, loss of energy
- Changes in eating habits or sleeping patterns
- Increased consumption of alcohol

These feelings, a normal part of grieving and recovering from any trauma, are also symptoms of situational or reactive depression. If these feelings persist for more than two weeks or begin to interfere with your daily living, if you are abusing alcohol or illegal drugs, or if you have thoughts of death or suicide, they are symptoms of a more serious episode of depression. This is a heightened reaction to an abnormal situation, not a character flaw or sign of personal weakness.

Depression is a treatable medical illness. Most people respond to treatment and are able to bring their lives back into balance. The number of traumatic events you have previously experienced may also affect your response. Pay attention to your own symptoms, and be ready to seek a doctor's help if your symptoms should persist or worsen. If you're not sure if your symptoms are part of your grieving or something more serious, seek the opinion of a doctor or therapist, early. Don't wait for your symptoms to become severe.

The healthiest things you can do for yourself and your loved ones are: be alert to changes in your feelings and moods, allow yourself time to heal and feel free to seek appropriate assistance. We know from a variety of studies that the chemistry in the brain changes in response to trauma. Seeking assistance from a health care professional after experiencing trauma is a reasonable response to a medical issue. The aftereffects of a traumatic experience are not something you can "pull yourself out of" or "toughen up" enough to "snap out of." The best response to trauma-related depression often involves three things: medical intervention, therapeutic assistance and peer support.

If you have thoughts of self-harm or suicide, contact your health care provider, a family member or friend, or call 911 immediately.

How to Cope with Depression After Trauma

The healing process after a traumatic event takes time, especially if you have experienced a personal loss. It is helpful to:

- Allow yourself time to grieve. Don't try to rush your own recovery or hide or deny your feelings.
- Talk to friends and family members about how you feel. Ask for support from people you trust.
- If the trauma you are coping with is prominent in the news media, limit your exposure to it. Get the facts you need, but try not to focus all of your energy on the disturbing event, reports and images of which may be repeated many times in the news.
- If you attend a support group, or have in the past, spend time at support group meetings or use other resources the group provides.
- Keep to your daily routine. Even if you don't feel like it, do your best to eat balanced meals and get plenty of rest.
- Continue taking any prescribed medications. Discontinuing medication or changing the amount you take can make your situation worse.
- Stay physically active. Even light exercise such as walking can help minimize physical effects of stress.
- Avoid making major life decisions during a time when you are under a lot of stress.
- Don't use alcohol or illegal drugs to cope with the stress. If you find you are unable to stop drinking or using, talk to a trusted friend, family member or a health care provider, or contact a recovery program such as Alcoholics Anonymous, whose phone number can be found in your local telephone book.
- Find out how you can help or get involved. Volunteer to give blood or donate money or clothing to a local charity. Contribute in any way that feels right to you.
- Spend time doing things you enjoy. Paint a picture, work in your garden, play a musical instrument, watch a movie, play with children, spend time with friends, or something

else that helps you. You may want to listen to music or read a book before going to sleep, rather than watching the news.

- Get help for yourself if you need it. Don't feel ashamed, afraid, or guilty about talking to a doctor, therapist, or member of the clergy if you need to. Be honest about all of your symptoms. You have every right to feel the way you do.

Psychotherapy, or "talk therapy" is an important part of treatment, which can work alone in some cases. A good therapist can help you work through the feelings you are having and develop skills to help with your recovery.

There are many effective medications available to treat depression today. Depression involves an imbalance of chemicals in the brain, and medications work on the brain to bring these chemicals back into balance. There is no more shame in taking medication for depression than there is in taking medication for diabetes, asthma, or other medical conditions.

How to help others cope
Sometimes friends and family may respond to a trauma differently than you do, even if they have experienced the same traumatic event. There is no right or wrong way to deal with a traumatic event. You may want to:

- Be on the lookout for others' signs of stress. Listen to others and allow them to express their feelings and reactions.
- Respect the fact that others may respond to trauma differently than you do. Seek ways to support them that work with their own unique experiences and responses.
- Give support and companionship. This involves understanding, patience and encouragement. Invite the person for walks, outings and other activities.
- Avoid telling someone to "get on with life" or that "things could have been worse."
- If a friend or family member is in need of a doctor or counselor's help, assist him or her in getting that help. This

may involve making an appointment and accompanying him or her to the appointment.

- Take any remarks about suicide seriously. Make sure the person discusses these feelings with his or her doctor immediately. Go with him or her to see a doctor or counselor if necessary. If you believe immediate self-harm is possible, call 911.

If you are experiencing stress or depression due to the trauma, you may be less able to help others. If so, be patient with yourself and seek others who can step in and assist your friend or family member who needs help.

Helping and talking with children

There is no way to completely shield children from events as they happen, but it is better for them to get their information from you than from someone else. Not knowing what is happening may contribute to their stress or make them imagine things are even worse than they are. Children absorb and process events just as you do, though they may not be able to express their feelings as easily. To help children and adolescents, you should:

- Help them to talk about their feelings. Let them know it is all right to feel sad or scared, and that there are no bad or wrong emotions.
- Explain what happened in easy-to-understand language, and answer questions honestly. If you don't know the answer to a question, it is all right to admit it. Keep conversations short and at a level that's appropriate for the child's age.
- If news media is replaying an event, make sure children are aware that what they are seeing is a repeat, and is not continually happening. Limit children's exposure to graphic news coverage, so they are less likely to see the event numerous times.
- Avoid discussions involving blame or retaliation for an event.
- Reassure children that they are safe, and that adults are working hard to take care of and protect people.

- Keep the family routine on schedule as much as possible.
- Remind children that you love them. Give them comfort and affection.
- Find ways for children and adolescents to help, such as choosing toys or clothing to donate to charity.
- Encourage children to draw pictures or play, and express their feelings in non-verbal ways.
- Create time for family events. Spend time together as a family.

As with all friends and loved ones, be aware of symptoms of depression in children or adolescents which linger or worsen, such as lack of interest in school or friends, increased or decreased eating or sleeping, excessive or uncontrollable crying and unexplained fears. If these symptoms are present for two or more weeks, or interfere with your child's day-to-day routine, consult your pediatrician or family doctor. He or she may be able to help or may refer you to a mental health professional with experience treating children or adolescents. Be especially aware of comments about self-harm or suicide. Take these comments very seriously and seek help immediately.

What Is Post-Traumatic Stress Disorder (PTSD)?

After exposure to an extremely distressing event, some people develop posttraumatic stress disorder (PTSD), which is characterized by:

- Having experienced an immediate response to a disturbing event which involved intense fear, helplessness or horror
- Continually re-experiencing the event ("flashbacks") through images, dreams, and/or a sense of re-living the experience
- Avoiding any reminders, thoughts or people associated with the event, or having memory loss associated with the event
- Symptoms of increased irritability, such as outbursts of anger, difficulty falling asleep or trouble concentrating
- A sense of heightened awareness, exaggerated response to being startled, feelings of impending doom or danger

- Symptoms that last longer than one month and impair functioning at work, in relationships or in other areas of life

When these symptoms occur within the first month after a traumatic experience, but lift within four weeks, they are known as acute stress disorder.

Post-traumatic stress disorder usually occurs within the first three months after a traumatic experience, but in some cases, there is a delay of more than six months before symptoms appear. Length of symptoms varies from person to person. Approximately half of the people affected by PTSD tend to recover within 3 months. For many others, however, symptoms last longer than one year and require treatment in order to improve.

Untreated PTSD can lead to other mental and physical illnesses. While talking about these symptoms may be very painful and confusing, these symptoms can be treated, and treatment can bring relief. Having symptoms that do not go away and needing to seek treatment are not character flaws or signs of personal weakness. If your symptoms continue, or if they interfere with your daily functioning, discuss them with your health care provider.

PTSD and depression

Rates of depression are very high in people who experience PTSD. In one study supported by the National Institute of Mental Health, 40 percent of people who had PTSD were experiencing depression one month and four months later. Early intervention is extremely helpful in treating PTSD and depression.

Preventing Suicide

After experiencing a traumatic event, some people may have thoughts of suicide. These thoughts are expressions of a treatable illness. If you are having thoughts of suicide, don't let feelings of shame or embarrassment keep you from talking about it with a friend, family member, clergy member or health care provider. Seek help right away.

- Tell your doctor or mental health professional immediately.
- Tell a friend, family member or other support person.
- Make sure you do not have access to guns, sharp objects, old medications or anything you could use to harm yourself. Have a family member lock them away or dispose of them completely.
- Instruct a close supporter to take away your car keys, credit cards and checkbook when you are having strong suicidal feelings.
- Keep pictures of your favorite people visible at all times to remind you that they are there to support you.
- If you need someone to stay with you, don't be afraid to ask.

If someone you know is having thoughts of suicide, take these thoughts seriously and help him or her to get help. Make sure he or she does not have access to weapons or medications and is not left alone. Go with him or her to a health care provider to seek medical and therapeutic assistance.

If You Live with Depression or Bipolar Disorder

If you live with depression or bipolar disorder (also known as manic depression), a stressful, traumatic event may be even more difficult to cope with. Be aware of the possibility of your depression worsening, or episodes of mania being triggered. Use resources that have given you relief and comfort in the past, and stay in touch with trusted friends and family members, your health care provider and your DBSA support group. Continue your treatment plan, take medications as prescribed and make healthy lifestyle choices. Let your health care provider know right away if your symptoms worsen, and discuss your treatment options. Talk with others about what you are experiencing.

The benefits of support groups for people with depression and bipolar disorder

With a grassroots network of over 1000 DBSA support groups, no one with depression or bipolar disorder needs to feel alone or ashamed. DBSA may offer one or more support groups in your community. Each group has a professional advisor and appointed facilitators. Members are people living with depression or bipolar disorder and their loved ones. Along with treatment, DBSA support groups:

- Can help individuals stick with their prescribed treatment plans and avoid hospitalization
- Provide a forum for mutual acceptance, understanding and self-discovery
- Help people understand that having depression or bipolar disorder does not define who they are
- Give people the opportunity to benefit from the experience of others who have "been there"

Returning Soldiers View PTSD Diagnoses as Self-Fulfilling Doom

David Dobbs

David Dobbs is a freelance science and medical writer in Montpelier, Vermont. His essays and features have appeared in well-respected magazines, including Scientific American, the Atlantic, New York Times Magazine and National Geographic.

In 2006, soon after returning from military service in Ramadi, Iraq, during the bloodiest period of the war, Captain Matt Stevens of the Vermont National Guard began to have a problem with PTSD, or post-traumatic stress disorder. Stevens's problem was not that he had PTSD. It was that he began to have doubts about PTSD: The condition was real, he knew, but as a diagnosis he saw it being dangerously overemphasized.

Stevens led the medics tending an armored brigade of 800 soldiers, and his team patched together GIs and Iraqi citizens almost every day. He saw horrific things. Once home, he had his share, he says, of "nights where I'd wake up and it would be clear I wasn't going to sleep again."

He was not surprised: "I would *expect* people to have nightmares for a while when they came back." But as he kept track of his unit in the U.S., he saw troops greeted by both a larger culture and a medical culture, especially in the Department of Veterans Affairs (VA), that seemed reflexively to view bad memories, nightmares and any other sign of distress as an indicator of PTSD.

"Clinicians aren't separating the few who really have PTSD from those who are experiencing things like depression or anxiety or social and reintegration problems, or who are just taking some time getting over it," says Stevens. He worries that many of these men and women are being pulled into a treatment and disability regime that will mire them in a self-fulfilling vision of a brain rewired, a psyche permanently haunted.

Stevens, now a major, and still on reserve duty while he works as a physician's assistant, is far from alone in worrying about the reach of PTSD. Over the last five years or so, a long-simmering academic debate over PTSD's conceptual basis and rate of occurrence has begun to boil over into the practice of trauma psychology and to roil military culture as well. Critiques, originally raised by military historians and a few psychologists, are now being advanced by a broad array of experts, including giants of psychology, psychiatry, diagnosis, and epidemiology such as Columbia's Robert Spitzer and Michael First, who oversaw the last two editions of the American Psychiatric Association's Diagnostic and Statistical Manual of Mental Disorders, the DSM-III and DSM-IV; Paul McHugh, the longtime chair of Johns Hopkins University's psychiatry department; Michigan State University epidemiologist Naomi Breslau; and Harvard University psychologist Richard McNally, a leading authority in the dynamics of memory and trauma, and perhaps the most forceful of the critics. The diagnostic criteria for PTSD, they assert, represent a faulty, outdated construct that has been badly overextended so that it routinely mistakes depression, anxiety, or even normal adjustment for a unique and particularly stubborn ailment.

This quest to scale back the definition of PTSD and its application stands to affect the expenditure of billions of dollars, the diagnostic framework of psychiatry, the effectiveness of a huge treatment and disability infrastructure, and, most important, the mental health and future lives of hundreds of thousands of U.S. combat veterans and other PTSD patients. Standing in the way of reform is conventional wisdom, deep cultural resistance and foundational concepts of trauma psychology. Nevertheless it is time, as Spitzer recently argued, to "save PTSD from itself."

Casting a Wide Net

The overdiagnosis of PTSD, critics say, shows in the numbers, starting with the seminal study of PTSD prevalence, the

1990 National Vietnam Veterans Readjustment Survey. The NVVRS covered more than 1,000 Vietnam veterans in 1988 and reported that 15.4 percent of them had PTSD at that time and 31 percent had suffered it at some point since the war. That 31 percent has been the standard estimate of PTSD incidence among veterans ever since.

In 2006, however, Columbia University epidemiologist Bruce Dohrenwend, hoping to resolve nagging questions about the study, reworked the numbers. When he had culled the poorly documented diagnoses, he found that the 1988 rate was 9 percent, and the lifetime rate just 18 percent.

McNally shares the general admiration for Dohrenwend's careful work. Soon after it was published, however, McNally asserted that Dohrenwend's numbers were still too high because he counted as PTSD cases those veterans with only mild, subdiagnostic symptoms, people rated as "generally functioning pretty well." If you included only those suffering "clinically significant impairment" — the level generally required for diagnosis and insurance compensation in most mental illness — the rates fell yet further, to 5.4 percent at the time of the survey and 11 percent lifetime. It was not 1 in 3 veterans that eventually got PTSD, but 1 in 9 — and only 1 in 18 had it at any given time. The NVVRS, in other words, appears to have overstated PTSD rates in Vietnam vets by almost 300 percent.

"PTSD is a real thing, without a doubt," says McNally. "But as a diagnosis, PTSD has become so flabby and overstretched, so much a part of the culture, that we are almost certainly mistaking other problems for PTSD, and thus mistreating them."

The idea that PTSD is overdiagnosed seems to contradict reports of resistance in the military and the VA to recognizing PTSD — denials of PTSD diagnoses and disability benefits, military clinicians discharging soldiers instead of treating them, and a disturbing increase in suicides among veterans of the Middle East wars. Yet the two trends are consistent. The VA's PTSD caseload has more than doubled since 2000, mostly owing to newly diagnosed

Vietnam veterans. The poor and erratic response to current soldiers and recent vets, with some being pulled in quickly to PTSD treatments and others discouraged or denied, may be the panicked stumbling of an overloaded system.

Overhauling both the diagnosis and the VA's care system, say critics, will ensure better care for genuine PTSD patients as well as those being misdiagnosed. But the would-be reformers face fierce opposition. "This argument," McNally notes, "tends to really piss some people off." Veterans send him threatening emails. Colleagues accuse him of dishonoring veterans, dismissing suffering, discounting the costs of war. Dean Kilpatrick, a University of South Carolina traumatologist who is president of the International Society for Traumatic Stress Studies (ISTSS), once essentially called McNally a liar.

A Problematic Diagnosis

The most recent Diagnostic and Statistical Manual (DSM-IV) defines PTSD as the presence of three symptom clusters — reexperiencing via nightmares or flashbacks; numbing or withdrawal; and hyperarousal, evident in irritability, insomnia, aggression, or poor concentration — that arise in response to a life-threatening event.

Both halves of this definition are suspect. To start with, the link to a traumatic event, which makes PTSD almost unique among complex psychiatric diagnoses in being defined by an external cause, also makes it uniquely problematic, for the tie is really to the memory of an event. When PTSD was first added to the DSM-III in 1980, traumatic memories were considered reasonably faithful recordings of actual events. But as research since then has repeatedly shown, memory is spectacularly unreliable and extraordinarily malleable. We routinely add or subtract people, details, settings, and actions to our memories. We conflate, invent, and edit.

In one study by Washington University memory researcher Elizabeth Loftus, one out of four adults who were told they were lost in a shopping mall as children came to believe it. Some insisted the event happened even after the ruse was exposed. Bounteous research since then has confirmed that such false memories are common. (*See,* "Creating False Memories" by Elizabeth Loftus, *Scientific American,* Sept 1997.)

Soldiers enjoy no immunity from this tendency. A 1990s study at the New Haven, Connecticut VA hospital asked 59 Gulf War veterans about their war experiences a month after their return and again two years later. The researchers asked about 19 specific types of potentially traumatic events, such as witnessing deaths, losing friends, and seeing people disfigured. Two years out, 70 percent of the veterans reported at least one traumatic event they had not mentioned a month after returning, and 24 percent reported at least three such events for the first time. And the veterans recounting the most "new memories" also reported the most PTSD symptoms.

To McNally, such results suggest that some veterans experiencing "late-onset" PTSD may be attributing symptoms of depression, anxiety, or other subtle disorders to a memory that has been elaborated and given new significance — or even unconsciously (and innocently) fabricated.

"This has nothing to do with gaming or working the system or consciously looking for sympathy," he says. "We all do this: We cast our lives in terms of narratives that help us understand them. A vet who's having a difficult life may remember a trauma, which may or may not have actually traumatized him, and everything makes sense."

To make PTSD diagnosis more rigorous, some have suggested that blood chemistry, brain imaging or other tests might be able to detect physiological signatures of PTSD. Studies of stress hormones in groups of PTSD patients show differences from normal subjects, but the overlap between the normal and the PTSD groups is huge, making individual profiles useless for diagnostics. Brain imaging has similar limitations, with the abnormal dynamics in PTSD heavily overlapping those of depression and anxiety.

With memory unreliable and biological markers elusive, diagnosis depends on clinical symptoms. But as a 2007 study showed starkly, PTSD's symptom profile is as slippery as the would-be biomarkers. Alexander Bodkin, a psychiatrist at Harvard's McLean Hospital, screened 90 clinically depressed patients separately for PTSD symptoms and for trauma, then compared the results. First he and a colleague used a standardized PTSD screening interview to assess PTSD symptoms. Then two other PTSD diagnosticians, ignorant of the symptom reports, used a standard interview to see which patients had ever experienced trauma fitting DSM-IV criteria.

If PTSD arose from trauma, the patients with PTSD symptoms should have histories of trauma, and those with trauma should show more PTSD. It was not so. While the symptom screens rated 70 of the 90 patients PTSD-positive, the trauma screens found only 54 who had suffered trauma; the diagnosed PTSD "cases" outnumbered those who had experienced traumatic events. Things got worse when Bodkin compared the diagnoses one-on-one. If PTSD required trauma, then the 54 trauma-exposed patients should account for most of the 70 PTSD-positive patients. But the PTSD-symptomatic patients –were equally distributed among the trauma-positive and the trauma-negative groups. The PTSD rate had zero relation to the trauma rate. It was, Bodkin observed, "a scientifically unacceptable situation."

More practically, as McNally points out, "To give the best treatment, you have to have the right diagnosis."

The most effective treatment for patients whose symptoms arose from trauma is exposure-based cognitive behavioral therapy (CBT), which concentrates on altering the response to a specific traumatic memory by repeated, controlled exposure to it. "And it works," says McNally. "If someone with genuine PTSD goes to the people who do this really well, they have a good chance of getting better." CBT for depression, in contrast, teaches the patient to recognize dysfunctional loops of thought and emotion and develop new responses to normal, present-day events. "If a depressed person takes on a PTSD interpretation of their troubles and gets exposure-based CBT, you're going to miss the boat," says McNally. "You're going to spend your time chasing this memory down instead of dealing with the way the patient misinterprets present events."

To complicate the matter, recent studies showing that traumatic brain injuries from bomb blasts, common among solders in Iraq, produce symptoms almost indistinguishable from PTSD. One more overlapping symptom set.

"The overlap issue worries me tremendously," says Gerald Rosen, a University of Washington psychiatrist who has worked extensively with PTSD patients. "We have to ask how we got here. We have to ask ourselves, 'What do *we* gain by having this diagnosis?'"

Disabling Conditions

Rosen is thinking of clinicians when he asks about gain. But what does a veteran gain with a PTSD diagnosis? One would hope, of course, that it grants access to effective treatment and support. This is not happening. In civilian populations, two-thirds of PTSD patients respond to treatment. But as psychologist Chris Frueh, who researched and treated PTSD for the VA from the early 1990s until 2006, notes, "In the two largest VA studies of combat veterans, neither showed a treatment effect. Vets getting PTSD treatment from the VA are no more likely to get better than they would on their own."

The reason, says Frueh, is the collision of the PTSD construct's vagaries with the VA's disability system, in which every benefit seems structured to discourage recovery.

The first benefit is healthcare. PTSD is by far the easiest mental health diagnosis to have declared "service-connected," a designation that often means the difference between little or no care and broad, lasting health coverage. Service connection also makes a vet eligible for monthly disability payments of up to $4,000. That link may explain why most veterans getting PTSD treatment from the VA report worsening symptoms until they are designated 100 percent disabled — at which point their use of VA mental health services drops by 82 percent. It may also help to explain why, although the risk of PTSD from a traumatic event drops as time passes, the number of Vietnam veterans applying for PTSD disability almost doubled between 1999 and 2004, driving total PTSD disability payments to more than $4 billion annually. Perhaps most disastrously, these payments continue only if you're sick. For unlike a vet who has lost a leg, a vet with PTSD loses disability benefits as soon as he recovers or starts working. The entire system seems designed to encourage chronic disability.

"In the several years I spent in VA PTSD clinics," says Frueh, "I can't think of a single PTSD patient who left treatment because he got better. But the problem is not the veterans. The problem is that the VA's disability system, which is 60 years old now, ignores all the intervening research we have on resilience, on the power of expectancy and the effects of incentives and disincentives. Sometimes I think they should just blow it up and start over." But with what?

Richard Bryant, an Australian PTSD researcher and clinician, suggests a disability system more like that Down Under. An Australian soldier injured in combat receives a lifelong "noneconomic" disability payment of $300 to $1,200 monthly. If the injury keeps her from working, she also gets an "incapacity" payment, as well as job training and help finding work. Finally — a crucial feature — she retains all these benefits for two years once she goes back to work. After that, her incapacity payments taper to zero over five years. But her noneconomic payments — a sort of financial Purple Heart — continue forever. And like all Australians, she gets free lifetime health care.

Australian vets come home to an utterly different support system from ours: Theirs is a scaffold they can climb. Ours is a low-hanging "safety net" liable to trap anyone who falls in.

Two Ways to Carry a Rifle

When a soldier comes home, he must try to reconcile his war experience with the person he was beforehand and the society and family he returns to. He must engage in what psychologist Rachel Yehuda, who researches PTSD at the Bronx VA hospital, calls "recontextualization" — the process of integrating trauma into normal experience. It is what we all do, on a smaller scale, when we suffer breakups, job losses, the deaths of loved ones. Initially the event seems an impossible aberration. Then slowly we accept the trauma as part of the complex context that is life.

Matt Stevens recognizes this can take time. Even after a year home, the war still occupies his dreams. Sometimes, for instance, he dreams that he is doing something completely normal — while carrying his combat rifle.

"One night I dreamt I was birdwatching with my wife. When we saw a bird, she would lift her binoculars, and I would lift my rifle and watch the bird through the scope. No thought of shooting it. Just how I looked at the birds."

It would be easy to read Stevens's dream as a symptom of PTSD, expressing fear, hypervigilance, and avoidance. Yet the dream can also be seen as demonstrating his success in recontextualizing his experience. He is reconciling the man who once used a gun with the man who no longer does.

Saving PTSD from itself, say Spitzer, McNally, Frueh, and other critics, will require a similar shift —seeing most post-combat distress not as a disorder but as part of normal, if painful, healing. This will involve, for starters, revising the PTSD diagnosis construct — presently under review for the new DSM-V due to be published in 2012 — so it accounts for the unreliability of memory and better distinguishes depression, anxiety, and phobia from true PTSD. Mental-health evaluations need similar revisions so they can detect genuine cases without leading patients to impose trauma narratives on other mental-health problems. Finally, Congress should replace the VA's disability regime with an evidence-based system that removes disincentives to recovery — and even go the extra mile and give all combat veterans, injured or not, lifetime healthcare.

These changes will be hard to sell in a culture that resists any suggestion that PTSD is not a common, even inevitable, consequence of combat. Mistaking its horror for its prevalence, people assume PTSD is epidemic, ignoring all evidence to the contrary.

The biggest longitudinal study of soldiers returning from Iraq and Afghanistan, led by VA researcher Charles Milliken and published in 2007, seemed to confirm that we should expect a high incidence of PTSD. It surveyed combat troops immediately on return from deployment and again about 6 months later and found around 20 percent symptomatically "at risk" of PTSD. But of those reporting symptoms in the first survey, half had improved by the second survey, and many who first claimed few or no symptoms later reported serious symptoms. How many of the early "symptoms" were just normal adjustment? How many of the later symptoms were the imposition of a trauma narrative onto other problems? Matt Stevens, for one, is certain these screens are mistaking many going through normal adjustment as dangerously at risk of PTSD. Even he, although functioning fine at work, home, and in society, scored positive in *both* surveys; he is, in other words, one of the 20 percent "at risk." Finally, and weirdly, both screens missed about 75 percent of those who actually sought counseling — a finding that raises further doubts about the screens' accuracy. Yet this study received prominent media coverage emphasizing that PTSD rates were probably being badly undercounted.

A few months later, another study — the first to track large numbers of soldiers through the war — provided a clearer and more consistent picture. Led by U.S. Navy researcher Tyler Smith and published in the British Medical Journal, the study monitored mental health and combat exposure in 50,000 U.S. soldiers from 2001 to 2006. The researchers took particular care to tie symptoms to types of combat exposure and demographic factors. Among the 20,000 troops who went to Iraq, 4.3 percent developed diagnosis-level symptoms of PTSD. The rate ran about 8 percent in those with combat exposure and 2 percent in those not exposed.

These numbers are about a quarter of the rates Milliken found. But they're a close match to PTSD rates seen in British Iraq War vets and to rates McNally calculated for Vietnam veterans. The contrast to the Milliken study, along with the consistency with British rates and with McNally's NVVRS calculation, should have made the Smith study big news. Yet the media, the VA, and the trauma psychology community almost completely ignored the study. "The silence," McNally wryly noted, "was deafening."

This silence may be merely a matter of good news going unremarked. Yet it supports McNally.

Extensive Research Results in New, Effective Diagnosis Guidelines

Tori DeAngelis

Tori DeAngelis is an award-winning freelance journalist and editor. For more than 30 years she has been writing magazine articles about psychology, health, medicine, culture, and other topics. She received her master's degree in magazine journalism from Syracuse University's Newhouse School of Public Communications.

Several psychological interventions help to significantly reduce post-traumatic stress disorder symptoms, say new guidelines.

It's a bittersweet fact: Traumatic events such as the Sept. 11 attacks, Hurricane Katrina, and the wars in Iraq and Afghanistan have enabled researchers to learn a lot more about how best to treat post-traumatic stress disorder (PTSD).

"The advances made have been nothing short of outstanding," says Boston University psychologist Terence M. Keane, PhD, director of the behavioral science division of the National Center for Posttraumatic Stress Disorder and a contributor to the original PTSD diagnosis. "These are very important times in the treatment of PTSD."

In perhaps the most important news, in November, the International Society for Traumatic Stress Studies (ISTSS), a professional society that promotes knowledge on severe stress and trauma, issued new PTSD practice guidelines. Using a grading system from "A" to "E," the guidelines label several PTSD treatments as "A" treatments based on their high degree of empirical support, says Keane, one of the volume's editors. The guidelines-the first since 2000-update and generally confirm recommendations of other major practice-related bodies, including the U.S. Department of Veterans Affairs (VA), the Department of Defense, the American

Psychiatric Association, and Great Britain's and Australia's national health-care guidelines, he says.

In other PTSD-treatment advances, researchers are adding medications and virtual-reality simulations to proven treatments to beef up their effectiveness. Clinical investigators are also exploring ways to treat PTSD when other psychological and medical conditions are present, and they are studying specific populations such as those affected by the Sept. 11 attacks.

Though exciting, these breakthroughs are somewhat colored by an October Institute of Medicine (IoM) report that concludes there is still not enough evidence to say which PTSD treatments are effective, except for exposure therapies. Many experts, however, disagree with that conclusion, noting that a number of factors specific to the condition, such as high dropout rates, can lead to what may seem like imperfect study designs.

Treatments That Make a Difference

The fact that several treatments made the "A" list is great news for psychologists, says Keane. "Having this many evidence-based treatments allows therapists to use what they're comfortable with from their own background and training, and at the same time to select treatments for use with patients with different characteristics," he says.

Moreover, many of these treatments were developed by psychologists, he notes.

They include:

- **Prolonged-exposure therapy**, developed for use in PTSD by Keane, University of Pennsylvania psychologist Edna Foa, PhD, and Emory University psychologist Barbara O. Rothbaum, PhD. In this type of treatment, a therapist guides the client to recall traumatic memories in a controlled fashion so that clients eventually regain mastery of their thoughts and feelings around the incident. While exposing people to the very events that caused their trauma may seem counterintuitive, Rothbaum emphasizes that it's done in a gradual, controlled and repeated manner, until the person can evaluate their circumstances realistically and understand they can safely return to the activities in their current lives that they had been avoiding. Drawing from PTSD best practices, the APA-initiated Center for Deployment Psychology includes exposure therapy in the training of psychologists and other health professionals who are or will be treating returning Iraq and Afghanistan service personnel (see "A unique training program").

- **Cognitive-processing therapy**, a form of cognitive behavioral therapy, or CBT, developed by Boston University psychologist Patricia A. Resick, PhD, director of the women's health sciences division of the National Center for PTSD, to treat rape victims and later applied to PTSD. This treatment includes an exposure component but places greater emphasis on cognitive strategies to help people alter erroneous thinking that has emerged because of the event. Practitioners may work with clients on false beliefs that the world is no longer safe, for example, or that they are incompetent because they have "let" a terrible event happen to them.

- **Stress-inoculation training**, another form of CBT, where practitioners teach clients techniques to manage and reduce anxiety, such as breathing, muscle relaxation and positive self-talk.

- **Other forms of cognitive therapy**, including cognitive restructuring and cognitive therapy.

- **Eye-movement desensitization and reprocessing**, or EMDR, where the therapist guides clients to make eye movements or follow hand taps, for instance, at the same time they are recounting traumatic events. It's not clear how EMDR works, and, for that reason, it's somewhat controversial, though the therapy is supported by research, notes Dartmouth University psychologist Paula P. Schnurr, PhD, deputy executive director of the National Center for PTSD.

- **Medications**, specifically selective serotonin reuptake inhibitors. Two in particular-paroxetine (Paxil) and sertaline (Zoloft)-have been approved by the Food and Drug Administration for use in PTSD. Other medications may be useful in treating PTSD as well, particularly when the person has additional disorders such as depression, anxiety or psychosis, the guidelines note.

Spreading the Word

So promising does the VA consider two of the "A" treatments-prolonged exposure therapy and cognitive-processing therapy-that it is doing national rollouts of them within the VA, notes psychologist Antonette Zeiss, PhD, deputy chief consultant for mental health at the agency.

"Enhancing our ability to provide veterans with the psychotherapies for PTSD that have the strongest evidence base is one of our highest priorities," Zeiss says. In fact, the VA began training psychologists to provide the two approaches more than a year before the Institute of Medicine released its report of successful treatments, she says. "We're pleased that the report confirms our emphasis on this training."

The VA system's structure and philosophy make it possible to test the results of treatments in large, realistic samples-a clinical researcher's dream, notes Schnurr, who has conducted a number of such studies, most recently in a study of female veterans that led to the rollout out of prolonged exposure therapy. That study was reported in the Feb. 28, 2007, issue of *The Journal of the American Medical Association* (Vol. 297, No. 8, pages 820-830).

"The VA was able to support the science, so the research didn't just sit around in a journal and get discussed," Zeiss says. "They put money toward it, and they asked us to help them do a major rollout of the treatment."

Boosting Effectiveness

Meanwhile, other researchers are experimenting with add-ons to these proven treatments to increase their effectiveness. Some are looking at how virtual reality might enhance the effects of prolonged-exposure therapy. By adding virtual reality, whereby clients experience 3-D imagery, sounds and sometimes smells that correspond with a traumatic event, "we think it might be a good alternative for people who are too avoidant to do standard exposure therapy, because it puts them right there," says Emory University's Rothbaum.

Other researchers are adding a small dose of an old tuberculosis drug, D-cycloserine, or DCS, to treatment to see if it can mitigate people's fear reactions. Rothbaum's team, which includes psychologist Mike Davis, PhD, and psychiatrist Kerry Ressler, MD, PhD, have recently shown that the drug helps to extinguish fear in animals, so they're hoping for a similar effect in people.

In one study with veterans of the current Iraq war, Rothbaum's team is giving all participants a type of virtual reality that simulates combat conditions in Iraq, then randomizing them into a drug condition where they get DCS, a placebo, or the anti-anxiety drug alprazolam (Xanax).

In a similar vein, researchers at the Program for Anxiety and Traumatic Stress Studies at Weill Cornell Medical College are using virtual reality and DCS to treat those directly affected by the 2001 World Trade Center attacks, including civilians who were in the towers or nearby buildings, witnesses, and firefighters and police officers who were first responders.

Participants receive standard cognitive behavioral treatment enhanced with virtual reality, where they see graded versions of a Twin Towers scenario, starting with simple images of the buildings on a sunny day, and progressing gradually to include the horrific sights and sounds of that day. They also randomly receive either a small dose of DCS or a placebo pill before each session.

While neither study is complete, the researchers say the treatments appear to significantly reduce participants' PTSD symptoms. Rothbaum has recently submitted a grant proposal for a study where she plans to compare traditional and virtual-reality exposure therapies-which hasn't yet been done-in combination with DCS or a placebo.

Addressing Comorbidity

Other psychologists are starting to think about ways to treat PTSD when it is accompanied by other psychiatric and health conditions. Psychologist John Otis, PhD, of Boston University and VA Boston, for instance, is testing an integrated treatment that aims to alleviate symptoms of both PTSD and chronic pain in Vietnam veterans and veterans of Operation Iraqi Freedom and Operation Enduring Freedom. The treatment combines aspects of cognitive processing therapy for trauma and cognitive behavioral therapy for chronic pain.

"We think these two conditions may interact in some [psychological] way that makes them more severe and challenging to treat," Otis says. In particular, he and others posit that "anxiety sensitivity"-fear of experiencing one's anxiety-related symptoms-may increase the odds that certain PTSD sufferers have more problems than others.

Again, while the study is not yet finished, results are encouraging, reports Otis. "Many of the veterans who are getting the integrated treatment are experiencing partial or complete remission of both kinds of symptoms," he says. On a broader scale, the National Center for PTSD's Keane believes that much more research is needed on treating PTSD and psychiatric co-morbidities such as depression, anxiety, substance abuse, personality disorders and psychosis — a common situation that escalates the more severe a person's PTSD symptoms are, he says.

He, for one, would like to examine possible applications to PTSD of the concept of a "unified protocol," a theory and methodology being developed by Boston University psychotherapy researcher David Barlow, PhD, to treat concurrent problems such as panic attacks, anxiety and phobias.

That said, the recent advances promise to help many more people suffering from a condition they did not bring on themselves, says Zeiss.

"While there is still more to learn, we have taken significant steps in developing treatments that have been shown to be effective and that will be increasingly provided both in VA and other mental health care settings," says Zeiss. "Those affected by combat stress and other traumas will be able to reach out for care without feeling ashamed or hopeless."

Iraq and Afghan War Vets Reap the Benefits of Technological Advances

Wayne Kinney

Wayne Kinney serves as a court-appointed special advocate, speaking for the best interests of abused and neglected children in court and other environments. He has a longstanding relationship with the U.S. Army in human resources, planning, and operations. He has an advanced degree in clinical psychotherapy and has been pursuing his doctorate in psychology.

Military personnel experiencing combat in Iraq and Afghanistan are suffering wounds that are much greater in number and variety than those endured by veterans of earlier wars. This circumstance is due, in part, to advances in medical science and technology. Soldiers, sailors and marines who suffered such severe wounds in earlier wars simply died because they were beyond the reach of then contemporary medicine or technology. In addition, in earlier wars, Post Traumatic Stress Syndrome was not even given a name, let alone recognized as a valid form of war-related casualty. Now, PTSD is thoroughly documented and a whole array of treatments are available to veterans of the Iraqi and Afghan Wars. Friedman (2006) summarized PTSD symptoms as being typified by numbing, evasion, hypervigilance, and re-experiencing of disturbing incidents via flashbacks. Veterans and other non-combatant participants in war who have outlived traumatic experiences typically suffer from PTSD.

PTSD is being reported in considerable numbers in service members returning from combat (Friedman 2006; Seal, Bertenthan, Miner, Saunak and Marmar, 2007). This is not surprising due to the chaotic nature of combat in the Iraqi and Afghan theatres. According to the Defense Manpower Data Center (2007), 65%

"Comparing PTSD Among Returning War Veterans," by Wayne Kinney, Journal of Military and Veterans' Health, August 2012. Reprinted by permission.

of Operation Enduring Freedom (OEF) and Operation Iraqi Freedom (OIF) casualties were caused by blasts, particularly those that resulted from improvised explosive devices (IEDs). Terrorist strikes, urban warfare, numerous and protracted combat operations and the pervasive hazard from roadside bombs are some of the distinctive characteristics of the OEF and OIF conflicts, which put particular stress on surviving military service members (Carlock, 2007).

A distinguishing pattern of wounds inflicted by explosive devices includes traumatic brain injury (TBI), burns, blindness and spinal cord injuries, along with the initial limb injuries that in time require amputation. This was, unfortunately, a major affliction among military personnel in these conflicts (Carlock, 2007). In order to explain the multifaceted and severe wounds to more than one body system, Eckholm (2006) and Scott, Belanger, Vanderpoeg, Massengale and Scholter (2006) used the term poly-trauma. Special care is given to veterans and service members who suffer from poly-trauma, which is specified as multiple injuries that cause physical, psychological, mental or psychosocial injuries and functional incapacity (Johnson, 2011).

The wounds endured by military personnel in Iraq and Afghanistan are much greater in number than those from earlier wars (Carlock, 2007). Most of the Iraqi War and Afghan War wounded are barely adult and they will need special treatment for more than fifty years (Blech, 2006). It cannot be denied that significant challenges still loom for physically and psychologically wounded Iraqi and Afghan War veterans. However, considering the existing political environment on the home front in the United States, the circumstances faced by the Iraqi and Afghan War veterans on their return is more conducive to healing and recovery as compared to that of the Vietnam War veterans (Hafemeister & Stockey, 2010). However, more Afghan War and Iraqi War veterans are afflicted with physical injuries and complex challenges than were the Vietnam War veterans. Nevertheless, numerous Afghan War and Iraqi War veterans have recovered and returned to combat and have served two or more tours. A majority of Vietnam veterans served only one tour. Also, it is important to note that while the Vietnam War had a 2.6 to 1 wounded-to-killed ratio, the Afghan and Iraqi Wars registered ratios of approximately 15 to [sic].

The survival of military personnel in Iraq and Afghanistan is close to 90%, generally because of developments in body armour and combat medicine as well as the promptness of evacuation (Gawande 2004). Numerous wounded service members, on the other hand, are enduring extremely debilitating injuries, which will require refined, all-inclusive, and frequently lifetime care. More than half of the 3,000 American soldiers wounded in Iraq and Afghanistan have suffered from brain damage and, unfortunately, the trauma will have a permanent effect on their memory, mood and behaviour as well as their ability to think and work (Blech, 2006).

Differences between Afghan War and Iraqi War veterans and Vietnam War veterans include age, gender and marital status. As compared to Vietnam War veterans, most Iraqi War and Afghan War veterans went to war at a younger age, included proportionately more females and more often they had held jobs before their enlistment. In addition, Iraqi War and Afghan War veterans are less likely to be married, separated, divorced or have a history of incarceration. According to Fontana and Rosenheck (2008), these disparities in the attributes and mental health of Iraqi War and Afghan War veterans as compared to the Vietnam War veterans may have significant consequences for the program and treatment planning of Veterans Affairs (VA). They reached this conclusion after comparing Iraqi and Afghan War veterans with four samples of outpatient and inpatient Persian Gulf War and Vietnam War veterans. Also, there are more women Iraqi War and Afghan War veterans than female Persian Gulf and Vietnam War veterans.

Iraqi War and Afghan War veterans also differ from Vietnam War veterans in terms of clinical status. Diagnosis with substance abuse disorders is less frequent among Iraqi War and Afghan War veterans than it had been among Vietnam War soldiers, marines, sailors and veterans. However, Iraqi War and Afghan War veterans were more prone to violent behaviour than Vietnam veterans. VA disability compensation rates due to PTSD are lower among Iraqi War and Afghan War veterans versus Vietnam War veterans. In terms of clinical status,Fontana and Rosenheck (2008) found that Iraqi War and Afghan War veterans filed fewer VA disability compensation rates due to PTSD.

Fontana, Rosenheck and Desai (2010) studied the noteworthy similarities and differences between female veterans of the Iraqi War and Afghan War and those of the Persian Gulf War.This comparison showed that female Persian Gulf War veterans suffered more sexual trauma and more noncombatant nonsexual trauma than did those of the Iraqi War and the Afghan War. The researchers concluded this might be a sign of more effective efforts to respond to military sexual abuse along with more wide-ranging preparation of female soldiers for their roles in combat. The comparative research also revealed the fact that Persian Gulf War female veterans suffer from more medical difficulties than the Iraqi War and Afghan War female veterans, especially in terms of general cognitive disability and drug abuse or dependence.

There are a number of differences in the medical problems experienced by Iraqi War and Afghan War male and female soldiers and veterans. Understanding these differences can be of help in planning treatment interventions for these war veterans.

Moreover, the differences of male and female soldiers who served in Iraq and Afghanistan in terms of threat exposure combine with gender differences in pathology (Fontana, Rosenheck, & Desai, 2010). Male soldiers are more often diagnosed with medical problems, alcohol abuse or dependence and PTSD than female soldiers. On the other hand, male soldiers are less often diagnosed with anxiety disorders if mood disorders and PTSD are excluded.

Female soldiers in Iraq and Afghanistan are less likely than male soldiers to be married and employed prior to their enlistment.

Veterans Administration and other researchers conclude female soldiers serving in Iraq and Afghanistan have more extensive social supports than do male soldiers. In general, ramifications of gender differences between male and female soldiers in Iraq and Afghanistan may be significant enough to support the contention that mixed-gender programs or independent programs for women be instituted (Fontana, Rosenheck and Desai, 2010).

Social functioning has mostly been left undamaged among modern war veterans diagnosed with PTSD and Fontana and Rosenheck (2008) saw an opportunity for improving and concentrating on treatment interventions that put emphasis on enabling returning war veterans to be assets to society.

Thus, it is important to analyse the differences between Iraqi War and Afghanistan War veterans and Persian Gulf and Vietnam War veterans in terms of PTSD diagnosis. As Iraqi War and Afghan War veterans, Persian Gulf and Vietnam War veterans alike make claims for Veterans Affairs (VA) Disability Compensation for disability benefits, an analysis of their differences in terms of PTSD diagnosis can help VA develop programs and treatment planning for them.

References

Blech, J. (2006). Severity of Injuries Requires New Forms of Rehabilitation. Der Spiegel Online http://www. spiegel.de/ international/spiegel/0,1518,443754,00.html, Date Accessed: May 29, 2012

Carlock, D. (2007). A Guide to Resources for Severely Wounded Operation Iraqi Freedom (OIF) and Operation Enduring Freedom (OEF) Veterans. Issues in Science and Technology Librarianship Online, http://drs.asu.edu/fedora/get/ asulib:142486/PDF-3, Date Accessed May 29, 2012.

Defense Manpower Data Center (2007). Global War on Terrorism Casualty Statistics by Reason. Retrieved from http://siadapp. dmdc.osd.mil/personnel/CASUALTY/gwot_reason.pdf

Eckholm, E. (2006). A new kind of care in a new era of casualties. New York Times

Fontana, A. and Rosenheck, R. (2008). Treatment-seeking veterans of Iraq and Afghanistan: comparison with veterans of previous wars. New England Mental Illness Research, Education and Clinical Center. Volume 196 - Issue 7 - pp 513-521

Fontana, A. Rosenheck, R. and Desai, R. (2010). Female Veterans of Iraq and Afghanistan Seeking Care from VA Specialized PTSD Programs: Comparison with Male Veterans and Female War Zone Veterans of Previous Eras. Journal of Women's Health. Vol. 22, No. 2, p. 1-9

Friedman, M. (2006). Posttraumatic stress disorder among military returnees from Afghanistan and Iraq. American Journal of Psychiatry. 163: 586-593

Gawande, A. (2004). Casualties of war--military care for the wounded from Iraq and Afghanistan. New England Journal of Medicine. 351:2471-2475

Hafemeister, T. L. and Stockey, N. A. (2010). Last Stand? The Criminal Responsibility of War Veterans Returning from Iraq and Afghanistan with Posttraumatic Stress Disorder. Indiana Law Journal. Vol. 85, Issue 1, Art.3, p. 87-141

Johnson, B. (2011). New 'home' fills a need for military families. Finance and Commerce

Scott, S.G., Belanger, H.G., Vanderpoeg, R.D., Massengale, J. and Scholter, J. (2006). Mechanism of injury approach to evaluating patients with blast related polytrauma. Journal of the American Osteopathic Association. vol. 106 no. 5, 265-270

Seal, K., Bertenthan, D., Miner, C., Saunak, S. and Marmar, C. (2007). Bringing the war back home: Mental health disorders among 103,788 US Veterans returning from Iraq and\Afghanistan seen at Department of Veterans Affairs facilities. Archives of Internal Medicine. Vol 167; p. 476-481

Be Aware of the New Standard for PTSD Diagnosis

Matthew J. Friedman

Dr. Matthew J. Friedman is the former executive director and now senior advisor at the U.S. Department of Veterans Affairs National Center for PTSD. He has worked with PTSD patients for more than 30 years. He is listed in The Best Doctors in America and is a Distinguished Fellow of the American Psychiatric Association. He has written or co-edited nearly 200 books, chapters, and journal articles.

A Brief History of the PTSD Diagnosis

The risk of exposure to trauma has been a part of the human condition since we evolved as a species. Attacks by saber tooth tigers or twenty-first century terrorists have probably produced similar psychological sequelae in the survivors of such violence. Shakespeare's Henry IV appears to meet many, if not all, of the diagnostic criteria for Posttraumatic Stress Disorder (PTSD), as have other heroes and heroines throughout the world's literature. The history of the development of the PTSD concept is described by Trimble (1).

In 1980, the American Psychiatric Association (APA) added PTSD to the third edition of its Diagnostic and Statistical Manual of Mental Disorders (DSM-III) nosologic classification scheme (2). Although controversial when first introduced, the PTSD diagnosis has filled an important gap in psychiatric theory and practice. From an historical perspective, the significant change ushered in by the PTSD concept was the stipulation that the etiological agent was outside the individual (i.e., a traumatic event) rather than an inherent individual weakness (i.e., a traumatic neurosis). The key to understanding the scientific basis and clinical expression of PTSD is the concept of "trauma."

"PTSD History and Overview," by Matthew J. Friedman, U.S. Department of Veterans Affairs, February 23, 2016.

Importance of traumatic events

In its initial DSM-III formulation, a traumatic event was conceptualized as a catastrophic stressor that was outside the range of usual human experience. The framers of the original PTSD diagnosis had in mind events such as war, torture, rape, the Nazi Holocaust, the atomic bombings of Hiroshima and Nagasaki, natural disasters (such as earthquakes, hurricanes, and volcano eruptions), and human-made disasters (such as factory explosions, airplane crashes, and automobile accidents). They considered traumatic events to be clearly different from the very painful stressors that constitute the normal vicissitudes of life such as divorce, failure, rejection, serious illness, financial reverses, and the like. (By this logic, adverse psychological responses to such "ordinary stressors" would, in DSM-III terms, be characterized as Adjustment Disorders rather than PTSD.) This dichotomization between traumatic and other stressors was based on the assumption that, although most individuals have the ability to cope with ordinary stress, their adaptive capacities are likely to be overwhelmed when confronted by a traumatic stressor.

PTSD is unique among psychiatric diagnoses because of the great importance placed upon the etiological agent, the traumatic stressor. In fact, one cannot make a PTSD diagnosis unless the patient has actually met the "stressor criterion," which means that he or she has been exposed to an event that is considered traumatic. Clinical experience with the PTSD diagnosis has shown, however, that there are individual differences regarding the capacity to cope with catastrophic stress. Therefore, while most people exposed to traumatic events do not develop PTSD, others go on to develop the full-blown syndrome. Such observations have prompted the recognition that trauma, like pain, is not an external phenomenon that can be completely objectified. Like pain, the traumatic experience is filtered through cognitive and emotional processes before it can be appraised as an extreme threat. Because of individual differences in this appraisal process, different people appear to have different trauma thresholds, some more protected from and some more vulnerable to developing clinical symptoms after exposure to extremely stressful situations. Although there is currently a renewed interest in subjective aspects of traumatic exposure, it must be emphasized that events such as rape, torture, genocide, and severe war zone stress are experienced as traumatic events by nearly everyone.

Revisions to PTSD diagnostic criteria

The DSM-III diagnostic criteria for PTSD were revised in DSM-III-R (1987), DSM-IV (1994), and DSM-IV-TR (2000) (2-5). A very similar syndrome is classified in ICD-10 (The ICD-10 Classification of Mental and Behavioural Disorders: Clinical Descriptions and Diagnostic Guidelines) (6). One important finding, which was not apparent when PTSD was first proposed as a diagnosis in 1980, is that it is relatively common. Recent data from the National Comorbidity Survey Replication indicates lifetime PTSD prevalence rates are 3.6% and 9.7% respectively among American men and women (7). Rates of PTSD are much higher in post-conflict settings such as Algeria (37%), Cambodia (28%), Ethiopia (16%), and Gaza (18%) (8).

DSM-IV Diagnostic criteria for PTSD included a history of exposure to a traumatic event and symptoms from each of three symptom clusters: intrusive recollections, avoidant/numbing symptoms, and hyper-arousal symptoms. A fifth criterion concerned duration of symptoms; and, a sixth criterion stipulated that PTSD symptoms must cause significant distress or functional impairment.

The latest revision, the DSM-5 (2013), has made a number of notable evidence-based revisions to PTSD diagnostic criteria, with both important conceptual and clinical implications (9). First, because it has become apparent that PTSD is not just a fear-based anxiety disorder (as explicated in both DSM-III and DSM-IV), PTSD in DSM-5 has expanded to include anhedonic/dysphoric presentations, which are most prominent. Such presentations are marked by negative cognitions and mood states as well as disruptive (e.g. angry, impulsive, reckless and self-destructive) behavioral symptoms. Furthermore, as a result of research-based changes to the diagnosis, PTSD is no longer categorized as an Anxiety Disorder. PTSD is now classified in a new category, Trauma- and Stressor-Related Disorders, in which the onset of every disorder has been preceded by exposure to a traumatic or otherwise adverse environmental event. Other changes in diagnostic criteria will be described below.

DSM-5 Criteria for PTSD Diagnosis

As noted above, the **"A" stressor criterion** specifies that a person has been exposed to a catastrophic event involving actual or threatened death or injury, or a threat to the physical integrity of him/herself or others (such as sexual violence). Indirect exposure includes learning about the violent or accidental death or perpetration of sexual violence to a loved one. Exposure through electronic media (e.g. televised images the 9/11 attacks on the World Trade Center) is not considered a traumatic event. On the other hand, repeated, indirect exposure (usually as part of one's professional responsibilities) to the gruesome and horrific consequences of a traumatic event (e.g. police personnel, body handlers, etc.) is considered traumatic.

Before describing the B-E symptom clusters, it is important to understand that one new feature of DSM-5 is that all of these symptoms must have had their onset or been significantly exacerbated after exposure to the traumatic event.

The **"B" or intrusive recollection criterion** includes symptoms that are perhaps the most distinctive and readily identifiable symptoms of PTSD. For individuals with PTSD, the traumatic event remains, sometimes for decades or a lifetime, a dominating psychological experience that retains its power to evoke panic, terror, dread, grief, or despair. These emotions manifest during intrusive daytime images of the event, traumatic nightmares, and vivid reenactments known as PTSD flashbacks (which are dissociative episodes). Furthermore, trauma-related stimuli that trigger recollections of the original event have the power to evoke mental images, emotional responses, and physiological reactions associated with the trauma. Researchers can use this phenomenon to reproduce PTSD symptoms in the laboratory by exposing affected individuals to auditory or visual trauma-related stimuli (10).

The **"C" or avoidance criterion** consists of behavioral strategies PTSD patients use in an attempt to reduce the likelihood that they will expose themselves to trauma-related stimuli. PTSD patients also use these strategies in an attempt to minimize the intensity of their psychological response if they are exposed to such stimuli. Behavioral strategies include avoiding any thought or situation which is likely to elicit distressing traumatic memories. In its extreme manifestation, avoidance behavior may superficially resemble agoraphobia because the PTSD individual is afraid to leave the house for fear of confronting reminders of the traumatic event(s).

Symptoms included in the **"D" or negative cognitions and mood criterion** reflect persistent alterations in beliefs or mood that have developed after exposure to the traumatic event. People with PTSD often have erroneous cognitions about the causes or consequences of the traumatic event which leads them to blame themselves or others. A related erroneous appraisal is the common belief that one is inadequate, weak, or permanently changed for the worse since exposure to the traumatic event or that one's expectations about the future have been permanently altered because of the event (e.g., "nothing good can happen to me," "nobody can be trusted," "the world is entirely dangerous," "people will always try to control me"). In addition to negative appraisals about past, present and future, people with PTSD have a wide variety of negative emotional states such as anger, guilt, or shame. Dissociative psychogenic amnesia is included in this symptom cluster and involves cutting off the conscious experience of trauma-based memories and feelings. Other symptoms include diminished interest in significant activities and feeling detached or estranged from others. Finally, although individuals with PTSD suffer from persistent negative emotions, they are unable to experience positive feelings such as love, pleasure or enjoyment. Such constricted affect makes it extremely difficult to sustain a close marital or otherwise meaningful interpersonal relationship.

Symptoms included in the **"E" or alterations in arousal or reactivity criterion** most closely resemble those seen in panic and generalized anxiety disorders. While symptoms such as insomnia and cognitive impairment are generic anxiety symptoms, hypervigilance and startle are more characteristic of PTSD. The hypervigilance in PTSD may sometimes become so intense as to appear like frank paranoia. The startle response has a unique neurobiological substrate and may actually be the most pathognomonic PTSD symptom. DSM-IV's Criterion D2, irritability or outbursts of anger, has been separated into emotional (e.g., D4) and behavioral (e.g., E1) components in DSM-5. Irritable and angry outbursts may sometimes be expressed as aggressive behavior. Finally reckless and self-destructive behavior such as impulsive acts, unsafe sex, reckless driving and suicidal behavior are newly included in DSM-5, as Criterion E2.

The **"F" or duration criterion** specifies that symptoms must persist for at least one month before PTSD may be diagnosed.

The **"G" or functional significance criterion** specifies that the survivor must experience significant social, occupational, or other distress as a result of these symptoms.

The **"H" or exclusion criterion** specifies that the symptoms are not due to medication, substance use, or other illness.

Assessing PTSD

Since 1980, there has been a great deal of attention devoted to the development of instruments for assessing PTSD. Keane and associates (10), working with Vietnam war-zone Veterans, first developed both psychometric and psychophysiological assessment techniques that have proven to be both valid and reliable. Other investigators have modified such assessment instruments and used them with natural disaster survivors, rape/incest survivors, and other traumatized individuals. These assessment techniques have been used in the epidemiological studies mentioned above and in other research protocols.

Neurobiology

Neurobiological research indicates that PTSD may be associated with stable neurobiological alterations in both the central and autonomic nervous systems. Psychophysiological alterations associated with PTSD include hyperarousal of the sympathetic nervous system, increased sensitivity and augmentation of the acoustic-startle eye blink reflex, and sleep abnormalities. Neuropharmacological and neuroendocrine abnormalities have been detected in most brain mechanisms that have evolved for coping, adaptation, and preservation of the species. These include the noradrenergic, hypothalamic-pituitary-adrenocortical, serotonergic, glutamatergic, thyroid, endogenous opioid, and other systems. Structural brain imaging suggests reduced volume of the hippocampus and anterior cingulate. Functional brain imaging suggests excessive amygdala activity and reduced activation of the prefrontal cortex and hippocampus. This information is reviewed extensively elsewhere (11-12).

Longitudinal expression

Longitudinal research has shown that PTSD can become a chronic psychiatric disorder and can persist for decades and sometimes for a lifetime. Patients with chronic PTSD often exhibit a longitudinal course marked by remissions and relapses. There is also a delayed variant of PTSD in which individuals exposed to a traumatic event do not exhibit the full PTSD syndrome until months or years afterward. DSM-IV's "delayed onset" has been changed to "delayed expression" in DSM-5 to clarify that although full diagnostic criteria may not be met until at least

6 months after the trauma, the onset and expression of some symptoms may be immediate. Usually, the prompting precipitant is a situation that resembles the original trauma in a significant way (for example, a war Veteran whose child is deployed to a war zone or a rape survivor who is sexually harassed or assaulted years later).

Co-occurring conditions
If an individual meets diagnostic criteria for PTSD, it is likely that he or she will meet DSM-5 criteria for one or more additional diagnoses (13). Most often, these comorbid diagnoses include major affective disorders, dysthymia, alcohol or substance abuse disorders, anxiety disorders, or personality disorders. There is a legitimate question whether the high rate of diagnostic comorbidity seen with PTSD is an artifact of our current decision-making rules for the PTSD diagnosis since there are not exclusionary criteria in DSM-5. In any case, high rates of comorbidity complicate treatment decisions concerning patients with PTSD since the clinician must decide whether to treat the comorbid disorders concurrently or sequentially.

Classification and subtypes
PTSD is no longer considered an Anxiety Disorder but has been reclassified as a Trauma and Stressor-Related Disorder because it has a number of clinical presentations, as discussed previously. In addition, two new subtypes have been included in the DSM-5. The Dissociative Subtype includes individuals who meet full PTSD criteria but also exhibit either depersonalization or de-realization (e.g. alterations in the experience of one's self and the world, respectively). The Preschool Subtype applies to children six years old and younger; it has fewer symptoms (especially in the "D" cluster because it is difficult for young children to report on their inner thoughts and feelings) and also has lower symptom thresholds to meet full PTSD criteria.

Questions to consider

Questions that remain about the syndrome itself include: what is the clinical course of untreated PTSD; are there other subtypes of PTSD; what is the distinction between traumatic simple phobia and PTSD; and what is the clinical phenomenology of prolonged and repeated trauma? With regard to the latter, Herman (14) has argued that the current PTSD formulation fails to characterize the major symptoms of PTSD commonly seen in victims of prolonged, repeated interpersonal violence such as domestic or sexual abuse and political torture. She has proposed an alternative diagnostic formulation, "complex PTSD," that emphasizes multiple symptoms, excessive somatization, dissociation, changes in affect, pathological changes in relationships, and pathological changes in identity. Although this formulation is attractive to clinicians dealing with individuals who have been repeatedly traumatized, scientific evidence in support of the complex PTSD formulation is sparse and inconsistent. For this reason, it was not included in the DSM-5 as subtype of PTSD. It is possible that the Dissociative Subtype, which has firm scientific support, will prove to be the diagnostic subtype that incorporates many or all of the symptoms first described by Herman.

PTSD has also been criticized from the perspective of cross-cultural psychology and medical anthropology, especially with respect to refugees, asylum seekers, and political torture victims from non-Western regions. Some clinicians and researchers working with such survivors argue that since PTSD has usually been diagnosed by clinicians from Western industrialized nations working with patients from a similar background, the diagnosis does not accurately reflect the clinical picture of traumatized individuals from non-Western traditional societies and cultures. It is clear however, that PTSD is a valid diagnosis cross-culturally (15). On the other hand, there is substantial cross-cultural variation and the expression of PTSD may be different in different countries and cultural settings, even when DSM-5 diagnostic criteria are met (16).

Treatment for PTSD

Most effective treatments for PTSD
The many therapeutic approaches offered to PTSD patients are presented in Foa, Keane, Friedman and Cohen's (2009) comprehensive book on treatment (17). The most successful interventions are cognitive-behavioral therapy (CBT) and medication. Excellent results have been obtained with CBT approaches such as prolonged exposure therapy (PE) and Cognitive Processing Therapy (CPT), especially with female victims of childhood or adult sexual trauma, military personnel and Veterans with war-related trauma, and survivors of serious motor vehicle accidents. Success has also been reported with Eye Movement Desensitization and Reprocessing (EMDR) and Stress Inoculation Therapy (SIT). Sertraline (Zoloft) and paroxetine (Paxil) are selective serotonin reuptake inhibitors (SSRIs) that are the first medications to have received FDA approval as indicated treatments for PTSD. Other antidepressants are also effective and promising results have recently been obtained with the alpha-1 adrenergic antagonist, prazosin (18).

A frequent therapeutic option for mildly to moderately affected PTSD patients is group therapy, although empirical support for this is sparse. In such a setting, the PTSD patient can discuss traumatic memories, PTSD symptoms, and functional deficits with others who have had similar experiences. This approach has been most successful with war Veterans, rape/incest victims, and natural disaster survivors. It is important that therapeutic goals be realistic because, in some cases, PTSD is a chronic, complex (e.g., with many comorbid diagnoses and symptoms), and severely debilitating psychiatric disorder that does not always respond to current available treatments. Resick, Nishith, and Griffin (2003) have shown however, that very good outcomes utilizing evidence-based Cognitive Processing Therapy (CPT) can be achieved, even with such complicated patients (19); and, more recently, group CPT has shown promising results (20-21). A remarkable recent finding is the effectiveness of group CPT, adapted for illiteracy and risk of ongoing violence, with sexual trauma survivors in the Democratic Republic of Congo (22). The hope remains, however, that our growing knowledge about PTSD will enable us to design other effective interventions for patients afflicted with this disorder.

Rapid interventions for trauma survivors

There is great interest in rapid interventions for acutely traumatized individuals, especially with respect to civilian disasters, military deployments, and emergency personnel (medical personnel, police, and firefighters). This has become a major policy and public health issue since the massive traumatization caused by the September 11 terrorist attacks on the World Trade Center, Hurricane Katrina, the Asian tsunami, the Haitian earthquake, the wars in Iraq and Afghanistan and other large-scale traumatic events. Currently, there is controversy about which interventions work best during the immediate aftermath of a trauma. Research on critical incident stress debriefing (CISD), an intervention used widely, has brought disappointing results with respect to its efficacy to attenuate posttraumatic distress or to forestall the later development of PTSD. The National Center for PTSD and the National Center for Child Traumatic Stress have developed an alternative early intervention, Psychological First Aid that is available online, but which has yet to be subjected to rigorous evaluation. On the other hand, brief cognitive behavioral therapy has proved very effective in randomized clinical trials (23).

Recommended Readings

Friedman, M. J. (2013). Finalizing PTSD in DSM-5: Getting here from there and where to go next (PDF). *Journal of Traumatic Stress, 26*, 548-556. doi: 10.1002/jts.21840 PILOTS ID: 87751

Brewin, C. R., (2013). "I wouldn't start from here" - An alternative perspective on PTSD from the ICD-11: Comment on Friedman

(2013). *Journal of Traumatic Stress, 26,* 557-559. doi: 10.1002/jts.21843 PILOTS ID: 87752

Maercker, A., & Perkonigg, A. (2013). Applying an international perspective in defining PTSD and related disorders: Comment on Friedman (2013). *Journal of Traumatic Stress, 26,* 560-562. doi: 10.1002/jts.21852 PILOTS ID: 87753

Kilpatrick, D. G. (2013) The DSM-5 got PTSD right: Comment on Friedman (2013). *Journal of Traumatic Stress, 26,* 563-566. doi: 10.1002/jts.21844 PILOTS ID: 87754

Friedman, M. J. (2013). PTSD in the DSM-5: Reply to Brewin (2013), Kilpatrick (2013), and Maercker and Perkonigg (2013) (PDF). *Journal of Traumatic Stress, 26,* 567-569. doi: 10.1002/jts.21847 PILOTS ID: 87755

Kilpatrick, D. G., Resnick, H. S., Milanak, M. E., Miller, M. W., Keyes, K. M., Friedman, M. J. (2013). National estimates of exposure to traumatic events and PTSD prevalence using DSM-IV and DSM-5 criteria (PDF). *Journal of Traumatic Stress, 26,* 537-547. doi: 10.1002/jts.21848 PILOTS ID: 87750

Footnotes

1. Trimble, M.D. (1985). Post-traumatic Stress Disorder: History of a concept. In C.R. Figley (Ed.), *Trauma and its wake: The study and treatment of Post-Traumatic Stress Disorder.* New York: Brunner/Mazel. Revised from Encyclopedia of Psychology, R. Corsini, Ed. (New York: Wiley, 1984, 1994)

2. American Psychiatric Association. (1980). *Diagnostic and statistical manual of mental disorders,* (3rd ed.). Washington, DC: Author.

3. American Psychiatric Association. (1987). *Diagnostic and statistical manual of mental disorders,* (Revised 3rd ed.). Washington, DC: Author.

4. American Psychiatric Association. (1994). *Diagnostic and statistical manual of mental disorders,* (4th ed.). Washington, DC: Author.

5. American Psychiatric Association. (2000). *Diagnostic and statistical manual of mental disorders,* (Revised 4th ed.). Washington, DC: Author.

6. World Health Organization. (1992). *The ICD-10 classification of mental and behavioural disorders.* Geneva, Switzerland: Author.

7. Kessler, R.C., Chiu, W. T., Demler, O., Merikangas, K. R., Walters, E. E. (2005). Prevalence, severity, and comorbidity of 12-month DSM-IV disorders in the National Comorbidity Survey Replication. *Archives of General Psychiatry,* 62, 617-627. doi: 10.1001/archpsyc.62.6.617

8. De Jong, J., Komproe, T.V.M., Ivan, H., von Ommeren, M., El Masri, M., Araya, M., Khaled, N.,van de Put, W., & Somasundarem, D.J. (2001). Lifetime events and Posttraumatic Stress Disorder in 4 postconflict settings. *Journal of the American Medical Association,* 286, 555-562. doi: 10.1001/jama.286.5.555

9. American Psychiatric Association. (2013). *Diagnostic and statistical manual of mental disorders,* (5th ed.). Washington, DC: Author.

10. Keane, T.M., Wolfe, J., & Taylor, K.I. (1987). Post-traumatic Stress Disorder: Evidence for diagnostic validity and methods of psychological assessment. *Journal of Clinical Psychology,* 43, 32-43. doi: 10.1002/1097-4679(198701)43:1<32::AID-JCLP2270430106>3.0.CO;2-X

11. Friedman, M.J., Charney, D.S. & Deutch, A.Y. (1995) *Neurobiological and clinical consequences of stress: From normal adaptation to PTSD*. Philadelphia: Lippincott-Raven.

12. Shiromani, P. J., Keane, T. M., & LeDoux, J. E. (Eds.). (2009). *Post-Traumatic Stress Disorder: Basic science and clinical practice*. New York: Humana Press.

13. Friedman, M. J., Resick, P. A., Bryant, R. A., & Brewin, C. R. (2011). *Considering PTSD for DSM-5. Depression and Anxiety*, 28, 750-769. doi: 10.1002/da.20767

14. Herman, J.L. (1992). *Trauma and recovery*. New York: Basic Books.

15. Hinton, D. E., & Lewis-Fernandez, R. (2011). The cross-cultural validity of Posttraumatic Stress Disorder: Implications for DSM-5. *Depression and Anxiety*, 28, 783-801. doi: 10.1002/da.20753

16. Marsella, A.J., Friedman, M.J., Gerrity, E. & Scurfield R.M. (Eds.). (1996). *Ethnocultural aspects of Post-Traumatic Stress Disorders: Issues, research and applications*. Washington, DC: American Psychological Association.

17. Foa, E.B., Keane, T.M., Friedman, M.J., & Cohen, J.A. (Eds.). (2009). *Effective treatments for PTSD, Second Edition*. New York, NY: Guilford.

18. Raskind, M. A., Peterson, K., Williams, T., Hoff, D. J., Hart, K., Holmes, H., Homas, D., Hill, J., Daniels, C., Calohan, J., Millard, S. P., Rohde, K., O'Connell, J., Pritzl, D., Feiszli, K., Petrie, E. C., Gross, C., Mayer, C. L., Freed, M. C.., Engel, C., & Peskind, E. R. (2013). A trail of prazosin for combat trauma PTSD with nightmares in active-duty soldiers returned from Iraq and Afghanistan. *American Journal of Psychiatry*, Advance online publication. doi: 10.1176/appi.ajp.2013.12081133

19. Resick, P. A., Nishith, P., & Griffin, M. G. (2003). How well does cognitive-behavioral therapy treat symptoms of complex PTSD? An examination of child sexual abuse survivors within a clinical trial. *CNS Spectrums*, 8, 340-355.

20. Alvarez, J., McLean, C., Harris, A. H. S., Rosen, C. S., Ruzek, J. I., & Kimerling, R. (2011). The comparative effectiveness of cognitive processing therapy for male Veterans treated in a VHA Posttraumatic Stress Disorder residential rehabilitation program. *Journal of Consulting and Clinical Psychology*, 79, 590-599. doi: 10.1037/a0024466

21. Chard, K. M., Ricksecker, E. G., Healy, E. T., Karlin, B. E., & Resick, P. A. (2011). Dissemination and experience with cognitive processing therapy. *Journal of Rehabilitation Research and Development*, 49, 667-678. doi: 10.1682/JRRD.2011.10.0198

22. Bass, J. K., Annan, J., McIvor Murray, S., Kaysen, D., Griffiths, S., Cetinoglu, T., Wachter, K., Murray, L. K., & Bolton, P. A. (2013). Controlled trial of psychotherapy for Congolese survivors of sexual violence. *New England Journal of Medicine*, 368, 2182-219. doi:10.1056/NEJMoa1211853

23. Bryant, R.A., Mastrodomenico, J., Felmingham, K.L., Hopwood, S., Kenny, L., Kandris, E., Cahill, C. & Creamer, M. (2008). Treatment of acute stress disorder: A randomized controlled trial. *Archives of General Psychiatry*, 65, 659-667. doi:10.1001/archpsyc.65.6.659

CHAPTER 3

Is PTSD a Valid Mental Health Disorder?

Overview: Literature, History, and the DSM All Document PTSD

Marc-Antoine Crocq and Louis Crocq

Marc-Antoine Crocq is a former psychiatrist at Centre Hospitalier de Rouffach in Rouffach, France, and FORENAP Institute for Research in Neuroscience and Neuropsychiatry in France. His specialties include clinical and biological psychiatry and DSM. His father, Louis Crocq, was a doctor at the Cellule d'Urgence Médico-Psychologique, SAMU de Paris, Hôpital Necker in Paris. Louis Crocq became a certified French military psychiatrist in 1962.

Abstract

The term posttraumatic stress disorder (PTSD) has become a household name since its first appearance in 1980 in the third edition of the Diagnostic and Statistical Manual of Mental Disorders (DSM-lll) published by the American Psychiatric Association, In the collective mind, this diagnosis is associated with the legacy of the Vietnam War disaster. Earlier conflicts had given birth to terms, such as "soldier's heart," "shell shock," and "war neurosis." The latter diagnosis was equivalent to the névrose de guerre and Kriegsneurose of French and German scientific literature. This article describes how the immediate and chronic consequences of psychological trauma made their way into medical literature, and how concepts of diagnosis and treatment evolved over time.

Epics and Classics

Mankind's earliest literature tells us that a significant proportion of military casualties are psychological, and that witnessing death can leave chronic psychological symptoms. As we are reminded in Deuteronomy 20:1-9, military leaders have long been aware

"From shell shock and war neurosis to posttraumatic stress disorder: a history of psychotraumatology," by L. Crocq and MA Crocq, Dialogues Clin Neurosci. 2000;2(1):47-55. ©Les Laboratoires Servier.

that many soldiers must be removed from the frontline because of nervous breakdown, which is often contagious:

> When thou goest out to battle against thine enemies, and seest horses, and chariots, and a people more than thou... the officers shall say, What man is there that is fearful and fainthearted? Let him go and return unto his house, lest his brethren's heart faint as well as his heart. (King James Version)

Mankind's first major epic, the tale of Gilgamesh, gives us explicit descriptions of both love and posttraumatic symptoms, suggesting that the latter are also part of human fundamental experience. After Gilgamesh loses his friend Enkidu, he experiences symptoms of grief, as one may expect. But after this phase of mourning, he races from place to place in panic, realizing that he too must die. This confrontation with death changed his personality. The first case of chronic mental symptoms caused by sudden fright in the battlefield is reported in the account of the battle of Marathon by Herodotus, written in 440 BC (*History,* Book VI, transl. George Rawlinson):

> A strange prodigy likewise happened at this fight. Epizelus, the son of Cuphagoras, an Athenian, was in the thick of the fray and behaving himself as a brave man should, when suddenly he was stricken with blindness, without blow of sword or dart; and this blindness continued thenceforth during the whole of his afterlife. The following is the account which he himself, as I have heard, gave of the matter: he said that a gigantic warrior, with a huge beard, which shaded all his shield, stood over against him; but the ghostly semblance passed him by, and slew the man at his side. Such, as I understand, was the tale which Epizelus told.

It is noteworthy that the symptoms are not caused by a physical wound, but by fright and the vision of a killed comrade, and that they persist ewer the years. The loss of sight has the primary benefit of blotting out the vision of danger, and the secondary benefit of procuring support and care. Frightening battle dreams are mentioned by Hippocrates (4607-377 bc), and in Lucretius' poem,

De Rerum Natura, written in 50 B.C. (Book IV, transl. William Ellery Leonard):

> The minds of mortals... often in sleep will do and dare the same... Kings take the towns by storm, succumb to capture, battle on the field, raise a wild cry as if their throats were cut even then and there. And many wrestle on and groan with pains, and fill all regions round with mighty cries and wild, as if then gnawed by fangs of panther or of lion fierce.

This text shows very vividly the emotional and behavioral reexperiencing of a battle in sleep. Besides Greco-Latin classics, old Icelandic literature gives us an example of recurring nightmares after battle: the *Gisli Súrsson Saga* tells us that the hero dreams so frequently of battle scenes that he dreads obscurity and cannot stay alone at night.

Jean Froissart was the most representative chronicler of the Hundred Years' War between England and France. He sojourned in 1388 at the court of Gaston Phoebus, Comte de Foix, and narrated the case of the Comte's brother, Pierre de Beam, who could not sleep near his wife and children, because of his habit of getting up at night and seizing a sword to fight oneiric enemies. The fact that soldiers are awakened by frightening dreams in which they experience past battles is a common theme in classical literature, as, for instance, Mercutio's account of Queen Mab in Shakespeare's *Romeo and Juliet* (I, iv):

> Sometime she driveth o'er a soldier's neck.
> And then dreams he of cutting foreign throats.
> Of breaches, ambuscadoes, Spanish blades,
> Of healths five fathom deep; and then anon
> Drums in his ear, at which he starts and wakes,
> And being thus frighted, swears a prayer or two,
> And sleeps again.

Etiologic hypotheses were put forward by army physicians during the French Revolutionary wars (1792-1800) and the Napoleonic wars (1800-1815). They had observed that soldiers collapsed into protracted stupor after shells brushed past them, although they emerged physically unscathed. This led to the description of the *"vent du boulet"* syndrome, where subjects were frightened by the wind of passage of a cannonball. The eerie sound of incoming shells was vividly described by Goethe, in his memoirs of the cannonade at the battle of Valmy in 1792[1] "The sound is quite strange, as if it were made up of the spinning of a top, the boiling of water, and the whistling of a bird." In the same text, Goethe gives an account of the feelings of derealization and depersonalization induced by this frightening environment:

> I could soon realize that something unusual was happening in me ... as if you were in a very hot place, and at the same time impregnated with that heat until you blended completely with the element surrounding you. Your eyes can still see with the same acuity and sharpness, but it is as if the world had put on a reddish-brown hue that makes the objects and the situation still more scary ... I had the impression that everything was being consumed by this fire ... this situation is one of the most unpleasant that you can experience.

The Dawn of Modern Psychiatry

The psychiatrist Pinel is often depicted as freeing the insane from their chains; in his treatise entitled *Nosographie Philosophique* (1798), he described the case of the philosopher Pascal who almost drowned in the Seine when the horses drawing his carriage bolted. During the remaining eight years of his life, Pascal had recurring dreams of a precipice on his left side and would place a chair there to prevent falling off his bed. His personality changed, and he became more apprehensive, scrupulous, withdrawn, and depressive. From his experience with patients shocked by the events and wars of the French Revolution, Pinel wrote the first precise descriptions of war neuroses — which he called "cardiorespiratory neurosis" — and acute stuporous posttraumatic states — which he called "idiotism."

The Industrial Revolution and the introduction of steam-driven machinery were to give rise to the first civilian man-made disasters and cases of PTSD outside the battlefield. The public's imagination was struck by the first spectacular railway disasters, and physicians at the time were puzzled by the psychological symptoms displayed by survivors. Very soon, a controversy pitted the proponents of the organic theory, according to which the mental symptoms were caused by microscopic lesions of the spine or brain (hence the names "railway spine" and "railway brain"), against those who held that emotional shock was the essential cause and that the symptoms were hysterical in nature. This controversy was to last until World War I. It seems that the first mention of the term "traumatic neurosis" dates from that time: it was the title given in 1884 by the German physician Hermann Oppenheim[2] to his book containing a description of 42 cases caused by railway or workplace accidents. This new diagnosis was vehemently criticized by Charcot who maintained that these cases were only forms of hysteria, neurasthenia, or hystero-neurasthenia[3]. After Charcot's death in 1893, the term traumatic neurosis made its way into French-language psychiatry: witness the Belgian psychiatrist Jean Crocq[4] who in 1896 reported 28 cases caused by railway accidents. It is at the time of Charcot's famous Tuesday's lectures that Janet (1889) and Freud (1893) discovered traumatic hysteria with all its correlates: the dissociation caused by trauma, the pathogenic role of forgotten memories, and "cathartic" treatment. This was a first glimpse of what would later be known as the unconscious.

The Russian-Japanese war (1904-5) was marked by the siege of Port Arthur and the naval battle of Tsushima. It was probably during this conflict that post-battle psychiatric symptoms were recognized for the first time as such by both doctors and military command. Russian psychiatrists — notably Avtocratov, who was in charge of a 50-bed psychiatric clearing hospital at Harbin in Manchuria — are credited with being the first to develop forward psychiatric treatment. This approach may have been a response to the difficulty of evacuating casualties over huge distances at a time when the Trans-Siberian Railway was not yet completed. Whatever the initial reason, forward treatment worked, and would again be confirmed as the best method during succeeding conflicts. The number of Russian psychiatric casualties was much larger than expected (1500 in 1904 and 2000 in 1905) and the Red Cross Society of Russia was asked to assist. The German physician Honigman served in this body, and he was the first to coin the term "war neurosis" *[Kriegsneurose]* in 1907 for what was previously called "combat hysteria" and "combat neurasthenia"; also, he stressed the similarity between these cases and those reported by Oppenheim after railway accidents[5].

World War I

World War I (WWI) was the first modern war fought with massive industrial means. This dubious distinction is also, to a lesser degree, shared by the American Civil War. In any event, WWI is certainly the period in history when "modern" warfare coincided with a "scientific" psychiatry that endeavored to define diagnostic entities as we understand them today. The role played by WWI in advancing the knowledge of psychotraumatology in European psychiatry may be compared to that of WWII and the Vietnam War in American psychiatry.

The mental distress of WWI soldiers was repeatedly described in literary autobiographies by English, German, and French authors such as Robert Graves (*Goodbye to All That*, 1929), Ernst Junger (*In Stahlgewittern [Storm of Steel]*, 1920), or Henri Barbusse (*Le Feu*, 1916). Junger wrote: "The state takes away our responsibility but cannot ease our grief, we have to carry it alone and it reaches deep within our dreams."

Shell shock

Psychiatric casualties were reported very early in the war, in numbers that no-one had anticipated. The French physician Milian reported four cases of "battle hypnosis" following military actions in 1914[6]. The well-known German psychiatrist Robert Gaupp reported in 1917:

> The big artillery battles of December 1914... filled our hospitals with a large number of unscathed soldiers and officers presenting with mental disturbances. From then on, that number grew at a constantly increasing rate. At first, these soldiers were hospitalized with the others ... but soon we had to open special psychiatric hospitals for them. Now, psychiatric patients make up by far the largest category in our armed forces ...The main causes are the fright and anxiety brought about by the explosion of enemy shells and mines, and seeing maimed or dead comrades ...The resulting symptoms are states of sudden muteness, deafness ... general tremor, inability to stand or walk, episodes of loss of consciousness, and convulsions[7].

In his review of 88 cases of mental disorder in 1915, the French psychiatrist Régis had expressed a very similar opinion about the etiological role of witnessing the horrible death of comrades: "20% only presented with a physical wound, but in all cases fright, emotional shock, and seeing maimed comrades had been a major factor." The clinical picture of war neuroses differed only slightly in the two World Wars.

In the British military, patients presenting with various mental disorders resulting from combat stress were originally diagnosed as cases of shell shock, before this diagnosis was discouraged in an attempt to limit the number of cases. It is not known when the term began to be used. According to Merskey[8], the first mention may be a story published in the *Times* on February 6, 1915, indicating that the War Office was arranging to send soldiers suffering from "shock" to be treated in special wards at the National Hospital for the Paralyzed and Epileptic, in Queen Square. Also in February 1915, the term shell shock was used by Charles Myers in an article in *The Lancet* to describe three soldiers suffering from "loss of memory, vision, smell, and taste."[9,10] Myers reported on three patients, admitted to a hospital in Le Touquet during the early phase of the war, between November 1914 and January

1915. These patients had been shocked by shells exploding in their immediate vicinity and presented with remarkably similar symptoms. According to Myers, these cases bore a close relation to "hysteria." The first two patients were transferred to England for further treatment after a couple of weeks (the third was still being treated in Le Touquet when the article was published). As we shall see below, these patients might not have been evacuated to the peaceful surroundings of their home country had they sustained their wounds a year later.

Forward treatment

Indeed, the experience of the first war months and the unexpected large influx of psychiatric casualties led to a change in treatment approaches. The evacuation of psychiatric casualties to the rear became less systematic as the experience of the remaining war years convinced psychiatrists that treatment should be carried out near the frontline, and that evacuation only led to chronic disability. It was noticed that soldiers treated in a frontline hospital, benefiting from the emotional support of their comrades, had a high likelihood of returning to their unit, whereas those who were evacuated often showed a poor prognosis, with chronic symptoms that ultimately led to discharge from the military. Also, it was discovered that prognosis was better if the convalescing soldiers remained in the setting of the military hierarchy, rather than in a more relaxed hospital environment. Thus, by the end of 1916, evacuations became rare and patients were treated instead in forward centers, staffed by noncommissioned officers (NCOs), within hearing distance of the frontline guns and with the expectation of prompt recovery[11]. Treatment in the forward area *(psychiatrie de l'avant)* became the standard treatment, along with the five key principles summarized in 1917 by the American physician Thomas W. Salmon[12], chief consultant in psychiatry with the American Expeditionary Forces in France: immediacy, proximity, expectancy, simplicity, and centrality. *Immediacy* meant treating as early as possible, before acute stress was succeeded by a latent period that often heralded the development of chronic symptoms; *proximity* meant treating the patient near the frontline, within hearing distance of the battle din, instead of evacuating him to the peaceful atmosphere of the rear, which he would, understandably, never wish to leave; *expectancy* referred to the positive expectation of a prompt cure, which was instilled into the patient by means of a persuasive psychotherapy; *simplicity* was the use of simple treatment means such as rest, sleep, and a practical psychotherapy that avoided exploring civilian and childhood traumas; finally, *centrality* was a coherent organization to regulate the flow of psychiatric casualties from the forward area to the rear, and a coherent therapeutic doctrine adopted by all medical personnel. Salmon's principles were discovered independently and applied universally by all warring sides; only to be forgotten, and rediscovered again, during World War II.

Among the many treatment applied to stress disorders, one was much used during WWI, and scarcely at all during WWII: the application of electrical current, also called faradization. This was probably because motor symptoms, such as tremor, paralysis, contractions, limping, or fixed postures, were common during WWI, and rare in WWII. Faradization was criticized in post-war Austria; Wagner Jauregg — a professor of psychiatry in Vienna who was awarded a Nobel prize in 1928 — was even accused of excessive cruelty in the administration of this treatment and had to appear before an investigation committee, in which Sigmund Freud had the more enviable role of testifying as an expert[13]. A most radical description of electrotherapy was published in 1916 by Fritz Kaufmann[14], in which he explained how war neuroses could be treated in one session only by combining suggestion, authority, and steadfast application of electricity until the symptoms subsided — a form of *fight at outrance*.

Concussion, fright, or malingering?

Etiology was a controversial question that was reflected by the choice of terms: shell shock or war neurosis? Soma or psyche?

The now obsolete term shell shock, harking back to the *vent du boulet* of the Napoleonic wars, implied a somatic etiology, such as microscopic brain lesions due to a vascular, meningeal, white or gray matter concussion. Other diagnoses were also used to express the belief that the cause was more an emotional stressor, rather that a physical concussion. Such diagnoses were, for instance, war neurasthenia and war psychoneurosis, in France.

Emil Kraepelin (1856-1926), without doubt one of the most influential psychiatrists of our times, wrote about his experience with war neuroses during WWI in his autobiography, published posthumously in German in 1983[15]:

> [As early as 1917], the question of war neuroses was raised. We alienists all agreed that we should try to limit an excessively liberal granting of compensations which might lead to a sharp rise in the number of cases and claims ... the fact that all kinds of more or less severe psychiatric symptoms could lead to a lengthy stay in a hospital, or even to a discharge from the military with a generous disability pension, had disastrous consequences. This was compounded by the population's feeling of pity for the seemingly severely ill "war-shakers" *[Kriegszilterer]*, who drew attention to themselves on street corners and used to be generously rewarded. In such circumstances, the number of those who believed that a "nervous shock," or, especially, having been buried alive, entitled them to discharge and continuous support, increased dramatically.

Kraepelin's comments typify the controversies that raged at the time: (i) were the mental symptoms nothing more than malingering, with the clear objective of getting away from the frontline? Some 346 British and Commonwealth soldiers were actually shot on the orders of military command and this number certainly included soldiers suffering from acute stress disorder who walked around dazed or confused and were accused of desertion or cowardice; (ii) Did posttraumatic symptoms have pathoanatomical explanations? For instance, were they produced by a concussion of the brain or strained nerve fibers, as had been hypothesized in previous decades for the "railway spine" resulting from train accidents? (iii) A third explanation was a psychological origin - in that case, was the psychological cause limited to the overwhelming fright constituting the trauma, or was it necessary to delve further into the patient's previous personality? The cases of war neurosis observed during WWI were indeed a challenge to psychoanalytical theories; it was simply unbelievable that all cases were caused by childhood traumas and it had to be admitted that psychological symptoms could be produced by recent traumas. Freud had postulated that dreams were a wish fulfillment. Not until 1920, in an address at an international congress of psychoanalysts, did he allow one exception: the case of traumatic dreams, dreams that recall recent accidents or childhood traumas. And even this turned out to be no real exception at all: Freud eventually understood traumatic dreams as fitting into his wish-fulfillment theory of dreams in that they embodied the wish to master the trauma by working it through[16].

World War II

A dreadful invention of WWII was the concept "total war," with the systematic targeting of civilian populations, as exemplified by the millions of deaths caused by the Holocaust, the air raids on cities to break the morale of civilian populations, and the atomic bombs dropped over Hiroshima and Nagasaki. Despite WWI, most armies were once again unprepared for the great number of psychiatric casualties and psychiatrists were often viewed as a useless burden, as exemplified by a memorandum addressed by Winston Churchill to the Lord President of the Council in December, 1942, in the following terms[17]:

> I am sure it would be sensible to restrict as much as possible the work of these gentlemen [psychologists and psychiatrists] ... it is very wrong to disturb large numbers of healthy normal men and women by asking the kind of odd questions in which the psychiatrists specialize.

American psychiatry

American psychiatrists made a major contribution to the study of combat psychiatry during WWII. In *Psychiatry in a Troubled World,* William C. Menninger[18] shows how the lessons of WWI seemed at first to have been entirely forgotten by the American military: "during the initial battles in Africa, psychiatric casualties were sent back to base hospitals, often hundreds of miles from the front. Only 5% of these were able to return to duty." As explained by Jones[19], American planners, under the guidance of Harry Stack Sullivan, had believed that potential psychiatric casualties could be screened out prior to being drafted. Correspondingly, no psychiatrists were assigned to combat divisions and no provision for special psychiatric treatment units at the field army level or communications zone had been made. The principles of forward treatment were rediscovered during the North Africa campaign in 1943. Advised by the psychiatrist Frederick Hanson, Omar N. Bradley issued a directive on 26 April 1943, which established a holding period of 7 days for psychiatric patients at the 9th Evacuation Hospital, and for the first time the term "exhaustion" was prescribed as initial diagnosis for all combat psychiatric cases[20]. This word was chosen because it was thought to convey the least implication of neuropsychiatric disturbance. Beginning in 1943, treatment in the forward area similar to that in WWI was the rule, with the result that between 50% to 70% of psychiatric casualties were able to return to duty. Here again, the sheer number of psychiatric casualties was staggering. For the total overseas forces in 1944, admissions for wounded numbered approximately 86 per 1000 men per year, and the neuropsychiatric rate was 43 per 1000 per year.

In 1941, the first year of the war for the United States, Abram Kardiner — famous for having been analyzed by Freud himself - published a book based on his treatment of WWI veterans at Veterans Hospital No. 81 between 1922 and 1925[21]. In the light of the experience with WWII soldiers, Kardiner published a revised edition of his book at the end of the war[22]. He wrote that "the real lesson of WWI and the chronic cases was that this syndrome must be treated immediately to prevent consolidation of the neurosis into its chronic and often intractable forms." He identified traumatic neurosis as a "physioneurosis," thereby stressing the concomitance of somatic and psychological symptoms. Kardiner developed his own concept of the "effective ego" and he postulated that "ego contraction" was a major mechanism. Posttraumatic psychiatric symptoms in military personnel fighting in WWII were reported as early as 1945 by the American psychiatrists Grinker and Spiegel[23]. Their book — *Men under Stress* — is an excellent reflection of psychiatric thinking of the time; it remained a classic treatise on war psychiatry because of its detailed description of 65 clinical cases, its reference to psychoanalytical theories, and the description of cathartic treatment by "narcosynthesis" using barbiturates. Grinker and Spiegel distinguished acute "reactions to combat" from delayed "reactions after combat." The latter included "war neuroses," designated by the euphemism "operational fatigue" syndrome in the Air Force. Other chronic consequences of combat included passive-dependent states, psychosomatic states, guilt and depression, aggressive and hostile reactions, and psychotic-like states.

European studies

Long-lasting psychological disorders were not tolerated in the German military during WWII, and official doctrine held that it was more important to eliminate weak or degenerate elements rather than allow them to poison the national community. Interviews we conducted with Alsatian veterans who had been forcibly drafted into the Wehrmacht taught us that soldiers who had suffered acute combat stress (such as being buried under a bunker hit by a bomb) were given some form of psychological assistance soon after rescue; they were typically sent to a forward area first aid station *(Verbandsplatz)* where they received milk and chocolate and were allowed to rest. The Soviet army evolved its own system of forward treatment, under the responsibility of the unit's political (ie, morale) officer[24]. A look at the textbook of psychiatry published by Gurevich and Sereyskiy[25] in Moscow immediately after the war in 1946, at the height of Stalin's power, shows the existence of a specific diagnostic label to classify posttraumatic disorders. The authors describe the "affective shock reactions" *(affeklivno-shokovye reaktsii)*, a subtype of psychogenic reactions, that are observed after wartime events, earthquakes, or railway accidents; these are characterized by acute (a few days) and subchronic (a few months) symptoms. These Russian authors tended to emphasize cardiovascular and vasomotor symptoms, which reminds us of Da Costa's "irritable heart" in American Civil War soldiers. The literature on Holocaust and concentration camp survivors is too abundant to be summarized here. The best known of all the early works studying concentration camp survivors is probably the article published by Eitinger.[26]

In contrast to WWI, the course of symptoms over decades and their chronic nature were extensively studied in WWII survivors. For instance, in 1988, we studied[27] a group of French civilians living in the Alsace-Lorraine region who were conscripted into the German army and later held in captivity in Russia. This population of Alsace-Lorraine was interesting because it was bilingual, French and German, and had cultural roots in both heritages. The analysis of 525 questionnaires showed that, after over four decades, 82% still experienced intrusive recollections and nightmares of their wartime captivity; 73% actively attempted to avoid thoughts or feelings associated with the trauma; 71% reported a foreshortened sense of the future; and nearly 40% reported survivor guilt. Beyond PTSD, these survivors from Alsace-Lorraine also suffered lasting personality changes. We believe that an aggravating factor was the fact that these individuals returned home uncelebrated, embittered, psychologically isolated, and that they were caught in a web of psychological ambiguity. They had fought in the German army against their will and under the threat of their families being deported, and were considered unreliable by the Germans. They were surprised to be treated as German soldiers upon their capture by the Soviet army. They were repatriated to a new post-war social environment in a French society that was itself plagued by the guilt of its early surrender to the Nazis, and they felt misunderstood by some of their countrymen who criticized their incorporation into the German military as a form of treason.

The Vietnam War

During the Vietnam War, the principles of treating psychiatric casualties in the forward area were successfully applied, with a correspondingly low level of acute psychiatric casualties (11.5 per 1000 men per year). In contrast, the incidence of alcoholism and drug abuse was high. Similarly, the late and delayed effects of combat exposure in the form of PTSD were a significant source of suffering and disability among veterans in the United States. An estimated 700 000 Vietnam veterans — almost a quarter of all soldiers sent to Vietnam from 1964 to 1973 — required some form of psychological help. The prevalence of delayed and chronic PTSD, in spite of the careful prevention of psychiatric casualties in Vietnam itself, was a rude awakening. Trying to explain this paradox called for new hypotheses, for instance, that PTSD might be a common form of psychiatric casualty in "low-level" warfare[28]. Similar profiles had been observed in the French post-colonial wars in Indochina and Algeria[29]. This post-Vietnam syndrome, increasingly diagnosed in veterans in the seventies, ultimately led to the adoption of PTSD as a diagnostic category in 1980 in *DSM-III*. It seems puzzling that no such category existed in *DSM-II,* which had even abandoned the former *DSM-I* category of so-called "gross stress reaction," when it was published in 1968, the year of the Communist Jet Offensive in Vietnam.

Retrospect

There is currently a measure of consensus on the diagnosis and phenomenological description of PTSD, which is recognized as a specific syndrome in individuals who have experienced a major traumatic event. Most modem textbooks concur in describing this syndrome as comprising three groups of symptoms: (i) the recurrent and distressing re-experiencing of the event in dreams, thoughts, or flashbacks; (ii) emotional numbing and avoidance of stimuli reminiscent of the trauma; (iii) and a permanent state of increased arousal. The first symptoms of PTSD are often delayed and they are separated from the trauma by a latency period; however, once installed, the disorder tends to follow a chronic course and the symptoms do not abate with time. DSM-IV[30] has the merit of clearly distinguishing PTSD, a chronic syndrome, from acute stress disorder, which is short-lived and appears soon after the trauma. We tend to abusively interpret the literature of previous decades as if today's diagnostic categories had always existed. However, a clear distinction between acute stress disorder and chronic PTSD is usually lacking in previous works. Also, there was little attempt to predict the risk of developing PTSD. Providing the trauma is severe enough, most individuals will go on to develop PTSD. However, one puzzling question is that many survivors seemingly do not develop symptoms even after a severe stressor[31]. Likewise, the historical literature on PTSD offers few clues concerning effective treatment, once the symptoms have become chronic. The practice of forward treatment aiming to prevent the development of chronic disorders may have inspired today's psychological debriefing of disaster victims.

Footnotes

1. Goethe JW. Werke. Hamburger Ausgabe. Munich, Germany: Deutscher Taschenbuch Verlag; 1998:X,234. (der Ton ist wundersam genug, als wär' er zusammengesetzt aus dem Brummen des Kreisels, dem Butteln des Wassers und dem Pfeifen eines Vogels... konnt' ich jedoch bald bemerken, daβ etwas Ungewöhnliches in mir vorgehe... es schien, als wäre man an einem sehr heiβen Orte, und zugleich von derselben Hitze völlig durchdrungen, so daβ man sich mit demselben Element, in welchem man sich befindet, vollkommen gleich fühlt. Die Augen verlieren nichts an ihrer Stärke, noch Deutlichkeit; aber es ist doch, als wenn die Welt einen braunrötlichen Ton hätte, der den Zustand sowie die Gegenstände noch apprehensiver rnacht... mir schien vielmehr alles in jener Glut verschlungen zu sein... Es gehört übrigens dieser Zustand unter die am wenigsten wünschenswerten).
2. Oppenheim H. *Die Traumatischen Neurosen. 2nd ed. Berlin, Germany: Hirschwald.* 1892
3. Crocq L. *Les Traumatisines Psychiques de Guerre. Paris, France: Odile Jacob.* 1999
4. Crocq J. *Les Névroses Traumatiques. Étude Pathogénique et Clinique. Brussels, Belgium: H. Lamertin.*1896
5. Ellis PS. The origins of the war neuroses. Part I. *J R Nav Med Serv.* 1984;70:168–177. [PubMed]
6. Milian G. L'hypnose des batailles. *Paris Med.* 1915 Jan 2;:265–270.

7. Ulrich B., Ziemann B. *Frontalltag im Ersten Weltkrieg. Wahn und Wirklichkeit. Frankfurt, Germany: Fischer.* 1994:102–103.
8. Merskey H. Post-traumatic stress disorder and shell shock - clinical section. In: Berrios GE, Porter R, eds. *A History of Clinical Psychiatry. London, UK: The Athlone Press.* 1995:490–500.
9. Myers CM. Contributions to the study of shell shock. *Lancet.* 1915;13:316–320.
10. Brown EM. Post-traumatic stress disorder and shell shock - social section. In: Berrios GE, Porter R, eds. *A History of Clinical Psychiatry. London, UK: The Athlone Press.* 1995:501–508.
11. Winter D. *Death's Men. Soldiers of the Great War. London, UK: Allen Lane.* 1978:136.
12. Salmon TW. Care and treatment of mental diseases and war neuroses (shell shock) in the British army. *Mental Hygiene.* 1917;1:509–547.
13. Eissler KR. *Freud und Wagner-Jauregg vor der Kommission zur Erhebung Militärischer Pflichtverletzungen. Vienna, Austria: Löcker Verlag.* 1979
14. Kaufmann F. Die planmäßige Heilung komplizierter psychogener Bewegungsstörungen bei Soldaten in einer Sitzung. *In: Feldärzt Beilage Münch Med Wochenschr.* 1916;63:802ff.
15. Kraepelin E. *Lebenserinnerung. Berlin, Germany: Springer Verlag.* 1983:189.
16. Freud S. *Supplements to the Theory of Dreams. London, UK: Standard Edition.* 1920;XVIII:4–5.
17. Ahrenfeldt RH. *Psychiatry in the British army in the second World War. New York, NY: Columbia University Press.* 1958:26.
18. Menninger WC. *Psychiatry in a Troubled World. New York, NY: Macmillan.* 1948
19. Jones FD., ed. *War psychiatry. Textbook of Military Medicine. Walter Reed Army Medical Center, Washington DC: Office of the Surgeon General USA.* 1995
20. Glass AJ. *Neuropsychiatry in World War II. Vol II. Overseas Theaters. Washington DC: Office of the Surgeon General, Dept of the Army.* 1973
21. Kardiner A. The traumatic neuroses of war. *Psychosomatic Medicine Monograph II III. Menasha, Wis: George Banta Publishing Company.* 1941
22. Kardiner A., Spiegel H. *War Stress and Neurotic Illness. New York, NY: Paul B. Hoeber Inc.* 1947
23. Grinker RR., Spiegel JP. *Men Under Stress. Philadelphia, Pa: Blakiston.* 1945
24. Gabriel R. *Soviet Military Psychiatry: The Theory and Practice of Coping With Battle Stress. Westport, Conn: Greenwood Press.* 1986:33–37.
25. Gurevich MO., Sereyskiy M Ya. *Uchebnik Psikhiatrii. Moscow, Russia: Medgiz.* 1946:376–377.
26. Eitinger L. Pathology of the concentration camp syndrome. *Arch Gen Psychiatry.* 1961;5:79–87.[PubMed]
27. Crocq MA., Macher JP., Barros-Beck J., Rosenberg SJ., Duval F. Post-traumatic stress disorder in World War II prisoners of war from Alsace-Lorraine who survived captivity in the USSR. In: Wilson JP, Raphael B, eds. *The International Handbook of Traumatic Stress Syndromes. Stress and Coping Series. New York, NY: Plenum Press.* 1992;(chap 21):253–261.
28. Belenky G (ed). *Contemporary Studies in Combat Psychiatry. Westport, Conn: Greenwood Press.*1987:4.
29. Crocq L., Crocq MA., Barrois C., Belenky G., Jones FD. Low-intensity combat psychiatry casualties. In: Pichot P, Berner P, eds. *Psychiatry, the State of the Art. New York, NY: Plenum Press.* 1985;6:545–550.
30. American Psychiatric Association. *Diagnostic and Statistical Manual of Mental Disorders, 4th ed. Washington DC: American Psychiatric Association.* 1994
31. Turner S. Place of pharmacotherapy in post-traumatic stress disorder. *Lancet.* 1999;354:1404–1405.[PubMed]

In Some Cultures, PTSD is Understood as a Part of War

Sebastian Junger

Sebastian Junger is a renowned American journalist and documentarian. The author of The Perfect Storm (1997), he also authored an award-winning account of the war in Afghanistan.

The first time I experienced what I now understand to be post-traumatic stress disorder, I was in a subway station in New York City, where I live. It was almost a year before the attacks of 9/11, and I'd just come back from two months in Afghanistan with Ahmad Shah Massoud, the leader of the Northern Alliance. I was on assignment to write a profile of Massoud, who fought a desperate resistance against the Taliban until they assassinated him two days before 9/11. At one point during my trip we were on a frontline position that his forces had just taken over from the Taliban, and the inevitable counterattack started with an hour-long rocket barrage. All we could do was curl up in the trenches and hope. I felt deranged for days afterward, as if I'd lived through the end of the world.

By the time I got home, though, I wasn't thinking about that or any of the other horrific things we'd seen; I mentally buried all of it until one day, a few months later, when I went into the subway at rush hour to catch the C train downtown. Suddenly I found myself backed up against a metal support column, absolutely convinced I was going to die. There were too many people on the platform, the trains were coming into the station too fast, the lights were too bright, the world was too loud. I couldn't quite explain what was wrong, but I was far more scared than I'd ever been in Afghanistan.

I stood there with my back to the column until I couldn't take it anymore, and then I sprinted for the exit and walked home. I had no idea that what I'd just experienced had anything to do with combat; I just thought I was going crazy. For the next several months I kept having panic attacks whenever I was in a small place with too many people—airplanes, ski gondolas, crowded bars. Gradually the incidents stopped, and I didn't think about them again until I found myself talking to a woman at a picnic who worked as a psychotherapist. She asked whether I'd been affected by my war experiences, and I said no, I didn't think so. But for some reason I described my puzzling panic attack in the subway. "That's called post-traumatic stress disorder," she said. "You'll be hearing a lot more about that in the next few years."

I had classic short-term (acute) PTSD. From an evolutionary perspective, it's exactly the response you want to have when your life is in danger: you want to be vigilant, you want to react to strange noises, you want to sleep lightly and wake easily, you want to have flashbacks that remind you of the danger, and you want to be, by turns, anxious and depressed. Anxiety keeps you ready to fight, and depression keeps you from being too active and putting yourself at greater risk. This is a universal human adaptation to danger that is common to other mammals as well. It may be unpleasant, but it's preferable to getting eaten. (Because PTSD is so adaptive, many have begun leaving the word "disorder" out of the term to avoid stigmatizing a basically healthy reaction.)

Because PTSD is a natural response to danger, it's almost unavoidable in the short term and mostly self-correcting in the long term. Only about 20 percent of people exposed to trauma react with long-term (chronic) PTSD. Rape is one of the most psychologically devastating things that can happen to a person, for example— far more traumatizing than most military deployments—and, according to a 1992 study published in the *Journal of Traumatic Stress*, 94 percent of rape survivors exhibit signs of extreme trauma immediately afterward. And yet, nine months later 47 percent of rape survivors have recovered enough to resume living normal lives.

Combat is generally less traumatic than rape but harder to recover from. The reason, strangely, is that the trauma of combat is interwoven with other, positive experiences that become difficult to separate from the harm. "Treating combat veterans is different from treating rape victims, because rape victims don't have this idea that some aspects of their experience are worth retaining," says Dr. Rachel Yehuda, a professor of psychiatry and neuroscience and director of traumatic-stress studies at Mount Sinai Hospital in New York. Yehuda has studied PTSD in a wide range of people, including combat veterans and Holocaust survivors. "For most people in combat, their experiences range from the best to the worst of times," Yehuda adds. "It's the most important thing someone has ever done—especially since these people are so young when they go in—and it's probably the first time they're ever free, completely, of their societal constraints. They're going to miss being entrenched in this very important and defining world."

Oddly, one of the most traumatic events for soldiers is witnessing harm to other people—even to the enemy. In a survey done after the first Gulf War by David Marlowe, an expert in stress-related disorders working with the Department of Defense, combat veterans reported that killing an enemy soldier—or even witnessing one getting killed—was more distressing than being wounded oneself. But the very worst experience, by a significant margin, was having a friend die. In war after war, army after army, losing a buddy is considered to be the most distressing thing that can possibly happen. It serves as a trigger for psychological breakdown on the battlefield and re-adjustment difficulties after the soldier has returned home.

Terrible as such experiences are, however, roughly 80 percent of people exposed to them eventually recover, according to a 2008 study in the *Journal of Behavioral Medicine*. If one considers the extreme hardship and violence of our pre-history, it makes sense that humans are able to sustain enormous psychic damage and continue functioning; otherwise our species would have died out long ago. "It is possible that our common generalized anxiety disorders are the evolutionary legacy of a world in which mild recurring fear was adaptive," writes anthropologist and neuroscientist Melvin Konner, in a collection called *Understanding Trauma*. "Stress is the essence of evolution by natural selection and close to the essence of life itself."

A 2007 analysis from the Institute of Medicine and the National Research Council found that, statistically, people who fail to overcome trauma tend to be people who are already burdened by psychological issues—either because they inherited them or because they suffered trauma or abuse as children. According to a 2003 study on high-risk twins and combat-related PTSD, if you fought in Vietnam and your twin brother did not—but suffers from psychiatric disorders—you are more likely to get PTSD after your deployment. If you experienced the death of a loved one, or even weren't held enough as a child, you are up to seven times more likely to develop the kinds of anxiety disorders that can contribute to PTSD, according to a 1989 study in the *British Journal of Psychiatry*. And according to statistics published in the *Journal of Consulting and Clinical Psychology* in 2000, if you have an educational deficit, if you are female, if you have a low I.Q., or if you were abused as a child, you are at an elevated risk of developing PTSD. These factors are nearly as predictive of PTSD as the severity of the trauma itself.

Suicide by combat veterans is often seen as an extreme expression of PTSD, but currently there is no statistical relationship between suicide and combat, according to a study published in April in the *Journal of the American Medical Association Psychiatry*. Combat veterans are no more likely to kill themselves than veterans who were never under fire. The much-discussed estimated figure of 22 vets a day committing suicide is deceptive: it was only in 2008, for the first time in decades, that the U.S. Army veteran suicide rate, though enormously tragic, surpassed the civilian rate in America. And even so, the majority of veterans who kill themselves are over the age of 50. Generally speaking, the more time that passes after a trauma, the less likely a suicide is to have anything to do with it, according to many studies. Among younger vets, deployment to Iraq or Afghanistan *lowers* the incidence of suicide because soldiers with obvious mental-health issues are less likely to be deployed with their units, according to an analysis published in *Annals of Epidemiology* in 2015. The most accurate predictor of post-deployment suicide, as it turns out, isn't combat or repeated deployments or losing a buddy but suicide attempts *before* deployment. The single most effective action the U.S. military could take to reduce veteran suicide would be to screen for pre-existing mental disorders.

It seems intuitively obvious that combat is connected to psychological trauma, but the relationship is a complicated one. Many soldiers go through horrific experiences but fare better than others who experienced danger only briefly, or not at all. Unmanned-drone pilots, for instance—who watch their missiles kill human beings by remote camera—have been calculated as having the same PTSD rates as pilots who fly actual combat missions in war zones, according to a 2013 analysis published in the *Medical Surveillance Monthly Report*. And even among regular infantry, danger and psychological breakdown during combat are not necessarily connected. During the 1973 Yom Kippur War, when Israel was invaded simultaneously by Egypt and Syria, rear-base troops in the Israeli military had psychological breakdowns at three times the rate of elite frontline troops, relative to their casualties. And during the air campaign of the first Gulf War, more than 80 percent of psychiatric casualties in the U.S. Army's VII Corps came from support units that took almost no incoming fire, according to a 1992 study on Army stress casualties.

Conversely, American airborne and other highly trained units in World War II had some of the lowest rates of psychiatric casualties of the entire military, relative to their number of wounded. A sense of helplessness is deeply traumatic to people, but high levels of training seem to counteract that so effectively that elite soldiers are psychologically insulated from even extreme risk. Part of the reason, it has been found, is that elite soldiers have higher-than-average levels of an amino acid called neuropeptide-Y, which acts as a chemical buffer against hormones that are secreted by the endocrine system during times of high stress. In one 1968 study, published in the *Archive of General Psychiatry*, Special Forces soldiers in Vietnam had levels of the stress hormone cortisol go down before an anticipated attack, while less experienced combatants saw their levels go up.

Shell Shock

All this is new science, however. For most of the nation's history, psychological effects of combat trauma have been variously attributed to neuroses, shell shock, or simple cowardice. When men have failed to obey orders due to trauma they have been beaten, imprisoned, "treated" with electroshock therapy, or simply shot as a warning to others. (For British troops, cowardice was a capital crime until 1930.) It was not until after the Vietnam War that the American Psychiatric Association listed combat trauma as an official diagnosis. Tens of thousands of vets were struggling with "Post-Vietnam Syndrome"—nightmares, insomnia, addiction, paranoia—and their struggle could no longer be written off to weakness or personal failings. Obviously, these problems could also affect war reporters, cops, firefighters, or anyone else subjected to trauma. In 1980, the A.P.A. finally included post-traumatic stress disorder in the third edition of the *Diagnostic and Statistical Manual of Mental Disorders*.

Thirty-five years after acknowledging the problem in its current form, the American military now has the highest PTSD rate in its history—and probably in the world. Horrific experiences are unfortunately universal, but long-term impairment from them is not, and despite billions of dollars spent on treatment, half of our Iraq and Afghanistan veterans have applied for permanent disability. Of those veterans treated, roughly a third have been diagnosed with PTSD. Since only about 10 percent of our armed forces actually see combat, the majority of vets claiming to suffer from PTSD seem to have been affected by something other than direct exposure to danger.

This is not a new phenomenon: decade after decade and war after war, American combat deaths have dropped steadily while trauma and disability claims have continued to rise. They are in an almost inverse relationship with each other. Soldiers in Vietnam suffered roughly one-quarter the casualty rate of troops in World War II, for example, but filed for disability at a rate that was nearly 50 percent higher, according to a 2013 report in the *Journal of Anxiety Disorders*. It's tempting to attribute this disparity to the toxic reception they had at home, but that doesn't seem to be the case. Today's vets claim three times the number of disabilities that Vietnam vets did despite a generally warm reception back home and a casualty rate that, thank God, is roughly one-third what it was in Vietnam. Today, most disability claims are for hearing loss, tinnitus, and PTSD—the latter two of which can be exaggerated or faked. Even the first Gulf War—which lasted only a hundred hours—produced nearly twice the disability rates of World War II. Clearly, there is a feedback loop of disability claims, compensation, and more disability claims that cannot go on forever.

Part of the problem is bureaucratic: in an effort to speed up access to benefits, in 2010 the Veterans Administration declared that soldiers no longer have to cite a specific incident—a firefight, a roadside bomb—in order to be eligible for disability compensation. He or she simply has to report being impaired in daily life. As a result, PTSD claims have reportedly risen 60 percent to 150,000 a year. Clearly, this has produced a system that is vulnerable to abuse and bureaucratic error. A recent investigation by the V.A.'s Office of Inspector General found that the higher a veteran's PTSD disability rating, the more treatment he or she tends to seek until achieving a rating of 100 percent, at which point treatment visits drop by 82 percent and many vets quit completely. In theory, the most traumatized people should be seeking more help, not less. It's hard to avoid the conclusion that some vets are getting treatment simply to raise their disability rating.

In addition to being an enormous waste of taxpayer money, such fraud, intentional or not, does real harm to the vets who truly need help. One Veterans Administration counselor I spoke with described having to physically protect someone in a PTSD support group because some other vets wanted to beat him up for faking his trauma. This counselor, who asked to remain anonymous, said that many combat veterans actively avoid the V.A. because they worry about losing their temper around patients who are milking the system. "It's the real deals—the guys who have seen the most—that this tends to bother," this counselor told me.

The majority of traumatized vets are *not* faking their symptoms, however. They return from wars that are safer than those their fathers and grandfathers fought, and yet far greater numbers of them wind up alienated and depressed. This is true even for people who didn't experience combat. In other words, the problem doesn't seem to be trauma on the battlefield so much as re-entry into society. Anthropological research from around the world shows that recovery from war is heavily influenced by the society one returns to, and there are societies that make that process relatively easy. Ethnographic studies on hunter-gatherer societies rarely turn up evidence of chronic PTSD among their warriors, for example, and oral histories of Native American warfare consistently fail to mention psychological trauma. Anthropologists and oral historians weren't expressly looking for PTSD, but the high frequency of warfare in these groups makes the scarcity of any mention of it revealing. Even the Israeli military—with mandatory national service and two generations of intermittent warfare—has by some measures a PTSD rate as low as 1 percent.

If we weed out the malingerers on the one hand and the deeply traumatized on the other, we are still left with enormous numbers of veterans who had utterly ordinary wartime experiences and yet feel dangerously alienated back home. Clinically speaking, such alienation is not the same thing as PTSD, but both seem to result from military service abroad, so it's understandable that vets and even clinicians are prone to conflating them. Either way, it makes one wonder exactly what it is about modern society that is so mortally dispiriting to come home to.

Soldier's Creed

Any discussion of PTSD and its associated sense of alienation in society must address the fact that many soldiers find themselves missing the war after it's over. That troubling fact can be found in written accounts from war after war, country after country, century after century. Awkward as it is to say, part of the trauma of war seems to be giving it up. There are ancient human behaviors in war—loyalty, inter-reliance, cooperation that typify good soldiering and can't be easily found in modern society. This can produce a kind of nostalgia for the hard times that even civilians are susceptible to: after World War II, many Londoners claimed to miss the communal underground living that characterized life during the Blitz (despite the fact that more than 40,000 civilians lost their lives). And the war that is missed doesn't even have to be a shooting war: "I am a survivor of the AIDS epidemic," a man wrote on the comment board of an online talk I gave about war. "Now that AIDS is no longer a death sentence, I must admit that I miss those days of extreme brotherhood ... which led to deep emotions and understandings that are above anything I have felt since the plague years."

What all these people seem to miss isn't danger or loss, per se, but the closeness and cooperation that danger and loss often engender. Humans evolved to survive in extremely harsh environments, and our capacity for cooperation and sharing clearly helped us do that. Structurally, a band of hunter-gatherers and a platoon in combat are almost exactly the same: in each case, the group numbers between 30 and 50 individuals, they sleep in a common area, they conduct patrols, they are completely reliant on one another for support, comfort, and defense, and they share a group identity that most would risk their lives for. Personal interest is subsumed into group interest because personal survival is not possible without group survival. From an evolutionary perspective, it's not at all surprising that many soldiers respond to combat in positive ways and miss it when it's gone.

There are obvious psychological stresses on a person in a group, but there may be even greater stresses on a person in isolation. Most higher primates, including humans, are intensely social, and there are few examples of individuals surviving outside of a group. A modern soldier returning from combat goes from the kind of close-knit situation that humans evolved for into a society where most people work outside the home, children are educated by strangers, families are isolated from wider communities, personal gain almost completely eclipses collective good, and people sleep alone or with a partner. Even if he or she is in a family, that is not the same as belonging to a large, self-sufficient group that shares and experiences almost everything collectively. Whatever the technological advances of modern society—and they're nearly miraculous—the individual lifestyles that those technologies spawn may be deeply brutalizing to the human spirit.

"You'll have to be prepared to say that we are not a good society—that we are an *anti-human* society," anthropologist Sharon Abramowitz warned when I tried this theory out on her. Abramowitz was in Ivory Coast during the start of the civil war there in 2002 and experienced, firsthand, the extremely close bonds created by hardship and danger. "We are not good to each other. Our tribalism is about an extremely narrow group of people: our children, our spouse, maybe our parents. Our society is alienating, technical, cold, and mystifying. Our fundamental desire, as human beings, is to be close to others, and our society does not allow for that."

This is an old problem, and today's vets are not the first Americans to balk at coming home. A source of continual embarrassment along the American frontier—from the late 1600s until the end of the Indian Wars, in the 1890s—was a phenomenon known as "the White Indians." The term referred to white settlers who were kidnapped by Indians—or simply ran off to them— and became so enamored of that life that they refused to leave.

According to many writers of the time, including Benjamin Franklin, the reverse never happened: Indians never ran off to join white society. And if a peace treaty required that a tribe give up their adopted members, these members would often have to be put under guard and returned home by force. Inevitably, many would escape to rejoin their Indian families. "Thousands of Europeans are Indians, and we have no examples of even one of those aborigines having from choice become European," wrote a French-born writer in America named Michel-Guillaume-Saint-Jean de Crèvecoeur in an essay published in 1782.

One could say that combat vets are the White Indians of today, and that they miss the war because it was, finally, an experience of human closeness that they can't easily find back home. Not the closeness of family, which is rare enough, but the closeness of community and tribe. The kind of closeness that gets endlessly venerated in Hollywood movies but only actually shows up in contemporary society when something goes wrong—when tornados obliterate towns or planes are flown into skyscrapers. Those events briefly give us a reason to act communally, and most of us do. "There is something to be said for using risk to forge social bonds," Abramowitz pointed out. "Having something to fight for, and fight through, is a good and important thing."

Certainly, the society we have created is hard on us by virtually every metric that we use to measure human happiness. This problem may disproportionately affect people, like soldiers, who are making a radical transition back home.

It is incredibly hard to measure and quantify the human experience, but some studies have found that many people in certain modern societies self-report high levels of happiness. And yet, numerous cross-cultural studies show that as affluence and urbanization rise in a given society, so do rates of depression, suicide, and schizophrenia (along with health issues such as obesity and diabetes). People in wealthy countries suffer unipolar depression at more than double the rate that they do in poor countries, according to a study by the World Health Organization, and people in countries with large income disparities—like the United States—run a much higher risk of developing mood disorders at some point in their lives. A 2006 cross-cultural study of women focusing on depression and modernization compared depression rates in rural and urban Nigeria and rural and urban North America, and found that women in rural areas of both countries were far less likely to get depressed than urban women. And urban American women—the most affluent demographic of the study—were the *most* likely to succumb to depression.

In America, the more assimilated a person is into contemporary society, the more likely he or she is to develop depression in his or her lifetime. According to a 2004 study in *The Journal of Nervous and Mental Disease,* Mexicans born in the United States are highly assimilated into American culture and have much higher rates of depression than Mexicans born in Mexico. By contrast, Amish communities have an exceedingly low rate of reported depression because, in part, it is theorized, they have completely resisted modernization. They won't even drive cars. "The economic and marketing forces of modern society have engineered an environment promoting decisions that maximize consumption at the long-term cost of well-being," one survey of these studies, from the *Journal of Affective Disorders* in 2012, concluded. "In effect, humans have dragged a body with a long hominid history into an overfed, malnourished, sedentary, sunlight-deficient, sleep-deprived, competitive, inequitable and socially-isolating environment with dire consequences."

For more than half a million years, our recent hominid ancestors lived nomadic lives of extreme duress on the plains of East Africa, but the advent of agriculture changed that about 10,000 years ago. That is only 400 generations—not enough to adapt, genetically, to the changes in diet and society that ensued. Privately worked land and the accumulation of capital made humans less oriented toward group welfare, and the Industrial Revolution pushed society further in that direction. No one knows how the so-called Information Age will affect us, but there's a good chance that home technology and the Internet will only intensify our drift toward solipsism and alienation.

Meanwhile, many of the behaviors that had high survival value in our evolutionary past, like problem solving, cooperation, and inter-group competition, are still rewarded by bumps of dopamine and other hormones into our system. Those hormones serve to reinforce whatever behavior it was that produced those hormones in the first place. Group affiliation and cooperation were clearly adaptive because in many animals, including humans, they trigger a surge in levels of a neuropeptide called oxytocin. Not only does oxytocin create a glow of well-being in people, it promotes greater levels of trust and bonding, which unite them further still. Hominids that were rewarded with oxytocin for cooperating with one another must have out-fought, out-hunted, and out-bred the ones that didn't. Those are the hominids that modern humans are descended from.

According to one study published in *Science* in June 2010, this feedback loop of oxytocin and group loyalty creates an expectation that members will "self-sacrifice to contribute to in-group welfare." There may be no better description of a soldier's ethos than that sentence. One of the most noticeable things about life in the military is that you are virtually never alone: day after day, month after month, you are close enough to speak to, if not touch, a dozen or more people. You eat together, sleep together, laugh together, suffer together. That level of intimacy duplicates our evolutionary past very closely and must create a nearly continual oxytocin reward system.

Hero's Welcome

When soldiers return to modern society, they must go through— among other adjustments—a terrific oxytocin withdrawal. The chronic isolation of modern society begins in childhood and continues our entire lives. Infants in hunter-gatherer societies are carried by their mothers as much as 50 to 90 percent of the time, often in wraps that keep them strapped to the mother's back so that her hands are free. That roughly corresponds to carrying rates among other primates, according to primatologist and psychologist Harriet J. Smith. One can get an idea of how desperately important touch is to primates from a landmark experiment conducted in the 1950s by a psychologist and primatologist named Harry Harlow. Baby rhesus monkeys were separated from their mothers and presented with the choice of two kinds of surrogates: a cuddly mother made out of terry cloth or an uninviting mother made out of wire mesh. The wire-mesh mother, however, had a nipple that would dispense warm milk. The babies invariably took their nourishment quickly in order to rush back and cling to the terry-cloth mother, which had enough softness to provide the illusion of affection. But even that isn't enough for psychological health: in a separate experiment, more than 75 percent of female baby rhesus monkeys raised with terry-cloth mothers—as opposed to real ones—grew up to be abusive and neglectful to their own young.

In the 1970s, American mothers maintained skin-to-skin contact with their nine-month-old babies as little as 16 percent of the time, which is a level of contact that traditional societies would probably consider a form of child abuse. Also unthinkable would be the common practice of making young children sleep by themselves in their own room. In two American studies of middle-class families during the 1980s, 85 percent of young children slept alone—a figure that rose to 95 percent among families considered "well-educated." Northern European societies, including America, are the only ones in history to make very young children sleep alone in such numbers. The isolation is thought to trigger fears that make many children bond intensely with stuffed animals for reassurance. Only in Northern European societies do children go through the well-known developmental stage of bonding with stuffed animals; elsewhere, children get their sense of safety from the adults sleeping near them.

More broadly, in most human societies, almost nobody sleeps alone. Sleeping in family groups of one sort or another has been the norm throughout human history and is still commonplace in most of the world. Again, Northern European societies are among the few where people sleep alone or with a partner in a private room. When I was with American soldiers at a remote outpost in Afghanistan, we slept in narrow plywood huts where I could reach out and touch three other men from where I slept. They snored, they talked, they got up in the middle of the night to use the piss tubes, but we felt safe because we were in a group. The Taliban attacked the position regularly, and the most determined attacks often came at dawn. Another unit in a nearby valley was almost overrun and took 50 percent casualties in just such an attack. And yet I slept better surrounded by those noisy, snoring men than I ever did camping alone in the woods of New England.

Many soldiers will tell you that one of the hardest things about coming home is learning to sleep without the security of a group of heavily armed men around them. In that sense, being in a war zone with your platoon feels safer than being in an American suburb by yourself. I know a vet who felt so threatened at home that he would get up in the middle of the night to build fighting positions out of the living-room furniture. This is a radically different experience from what warriors in other societies go through, such as the Yanomami, of the Orinoco and Amazon Basins, who go to war with their entire age cohort and return to face, together, whatever the psychological consequences may be. As one anthropologist pointed out to me, trauma is usually a group experience, so trauma recovery should be a group experience as well. But in our society it's not.

"Our whole approach to mental health has been hijacked by pharmaceutical logic," I was told by Gary Barker, an anthropologist whose group, Promundo, is dedicated to understanding and preventing violence. "PTSD is a crisis of connection and disruption, not an illness that you carry within you."

This individualizing of mental health is not just an American problem, or a veteran problem; it affects everybody. A British anthropologist named Bill West told me that the extreme poverty of the 1930s and the collective trauma of the Blitz served to unify an entire generation of English people. "I link the experience of the Blitz to voting in the Labour Party in 1945, and the establishing of the National Health Service and a strong welfare state," he said. "Those policies were supported well into the 60s by all political parties. That kind of cultural cohesiveness, along with Christianity, was very helpful after the war. It's an open question whether people's problems are located in the individual. If enough people in society are sick, you have to wonder whether it isn't actually society that's sick."

Ideally, we would compare hunter-gatherer society to post-industrial society to see which one copes better with PTSD. When the Sioux, Cheyenne, and Arapaho fighters returned to their camps after annihilating Custer and his regiment at Little Bighorn, for example, were they traumatized and alienated by the experience—or did they fit right back into society? There is no way to know for sure, but less direct comparisons can still illuminate how cohesiveness affects trauma. In experiments with lab rats, for example, a subject that is traumatized—but not injured— after an attack by a larger rat usually recovers within 48 hours *unless it is kept in isolation,* according to data published in 2005 in *Neuroscience & Biobehavioral Reviews.* The ones that are kept apart from other rats are the only ones that develop long-term traumatic symptoms. And a study of risk factors for PTSD in humans closely mirrored those results. In a 2000 study in the *Journal of Consulting and Clinical Psychology,* "lack of social support" was found to be around two times more reliable at predicting who got PTSD and who didn't than the severity of the trauma itself. You could be mildly traumatized, in other words—on a par with, say, an ordinary rear-base deployment to Afghanistan—and experience long-term PTSD simply because of a lack of social support back home.

Anthropologist and psychiatrist Brandon Kohrt found a similar phenomenon in the villages of southern Nepal, where a civil war has been rumbling for years. Kohrt explained to me that there are two kinds of villages there: exclusively Hindu ones, which are extremely stratified, and mixed Buddhist/Hindu ones, which are far more open and cohesive. He said that child soldiers, both male and female, who go back to Hindu villages can remain traumatized for years, while those from mixed-religion villages tended to recover very quickly. "PTSD is a disorder of recovery, and if treatment only focuses on identifying symptoms, it pathologizes and alienates vets," according to Kohrt. "But if the focus is on family and community, it puts them in a situation of collective healing."

Israel is arguably the only modern country that retains a sufficient sense of community to mitigate the effects of combat on a mass scale. Despite decades of intermittent war, the Israel Defense Forces have a PTSD rate as low as 1 percent. Two of the foremost reasons have to do with national military service and the proximity of the combat—the war is virtually on their doorstep. "Being in the military is something that most people have done," I was told by Dr. Arieh Shalev, who has devoted the last 20 years to studying PTSD. "Those who come back from combat are re-integrated into a society where those experiences are very well understood. We did a study of 17-year-olds who had lost their father in the military, compared to those who had lost their fathers to accidents. The ones whose fathers died in combat did much better than those whose fathers hadn't."

According to Shalev, the closer the public is to the actual combat, the better the war will be understood and the less difficulty soldiers will have when they come home. The Israelis are benefiting from what could be called the shared public meaning of a war. Such public meaning—which would often occur in more communal, tribal societies—seems to help soldiers even in a fully modern society such as Israel. It is probably not generated by empty, reflexive phrases—such as "Thank you for your service"—that many Americans feel compelled to offer soldiers and vets. If anything, those comments only serve to underline the enormous chasm between military and civilian society in this country.

Another Israeli researcher, Reuven Gal, found that the perceived legitimacy of a war was more important to soldiers' general morale than was the combat readiness of the unit they were in. And that legitimacy, in turn, was a function of the war's physical distance from the homeland: "The Israeli soldiers who were abruptly mobilized and thrown into dreadful battles in the middle of Yom Kippur Day in 1973 had no doubts about the legitimacy of the war," Gal wrote in the *Journal of Applied Psychology* in 1986. "Many of those soldiers who were fighting in the Golan Heights against the flood of Syrian tanks needed only to look behind their shoulders to see their homes and remind themselves that they were fighting for their very survival."

In that sense, the Israelis are far more like the Sioux, Cheyenne, and Arapaho at Little Bighorn than they are like us. America's distance from her enemies means that her wars have generally been fought far away from her population centers, and as a result those wars have been harder to explain and justify than Israel's have been. The people who will bear the psychic cost of that ambiguity will, of course, be the soldiers.

A Bright Shining Lie

'I talked to my mom only one time from Mars," a Vietnam vet named Gregory Gomez told me about the physical and spiritual distance between his home and the war zone. Gomez is a pure-blooded Apache who grew up in West Texas. He says his grandfather was arrested and executed by Texas Rangers in 1915 because they wanted his land; they strung him from a tree limb, cut off his genitals, and stuffed them in his mouth. Consequently, Gomez felt no allegiance to the U.S. government, but he volunteered for service in Vietnam anyway. "Most of us Indian guys who went to Vietnam went because we were warriors," Gomez told me. "I did not fight for this country. I fought for Mother Earth. I wanted to experience combat. I wanted to know how I'd do."

Gomez was in a Marine Corps Force Recon unit, one of the most elite designations in the U.S. military. He was part of a four-man team that would insert by helicopter into enemy territory north of the DMZ and stay for two weeks at a time. They had no medic and no backup and didn't even dare eat C rations, because,

Gomez said, they were afraid their body odor would give them away. They ate Vietnamese food and watched enemy soldiers pass just yards away in the dense jungle. "Everyone who has lived through something like that has lived through trauma, and you can never go back," he told me. "You are 17 or 18 or 19 and you just hit that wall. You become very old men."

American Indians, proportionally, have provided more soldiers to America's wars than almost any other ethnic group in this country. They are also the product of an ancient and vibrant warring culture that takes great pains to protect the warrior from society, and vice versa. Although those traditions have obviously broken down since the end of the Indian Wars, there may be something to be learned from the principles upon which they stand. When Gomez came home he essentially isolated himself for more than a decade. He didn't drink, and he lived a normal life except that occasionally he'd go to the corner store to get a soda and would wind up in Oklahoma or East Texas without any idea how he got there.

He finally started seeing a therapist at the V.A. as well as undergoing traditional Indian rituals. It was a combination that seemed to work. In the 1980s, he underwent an extremely painful ceremony called the Sun Dance. At the start of the ceremony, the dancers have wooden skewers driven through the skin of their chests. Leather thongs are tied to the skewers and then attached to the top of a tall pole at the center of the dance ground. To a steady drumbeat, the dancers move in a circle while leaning back on the leather thongs until, after many hours, the skewers finally tear free. "I dance back and I throw my arms and yell and I can see the ropes and the piercing sticks like in slow motion, flying from my chest towards the grandfather's tree," Gomez told me about the experience. "And I had this incredible feeling of euphoria and strength, like I could do anything. That's when the healing takes place. That's when life changes take place."

America is a largely de-ritualized society that obviously can't just borrow from another society to heal its psychic wounds. But the spirit of community healing and empowerment that forms the basis of these ceremonies is certainly one that might be converted to a secular modern society. The shocking disconnect for veterans isn't so much that civilians don't know what they went through—it's unrealistic to expect anyone to fully understand another person's experience—but that what they went through doesn't seem relevant back home. Given the profound alienation that afflicts modern society, when combat vets say that they want to go back to war, they may be having an entirely healthy response to the perceived emptiness of modern life.

One way to change this dynamic might be to emulate the Israelis and mandate national service (with a military or combat option). We could also emulate the Nepalese and try to have communities better integrate people of different ethnic and religious groups. Finally, we could emulate many tribal societies—including the Apache—by getting rid of parades and replacing them with some form of homecoming ceremony. An almost universal component of these ceremonies is the dramatic retelling of combat experiences to the warrior's community. We could achieve that on Veterans Day by making every town and city hall in the country available to veterans who want to speak publicly about the war. The vapid phrase "I support the troops" would then mean actually showing up at your town hall every Veterans Day to hear these people out. Some vets will be angry, some will be proud, and some will be crying so hard they can't speak. But a community ceremony like that would finally return the experience of war to our entire nation, rather than just leaving it to the people who fought.

It might also begin to re-assemble a society that has been spiritually cannibalizing itself for generations. We keep wondering how to save the vets, but the real question is how to save ourselves. If we do that, the vets will be fine. If we don't, it won't matter anyway.

Many Different Factors Can Cause PTSD

Sally Satel

Sally Satel is an American psychiatrist in Washington, D.C. She serves as a lecturer at the Yale University School of Medicine. Her articles have appeared in major magazines and newspapers, including The New Republic, the Wall Street Journal, and the New York Times. Her topics include psychiatry and addiction.

M ilitary history is rich with tales of warriors who return from battle with the horrors of war still raging in their heads. One of the earliest known observations was made by the Greek historian Herodotus, who described an Athenian warrior struck blind "without blow of sword or dart" when a soldier standing next to him was killed. The classic term—"shell shock"—dates to World War I; "battle fatigue," "combat exhaustion" and "war stress" were used in Word War II.

Modern psychiatry calls these invisible wounds post-traumatic stress disorder. And along with this diagnosis, which became widely known in the wake of the Vietnam War, has come a new sensitivity to the causes and consequences of being afflicted with it.

Veterans with unrelenting PTSD can receive disability benefits from the Department of Veterans Affairs. As retired Army Gen. Eric K. Shinseki, secretary of Veterans Affairs, said last week, the mental injuries of war "can be as debilitating as any physical battlefield trauma." The occasion for his remark was a new VA rule allowing veterans to receive disability benefits for PTSD if, as non-combatants, they had good reason to fear hostile activity, such as firefights or explosions. In other words, veterans can now file a benefits claim for being traumatized by events they did not actually experience.

"The Battle Over Battle Fatigue," by Sally Satel, Mental Illness Policy Org., July 17, 2010. Reprinted by permission.

The very notion that one can sustain an enduring mental disorder based on anxious anticipation of a traumatic event that never materializes is a radical departure from the clinical—and common-sense—understanding that disabling stress disorders are caused by traumatic events that actually do happen to people. This is not the first time that controversy has swirled around the diagnosis of PTSD.

In brief, the symptoms of PTSD fall into three categories: re-experiencing (e.g., relentless nightmares; unbidden waking images; flashbacks); hyper-arousal (e.g., enhanced startle, anxiety, sleeplessness); and phobias (e.g., fear of driving after having been in a crash). Symptoms must last at least one month and impair the normal functioning to some degree. Overwhelming calamity, not only combat exposure, can lead to PTSD, including natural disasters, rape, accidents and assault.

Not everyone who confronts horrific circumstances develops PTSD. Among the survivors of the Oklahoma City bombing, 34% developed PTSD, according to a study by psychiatric epidemiologist Carol North. After a car accident or natural disaster, fewer than 10% of victims are affected, while among rape victims, well over half are affected. The reassuring news is that, as with grief and other emotional reactions to painful events, most sufferers get better with time, though periodic nightmares and easy startling may linger for additional months or even years.

Large-scale data on veterans are harder to come by. According to the major study of Vietnam veterans, the 1988 National Vietnam Veterans' Readjustment Study, 50% of those whose stress reactions were diagnosed as PTSD recovered fully over time. A re-analysis of the data, published in Science in 2006, found that 18.7% of Vietnam veterans suffered PTSD at some point after returning from war, but half had recovered by the time the study was conducted in the mid-1980s.

A 2010 article in the Journal of Traumatic Stress summarized over two dozen studies and found that among servicemen and women previously deployed to Iraq and Afghanistan, between 5% and 20% have been diagnosed with PTSD.

The story of PTSD starts with the Vietnam War. In the late 1960s, a band of self-described antiwar psychiatrists—led by Chaim Shatan and Robert Jay Lifton, who was well known for his work on the psychological damage wrought by Hiroshima—formulated a new diagnostic concept to describe the psychological wounds that the veterans sustained in the war. They called it "Post-Vietnam Syndrome," a disorder marked by "growing apathy, cynicism, alienation, depression, mistrust, and expectation of betrayal as well as an inability to concentrate, insomnia, nightmares, restlessness, uprootedness, and impatience with almost any job or course of study." Not uncommonly, Messrs. Shatan and Lifton said, the symptoms did not emerge until months or years after the veterans returned home.

This vision inspired portrayals of the Vietnam veteran as the kind of "walking time bomb" as immortalized in films such as "Taxi Driver" and "Rambo." In the summer of 1972, the *New York Times* ran a front-page story on Post-Vietnam Syndrome. It reported that 50% of all Vietnam veterans—not just combat veterans—needed professional help to readjust, and contained phrases such as "psychiatric casualty," "emotionally disturbed" and "men with damaged brains." By contrast, veterans of World War II were heralded as heroes. They fought in a popular war, a vital distinction in understanding how veterans and the public give meaning to their wartime hardships and sacrifice.

Psychological casualties are as old as war itself, but historians and sociologists note that the high-profile involvement of civilian psychiatrists in the wake of the Vietnam War set those returning soldiers apart. "The suggestion or outright assertion was that Vietnam veterans have been unique in American history for their psychiatric problems," writes the historian Eric T. Dean Jr. in "Shook over Hell: Post-Traumatic Stress, Vietnam, and the Civil War." As the image of the psychologically injured veteran took root in the national conscience, the psychiatric profession debated the wisdom of giving him his own diagnosis. During the Civil War, some soldiers were said to suffer "irritable heart" or "Da Costa's Syndrome"—a condition marked by shortness of breath, chest discomfort and pounding palpitations that doctors could not attribute to a medical cause. In World War I, the condition became known as "shell shock" and was characterized as a mental problem. The inability to cope was believed to reflect personal weakness—an underlying genetic or psychological vulnerability; combat itself, no matter how intense, was deemed little more than a precipitating factor. Otherwise well-adjusted individuals were believed to be at small risk of suffering more than a transient stress reaction once they were removed from the front.

In 1917, the British neuroanatomist Grafton Elliot Smith and the psychologist Tom Pear challenged this view, attributing the cause more to the experiences and less on those who suffered them. "Psychoneurosis may be produced in almost anyone if only his environment be made 'difficult' enough for him," they wrote in their book "Shell Shock and Its Lessons." This triggered a feisty debate within British military psychiatry, and eventually the two sides came to agree that both the soldier's predisposition to stress and his exposure to hostilities contributed to breakdown. By World War II, then, military psychiatrists believed that even the bravest and fittest soldier could endure only so much. "Every man has his breaking point," as the saying went.

In 1980, the American Psychiatric Association adopted post-traumatic stress disorder (rather than the narrower Post-Vietnam Syndrome) as an official diagnosis in the third edition of its Diagnostic and Statistical Manual. A patient could be diagnosed with PTSD if he experienced a trauma or "stressor" that, as DSM described it, would "evoke significant symptoms of distress in almost everyone." Rape, combat, torture and fires were those deemed to fall, as the DSM III required, "generally outside the range of usual human experience." Thus, while the stress was unusual, the development of PTSD in its wake was not.

No longer were prolonged traumatic reactions viewed as a reflection of constitutional vulnerability. They became instead a natural process of adaptation to extreme stress. The influence of individual differences shaping response to crisis gave way to the profound impact of the trauma, with its leveling effect on all human response.

If the pendulum swung too far, obliterating the role of an individual's own characteristics in the development of the condition, it served a political purpose. As British psychiatrist Derek Summerfield put it, the newly minted diagnosis of PTSD "was meant to shift the focus of attention from the details of a soldier's background and psyche to the fundamentally traumatic nature of war."

Messrs. Shatan and Lifton clearly saw PTSD as a normal response. "The placement of post-traumatic stress disorder in [the DSM] allows us to see the policies of diagnosis and disease in an especially clear light," writes combat veteran and sociologist Wilbur Scott in his detailed 1993 account "The Politics of Readjustment: Vietnam Veterans Since the War." PTSD is in DSM, Mr. Scott writes, "because a core of psychiatrists and Vietnam veterans worked conscientiously and deliberately for years to put it there… at issue was the question of what constitutes a normal reaction or experience of soldiers to combat." Thus, by the time PTSD was incorporated into the official psychiatric lexicon, it bore a hybrid legacy—part political artifact of the antiwar movement, part legitimate diagnosis.

While the major symptoms of PTSD are fairly straightforward— re-experiencing, anxiety and avoidance—what counted as a traumatic experience turned out to be a moving target in subsequent editions of the DSM.

In 1987, the DSM III was revised to expand the definition of a traumatic experience. The concept of stressor now included a secondhand experience. In the fourth edition in 1994, the range of "traumatic" events was expanded to include hearing about the unexpected death of a loved one or receiving a fatal diagnosis such as terminal cancer. No longer did one need to experience a life-threatening situation directly or be a close witness to a ghastly accident or atrocity. Experiencing "intense fear, helplessness, or horror" after watching the Sept. 11 terrorist attacks on television, for example, could qualify an individual for PTSD.

There is pitched debate among trauma experts as to whether a stressor should be defined as whatever traumatizes a person. True, a person might feel "traumatized" by, say, a minor car accident—but to say that a fender-bender counts as trauma alongside such horrors as concentration camps, rape or the Bataan Death March is to dilute the concept. "A great deal rides on how we define the concept of traumatic stressor, says Harvard psychologist Richard J. McNally, author of "Remembering Trauma." In the civilian realm, Mr. McNally says, "the more we broaden the category of traumatic stressors, the less credibly we can assign causal significance to a given stressor itself and the more weight we must place on personal vulnerability."

For some non-combat servicemen and women, anticipatory fear of being in harm's way can turn into a crippling stress reaction. But how often symptoms fail to dissipate after separation from the military and subsequently morph into a lasting disability is unknown.

Americans are deeply moved by the men and women who fight our wars. We have an incalculable moral debt, as Abraham Lincoln said, "to care for him who shall have borne the battle." Yet rather than broaden the definition of PTSD, it would do our veterans better to ensure they first receive quality treatment and rehabilitation before applying for disability status. Otherwise, how can we assess their prospects for meaningful recovery no matter their diagnosis?

The new regulations announced by Mr. Shinseki take the definition of PTSD further than any of his predecessors surely imagined.

Identifying Psychological Injury Helps Diagnosis and Treatment

David Forbes

David Forbes is Director, Australian Centre for Posttraumatic Mental Health. He also serves as professor of psychiatry at the University of Melbourne in Australia.

S erving on operational deployments in conflict zones carries not only the obvious physical threats, it also poses significant mental health risks. While depression and anxiety disorders are common among returned service personnel, post-traumatic stress disorder (PTSD) is perhaps the most commonly considered mental disorder in this group.

Approximately 8% of Australian Defence Force (ADF) members report current PTSD, though the rates of PTSD following specific deployments have not yet been published.

A parliamentary committee is currently investigating this issue as part of its inquiry into the care of ADF personnel injured on operations. The release date of the final report hasn't been confirmed, but so far submissions and public hearings have raised concerns about the risks of PTSD, disclosure of mental health problems and when it's safe to redeploy soldiers who have experienced mental ill health.

What is PTSD?

PTSD is a potentially debilitating mental condition characterised by intrusive recollections of a traumatic event. This might include repetitive nightmares and distress when faced with sights and sounds that remind the person of the trauma. People with PTSD are constantly on guard and look for threatening situations, meaning they're in a constant state of high physiological arousal.

Given the distress these trauma memories can evoke, survivors try hard to avoid thinking about them or coming into contact with related reminders, sometimes going to great lengths to move to more remote areas to stay away from possible cues. Avoidance can also take the form of emotional numbing, where the person with PTSD experiences an emotional "shutdown", with difficulty feeling love or happiness.

Survivors also may use alcohol or other substances to dampen levels of anxiety and blot out the nightmares and distressing memories. Such substance abuse, combined with emotional numbing, can significantly affect relationships with partners, families and friends.

Risk to Australian Soldiers

The years between the withdrawal of the last Australian soldier from Vietnam in 1973 and the conflict in East Timor in 1999 were relatively quiet for ADF members, with the exception of a number of briefer deployments in Cambodia (1991-93), Somalia (1992-95) and Rwanda (1994-5).

Over the past 13 years we've seen a significant change in the ADF's "operational tempo", with frequent military deployment to conflict zones. So it's likely that as a serving member of the ADF – whether soldier, sailor or airman – you have been deployed to a conflict zone on at least one, and often more than one, occasion. These deployments vary quite significantly in the level of risk and conflict confronted.

Importantly, current research informs us that the risk for mental health problems does not rise with increased deployments per se. Rather, the risk of PTSD is determined by the frequency and severity of the potentially traumatic events to which serving members may be exposed on these deployments.

PTSD Treatment

PTSD and other mental health problems that emerge in the context of deployment are treatable. We have very effective psychological and pharmacological treatments available, particularly if people can access these treatments early.

But serving members who experience these mental health problems on return from deployment face the dilemma about whether to step forward and report them to Defence medical personnel. Many ADF members, particularly in this heightened operational environment, are keen to be redeployed and fear that acknowledging a mental health problem will reduce their likelihood of being redeployed and will negatively affect their military career.

Of course, this is not a simple issue to address. The ADF has made significant efforts, particularly in recent years, to de-stigmatise mental health problems. It has tried to make clear to members that their psychological injuries will be regarded and treated the same as physical injuries: the aim is effective treatment followed by a rapid return to their military roles.

This task is made difficult in organisations such as defence forces, where globally and historically the culture has stigmatised people with mental health disorders. Such policy and culture changes take time to work their way through to the day-to-day experience of the serving member on the ground.

The desire to look after the interests of an ADF member with a mental health concern, however, must also be balanced against the need to protect the safety of this individual member and those with whom he or she may be deployed. Just as physical fitness to perform a role has to be assessed prior to deployment, a person's mental fitness to perform a role must also be assessed.

As with physical injuries, there are decisions to be made about the degree to which the mental health problem may interfere with functioning, and limit the capacity of the member to respond to the kinds of scenarios faced on deployment.

Redeployment After Mental Illness

We know that a history of prior mental health problems is a risk factor for development of future mental health problems. However, making this a "rule out" for future deployment is a sure fire path to reducing self-disclosure and further stigmatising mental health.

And many members recover well from a transient mental health disorder, so any risks posed by their previous psychological injuries are minimised.

Redeployment decisions, therefore, need to be made on a case-by-case basis, with careful consideration of the nature of the person's recovery and their future risk.

Over the years, the ADF has gained expertise in identifying psychological injury in its members and offering prompt treatment that in some cases allows the member to return to deployment if they wish.

Stigma around mental health still exists within the defence forces but this is slowly changing. Hopefully with time we can find a balance between protecting the safety of all members on deployment and encouraging open disclosure and acceptance of psychological injuries.

PTSD Is Not a Mental Illness

Denise Williams

Denise Williams is a freelance writer based in Chicago who advocates for the military and veterans.

P ost Traumatic Stress Disorder is not a mental illness. Unfortunately, the best treatment for PTS is mental health counseling. Fortunately, mental health counseling is the best treatment for PTS. Those two opposing statements are equally valid.

It is unfortunate in that because the treatment falls under the profession of mental health, too many make the seemingly natural assumption that the ailment or issue is a mental illness. There is no question that the symptoms of this physiological disease present as emotional or psychological problems. There have been other diseases that historically were considered purely psychological or emotional that are now understood to be purely physical, too.

Take for example, menopause and pre-menstrual syndrome. Throughout the history of modern medicine, the opinion of nearly every doctor, backed by medical literature, classified these as 'hysteria'. It wasn't too long ago that a woman experiencing extreme pain and mood swings was told it was all in her head. Thankfully, after years of research, and more importantly, education, no one now disputes that these are biological, physiological conditions with emotional and/or psychological presentations.

The contradictory statement, it is fortunate that mental health counseling is the only treatment for PTS, is a harder sell to the military and veteran mind. Even in the wider civilian society, mental health problems are too often viewed as weakness, or even a choice. To those who have spent years training to be mentally and physically tough, admitting to a mental health disorder is particularly tough.

"Post Traumatic Stress Disorder Is Not a Mental Illness," by Denise Williams, Chicago Tribune Media Group, June 10, 2014. Reprinted by permission.

From day one of Basic training, troops are taught to be strong, mentally and physically. This is an absolute requirement of military training, and frankly, one that cannot and should not change. Having an Army of hypochondriacs who run crying for a bandage every time they scrape their knee would seriously undermine the capabilities of our Armed Forces. But recognizing that when the bone is sticking out through your shin that it might be time to go see the medic is just as critical; as critical as it is to understanding PTS is a physical malady.

There is no stigma attached to having a broken leg, a torn ligament or a dislocated disc. A part of your body has succumbed to the unnatural stresses placed on it. Just as no one blames a soldier who lands in a drop zone from a static line jump twenty times but on the twenty-first, his leg snaps, no one can be looked down upon when the electrical and chemical signals in the brain short out the synapses.

The fix for the broken leg is immobilization, rest and then careful rebuilding of the leg until it can again hold the weight of the body. At the very least, the treatment will include not doing that which caused the bone to fracture in the first place until it is healed. Not following this prescription just about guarantees permanent damage. If not treated promptly and with the necessary interventions later treatments may never be able to restore full use, or only do so after extensive reconstruction and therapy. This is an important corollary to keep in mind.

Equally important is the difference between a treatment and a cure. With prompt attention and care, it is possible to effect a functional cure, even of a bone break so severe, surgery is required. The cure is not the surgery, it is what happens naturally. Properly cared for and nutured, the body, not being subjected to further insult to the injured part, can heal.

Of course, when you break a leg, blow out your knee or tear a rotator cuff, you are also given a pill. Usually, many pills to address different parts of the injury. Pain pills, anti-inflammatories, even sleeping aids to ensure your body gets the rest it needs. These pills, like the surgery are not the cure. The cure is what our bodies do after medical intervention. That happens organically.

When discussing PTS as a medical condition, we need to address the symptoms. Take a look at this list:

- Trouble Sleeping
- Hallucinations
- Manic Episodes
- Personality Changes
- Loss of Reality
- Suicidal Thoughts
- Restlessness
- Easily Annoyed/Angered

This is actually not a list of PTS symptoms, they are just a few of the most commonly reported side effects of the drugs used to treat the symptoms of PTS.

On the one hand, it is critical to understand that Post-Traumatic Stress is not a mental illness but we cannot treat the disease as we do most illnesses with a pill. We must see this disease as a biological, physiological problem but treat it with mental health modalities. Otherwise, all we are doing is making the symptoms worse, turning our vets into zombies and further damaging their already compromised nervous systems.

Each drug a vet receives for a symptom acts by either suppressing neural reactions or adding synthetic hormones that act on the nervous system. Prescribing something that places further stress on an already damaged central nervous system is like trying to fix a broken leg by walking on it.

All of this is the long way of saying while PTS is not a mental illness, the best course of treatment is mental health counseling.

Pre-Wartime Experiences Contribute to PTSD

Morena Lauth-Lebens and Gerhard W. Lauth

Morena Lauth-Lebens and Gerhard W. Lauth are both associated with the Department of Special Education and Rehabilitation Science at the University of Cologne in Germany.

Phenomenology and Diagnosis

PTSD represents the only psychiatric condition where the exposure to a situational stressor and the subsequent reaction constitutes a diagnostic criterion. The ICD–10 criteria for diagnosing PTSD require that the individual [1] has been exposed to a traumatic incident [2] suffers from distressing re-experiencing symptoms elicited by the trauma. According to the DSM, three clusters of symptoms – intrusive memories, avoidance and arousal - must have been experienced for a period of at least one month. The apparent differences between the two diagnostic systems have been discussed more extensively in the guidelines published by the National Institute of Clinical Excellence[1]. However, the three-factorial DSM–IV framework raised controversies and a revision of diagnostic criteria has been proposed for the DSM-V[2]. Investigating a non-clinical sample, Elhai et al.[3] found that 67% of the healthy participants reported at least one traumatic event as defined in the DSM-IV, while 59% would meet the trauma criteria proposed in the DSM-V. Similarly, converging lines of evidence have called into question the conceptual distinction between delayed-onset and immediate-onset forms of PTSD introduced in the DSM-III[4].

To date, the diagnostic classification approaches forwarded by the ICD and DSM primarily operate on a categorical basis. They are almost exclusively focused on the presence or absence of symptoms

"Risk and Resilience Factors of Post-Traumatic Stress Disorder: A Review of Current Research", by Morena Lauth-Lebens and Gerhard W. Lauth, Clinical and Experimental Psychology, April 20, 2016. http://www.omicsonline.org/open-access/risk-and-resilience-factors-of-posttraumatic-stress-disorder-a-reviewof-current-research-2471-2701-1000120.pdf. Licensed Under CC BY-ND 4.0 International.

within a specified period and not yet sensitive for different trajectories. In response to dissatisfaction with the traditional paradigm, a new line of research emerged that departs from a categorical understanding of PTSD and shifts attention towards its developmental mechanisms. A veritable amount of literature has now been generated on the diverse avenues and outcomes of PTSD As a comprehensive review of 54 studies indicates, several dimensions traditionally conceived as symptoms might actually be antecedents of PTSD[5]. Even some of the hallmark features such as arousal have been designated as pretrauma factors that may contribute to the aetiology of PTSD. Further research is required then for discerning the antecedents from the consequences of PTSD research.

In an effort to systematize the heterogeneous pathways of PTSD, Bering[6] forwarded an empirically-derived typology that divides between the dependent, paranoid-hallucinating, suicidal and pain-related phenomenological subtypes of PTSD. They can be distinguished with respect to the presentation, duration and severity of their symptoms and potential comorbidities. Patients who belong to the dependent trajectory class tend to misuse substances in an effort to cope with traumatic experiences. Those within the paranoid-hallucinating class were vulnerable to borderline and paranoid personality disorders and delusions. Suicidal trajectories are associated with parasuicidal tendencies. Persons with a pain-related trajectories suffered from somatic problems, including lower back pain. Each of these pathways develops in response to a specific interaction of antecedent and situational factors and is then maintained by individual's habitual coping style. Fully consonant with the paradigm of multifinality and quality, the constellation of individual predisposition and situational stressors can elicit entirely different trauma pathways. Clinical and empirical evidence has been obtained that substantiates this compelling and intuitively appealing framework.

Aetiology of PTSD

While the vulnerability-stress model applies to almost every psychiatric disorder, its explanatory power becomes evident when considering the aetiology of PTSD. As has been pervasively demonstrated in past studies, exposure to a traumatic event constitutes a necessary but not the singular condition for PTSD. Some individuals never display clinically meaningful symptoms, despite having experienced a severe trauma[7]. Indeed, the majority of trauma victims seem to adjust in the aftermath of the critical event and less than 10% of them develop PTSD[8]. One compelling explanation for the differential effects relates to the well-documented principles of multifinality and equifinality, derived from extensive research on developmental psychopathology[9]. Since its very inception, the notion of multifinality and equifinality attracted considerable research interested and has been transferred to PTSD. According to the notion of multifinality, a certain stressor does not invariably result in the expression of a disorder but can evoke a range of responses. These are a function of individual differences in vulnerability, which predisposes for specific disorders. Equifinality describes the mechanisms whereby a variety of developmental pathways and antecedent condition result in the same end state[10]. With respect to the aetiology of PTSD, different types of trauma can elicit the same symptom clusters. Conversely, exposure to the same traumatic stressor can result in entirely different responses, ranging from subclinical to pathological ones. By implication, the traumatic stressor itself seems to be a catalyst that exacerbates the vulnerability conferred by biological, behavioural and social risk factors.

There has been extensive research on risk factors beyond the traumatic experience itself that might precede chronic forms of PTSD. Protective factors go beyond the mere absence of risks and actively operate under adverse conditions. They possess a unique protective value that contributes to positive developmental and mental health outcomes in high-risk contexts[11]. Therefore, protective and risk are currently discussed as orthogonal rather than oppositional constructs. Traditionally, these predictors of PTSD have been stratified into pretrauma, peritrauma and posttrauma risk factors[12]. More recently, the specification of variables that precede and predict different PTSD trajectories has attracted extensive research coverage. Longitudinal data from a carefully designed study on the trajectories of PTSD in former political prisoners reveal some of the predictors of resilience and vulnerability[13]. To examine the prevalence and patterns of different trajectories, interviews were administered at two measurement points during a 14-year interval. A parsimonious and convincing four-factorial solution emerged from the data analysis and differentiates between chronic, resilient, recovered and delayed trajectories of PTSD. Among the sample consisting of 86 former political prisoners, the chronic course was the most prevalent one (36%). A similar number of resilient (27%) and recovered (26%) trajectories have been detected, while delayed courses of PTSD appear to be less common (12%). In response to notable changes in symptom presentation, 38% of the participants were removed from their initial trajectory class and assigned to a different one. Hence, the diagnosis of a particular trajectory is not an ultimate and invariant one. Indeed, there is considerable variation in the phenomenology and symptom presentation between individuals and over prolonged periods. To explain this variability, the study investigated how pre-, peri- and posttrauma factors contribute to the course of PTSD.

Essentially, chronic trajectories were frequently observed in patients with severe trauma experiences, higher numbers of intermediate comorbidities, lower education levels and reduced availability of social support. Conversely, the recovered pathway was predicted by fewer comorbid diagnoses and higher levels of social support. Resilient trajectories were only preceded by factors operating subsequent rather than prior to or during the trauma; the predictors implicated in resilient pathways include a lower number of comorbidities and an alleviated impulse to disclose about the trauma. Individuals who experienced social support were more likely to belong to recover, whereas maladaptive self-disclosure decreased the probability of resilient pathways. Interestingly, participants with a lower treatment frequency and self-disclosure tendency were more likely to belong to the resilient group. These observations might be a function of reduced symptom severity; the resilient participants seem to experience less strain from the onset and therefore exhibit a reduced demand for treatment and self-disclosure. Overall, the longitudinal data underscores the contribution of specific risk factors to the development and long-term trajectories of PTSD. To elaborate these risk and resilience mechanisms, the following sections provide an outline of current research on different PTSD predictors.

Pretrauma Risk Factors

Regarding the pretrauma and demographic factors of PTSD, the disorder seems to be more prevalent among trauma survivors with premorbid trauma experiences[14], a low educational level, lack of subjective preparedness and a history of childhood adversity[15]. A 4-year long longitudinal study on the factors that precipitate PTSD in a military sample reported a greater prevalence of the disorder among individuals with premorbid mental health problems. However, their unique contribution to PTSD risk is relatively weak compared to that of group cohesion and combat exposure. When controlling for the effect of baseline psychic symptoms, the amount of variance explained by the other two predictors did not change significantly[16]. By implication, the mental health status is not necessarily predictive for PTSD susceptibility and expression. A similar conclusion applies to the risk conveyed by prior trauma that has only been associated with increased PTSD risk if the trauma survivor already developed the disorder in response to the first trauma[17]. Interestingly, the relationship status at the time of deployment seems to be predictive for PTSD development in military samples: an increased risk has been observed among military service individuals who were single, divorced or separated[15].

One of the most consistent findings in PTSD research is the higher risk of this disorder in women. There is considerable support for a greater PTSD prevalence in female trauma survivors[17, 18]. Tolin and Foa[19] conducted a comprehensive meta-analysis of gender differences in PTSD and observed a twofold risk for women. Compared to males, females were twice as likely to fulfil the diagnostic criteria for PTSD. By implication, exposure to a traumatic event appears to induce a higher PTSD risk in women than in men. However, the evidence for significant gender differences is mixed and inconclusive to date. While researchers reported a twofold risk for PTSD among female survivors of an industrial disaster[20], others detected considerable[21,22,23] or no gender differences in the military[15, 24] but not in the civilian population[25]. Overall, contribution of gender to PTSD susceptibility and expression seems to depend on its interaction with other moderating factors such as trauma type. When comparing gender differences in PTSD across different types of trauma, only those involving physical or sexual assault seem place women at a greater risk than men[8]. Somewhat contrasting findings have been observed in a military sample, where males developed more severe symptoms of PTSD and distress than females in response to sexual abuse[26]. A closer inspection of the available findings reveals potential moderating factors that might account for the gender specific PTSD risks. Compared to women, men are more inclined to consume alcohol as a maladaptive coping strategy and this might confound disclosure and diagnosis of PTSD symptoms[26]. Also, there is ample evidence for the contribution of increased trait anxiety and subjective threat perceptions to PTSD and these predictors are more pronounced in females than in males. Complex interactions between multiple risk factors rather than linear gender effects can predispose females to develop PTSD. Women might not be inherently vulnerable to the disorder but exposed to specific conditions that amplify their risk for PTSD susceptibility and expression. To account for the gender differential in PTSD risk, a consideration of the distinctive predictors and vulnerability mechanisms in males and females is paramount. While rape and intimate partner violence have been investigated extensively among women, the risks they convey for men merits future research.

With respect to biological predisposition, an empirical synthesis of twin studies identified pretrauma reduced hippocampal volume, lower general intellectual ability and deficits in executive function, attention and declarative memory as prominent risk factors. Zhou et al.[26] screened 14.798 adult survivors six months after a severe earthquake and observed that old age, female gender and living alone represent salient risk factors for PTSD. Using standardized psychiatric instruments, Naeem et al.[27] obtained data from 1200 adult survivors of a severe earthquake in Pakistan and pervasively demonstrated that living in a joint family predicted resilience against PTSD. Results from a comprehensive meta-analysis inform about the risk conveyed by a set of pre-, peri- and posttrauma variables[28]. A total of 64 studies with 32,238 participants aged 6-18 have been selected from the extant literature. Pretrauma and demographic parameters such as age and premorbid psychiatric status yielded small to moderate effects and seem only weakly implicated in PTSD development. Consequently, their value as a predictor and target variable for screening is deemed as low. Discrepant findings on the predictive power of pretrauma psychopathology have been obtained by another meta-analysis, that examined predictive and protective factors of accident related PTSD in children and adolescents[29]. As the meta-analysis was exclusively focused on PTSD following, only 14 single studies fulfilled the inclusion criteria. From the range of predictors that have been examined, pretrauma psychopathology emerged as a prominent risk factor for PTSD. Given the restricted scope and sample size of the study, the outcomes need to be interpreted with caution and may not apply to other trauma types and populations. By implication, only a subset of pretrauma risk and demographic factors has been consistently associated PTSD development. As these variables seem relatively invariant and difficult to change, they may not be an effective target for intervention but potentially helpful for screening purposes.

Peritrauma Risk Factors

Of the factors that predict the development of PTSD, those operating during the event are among the principal ones. Trauma type, frequency and impact of the event as well as level of perceived distress are well-documented peritrauma risk factors in the military population[7]. Based on an examination 4762 military service individuals, perceived threat to life and the length of the traumatic episode have been designated as a major predictors of PTSD symptoms[15]. Concordantly, a meta-analysis comprising 45 single studies and a total of 31,422 subjects revealed trauma severity and peritrauma dissociation as prominent risk factors[14]. In a meta-analysis of PTSD predictors in children and adolescents, perceived trauma severity generated medium to large effect sizes. Subjective appraisals of trauma severity then appear to be associated with PTSD risk in younger sample. In response to consistent findings on the profound effect of trauma severity on PTSD susceptibility and expression, a dose- response model has been formulated[30, 31]. Advocates of this model implicate the magnitude of a traumatic event in the aetiology of PTSD and conceive it as a major predictor for symptom severity[18, 32]. While the dose-response model seems intuitively appealing and not without empirical support, the measures of trauma magnitude used in previous studies are inconsistent and complicated further by subjective appraisals of the critical event. Additionally, the dose-response model suggests a linear and direct effect of trauma severity on symptom presentation without sufficiently taking other well-documented social and cognitive influences into the equation[33, 34]. Indeed, the extent of social cohesion within a military unit seems to be a protective moderating factor that attenuates the risk conveyed by trauma dose[35].

Recent work departs from an almost exclusive concern with trauma magnitude and shifts research attention to the types of trauma, as these seem to possess a greater predictive utility for PTSD. More specifically, trauma types have been divided with respect to the degree of intentionality. Compared to traumatic incidences without human contributions such as natural disasters and motor vehicle accidents, rape and assault that implicate conscious harmful actions are significantly more likely to result in PTSD[36]. A systematic review compared the prevalence and trajectories of PTSD in non-intentional and intentional trauma exposed populations[37]. Measures of PTSD were compared one month and one year after trauma exposure. Overall, the mean prevalence of PTSD across all samples trended down from the first (28.8%) to the second measurement point 17.0%. A closer inspection of the data revealed a differential effect of trauma type on prevalence rates: Whereas a decline in PTSD rates has been observed among survivors of non-intentional trauma develop, the prevalence increased from 11.8% to 23.3%. Additionally, intentional trauma events have been associated with chronic courses of PTSD. In effect, the differentiation between intentional and non-intentional traumata might assist screening and intervention planning. Regarding the risk conferred by dissociation during the traumatic event, the data are discrepant and yet inconclusive. According to some scholars, the dissociative subtype constitutes a unique form of PTSD with distinctive clinical features that are invariably concealed in the traditional classification systems[38,39]. To others, the association between peritrauma dissociation and symptom severity is not yet sufficiently specified and the dissociation subtype of dubious value[40]. While numerous studies related peri-trauma dissociation to negative PTSD outcomes[41], others were unable to detect a clinically meaningful effect and reported at moderate associations at best[42, 43].

To clarify the apparently inconsistent findings, a meta-analysis has addressed this issue and explored the outcomes of carefully selected studies. In essence, the variability observed in PTSD symptoms seems to be a function of methodological differences rather than dissociation[44]. Consequently, there is no consensus regarding the classification of peri-traumatic dissociation as a global risk factor for PTSD[26]. Recent evidence lends support to a differential effect of peri-trauma dissociation that appears to be moderated by individual characteristics including gender and prior learning experience[45]. In effect, the risk conferred by peri-trauma dissociation might be expressed in a subset of patients with specific features. More specifically, it is vital to consider gender differences in the expression of peri-trauma dissociation. Women are at a greater risk for sexual assault and might be predisposed to dissociate during the trauma; the interplay of these vulnerability conditions together with their differential effects need to be elaborated in future studies. Compared to pretrauma factors, the stressors that operate during the trauma seem to be more predictive for PTSD.

Posttrauma Risk Factors

Compared to other parameters, posttrauma risk factors were ranked as the most powerful predictor for the outcome of PTSD across different trajectory types[46]. Within the group of posttrauma factors, the provision of social support appears to be the principal one[12, 27]. An elevated risk for PTSD has been observed in veterans with problematic relationship and reduced social support[47]. Further evidence for the significance of psychosocial factors emerged from a compelling study with 272 veterans of the military operations "Enduring Freedom" and "Iraqi Freedom." Rigorous measures for screening PTSD, social support and resilience revealed a strong association between social support and PTSD[48]. Similar results been obtained from a longitudinal study on military service individuals deployed in Iraq. In essence, low social support was associated with an increased PTSD risk[15]. While the extant literature on social support and PTSD is intriguing, the relationship between these parameters remains to be elobarated and validated by future research. Specifically the association between the quality of personal or intimate relationships and symptom presentation remains to be investigated further. Capitalizing on the findings obtained in past research, PTSD seems associated with negative forms of dyadic coping that can perpetuate the disorder.

Higher levels of co-morbidity were designated as another principal risk factor for PTSD in diverse populations such as former political prisoners[49] children and adolescents[31] and military personnel[50]. Data gathered from a meta-analysis on PTSD risks in children and adolescents revealed substantial effect sizes for posttrauma parameters, including social support and co-morbidity. From various comorbid disorders, depression confer the greatest risk for PTSD[31]. Interestingly, the risk conferred by co-morbid disorders has been moderated by the type of trauma and was greater in intentional than in unintentional ones[31]. Alternatively, the differential effect of comorbid disorders could be attributed to social context variables. Such an interpretation is not without rationale, as the young survivors of intentional and interpersonal trauma might be exposed to adverse environmental conditions. Together with posttrauma variables, those related to the trauma itself seem paramount in the development of PTSD. Overall, posttrauma risk factors have a considerable predictive utility as targets for screening tools[31]. Contrary to these results, a meta-analysis encompassing 32 studies revealed no significant association between comorbidity and combat-related PTSD risk. One explanation for the mixed findings refers to the heterogeneous sample composition across studies; the meta-analysis on the antecedents of combat-related PTSD has exclusively investigated data from military population[33]. Another reservation concerns the classification of comorbidity as a pretrauma or posttrauma factor. While comorbid psychological problems are frequently conceived as posttrauma variables, they might belong to the predisposing conditions. Data from previous studies report disparate findings as to whether comorbid psychological problems precede or follows PTSD[51]. Further research is warranted and necessary to reveal the causal ordering of comorbidity and PTSD.

A similar caveat applies to cognitions dimensions that have been implicated in the development and maintenance of PTSD. There is pervasive evidence for an association between dysfunctional cognitions and PTSD: Elsesser and Sartory[49] investigated dysfunctional cognitions in a group of recent trauma victims, PTSD patients and controls. Compared to controls and trauma-exposed controls, PTSD patients were more likely to express more negative appraisal and more dysfunctional thought control strategies. However, these tendencies might have already been present prior to the trauma and a contributor rather than a response to PTSD. Findings on the predictive power of posttrauma factors such as social support have practical implications because these are potentially modifiable and a promising treatment target.

Discussion and Conclusion

As has been vigorously documented in past research, a traumatic incidence alone is not sufficient to produce PSTD. To become pathogenic, a traumatic experience requires antecedent conditions that potentiate and release its effects. Individuals with traumatic experiences may be predisposed to develop PTSD but whether or not the disorder is actually expressed depends on the frequency, nature and intensity of several parameters ranging from biological to psychosocial ones[50]. Such insights underscore the need to introduce vulnerability and protective factors into the equation. Compared to other classes of factors, those operating subsequently to the trauma seem to possess considerable explanatory power. These are located within the scope of psychosocial interventions and more adaptive to treatment than relative static factors, such as demographic variables. In effect, the results on the predictive value of posttrauma parameters point to an optimistic message concerning PTSD treatment and symptom reduction.

A major objection that can be raised against prior research relates to methodological inconsistencies, as exemplified by the diverse sample and measures. Self-reports are among the most widely used measures, but subject to inherent limitations such as recall and selection biases and therefore of questionable methodological value[13, 33]. While it arguably difficult to attain objective data, the line of research on risk factors might benefit from using more standardized self-reports. Only a few risk factors have been regularly and systematically examined across studies. Therefore, discrepancies observed in prior studies accentuate the need for a more systematic research strategy. Different factors have been assessed with a variety of measures and different samples, resulting in inconclusive results. Given these large methodological variations between the available studies, different outcomes are simply to be expected and do not necessarily implicate opposing results. Also, many insights into the risk and resilience factors are drawn from military samples and may apply less to other subsets of the population. Hence, the conclusion derived from combat-related PTSD might be tentative sampling biases need to be taken into consideration. To arrive at a more conclusive evidence base, the use of standardised and robust methods across different samples is advocated.

Several intriguing research avenues emerge from this review and merit further investigation. First, there remains a strong need for additional research on processes of multifinality and equifinality implicated in PTSD. While the majority of risk and resilience factors reviewed here have been extrapolated from a veritable body of pervasive studies, a specification their interactive and differential effects is necessary. An inherent complexity associated with the identification of risk factors relates to their chronological ordering. By implication, the differential and interactive effects conferred by multiple risk factors together with the heterogeneous expression of PTSD confound attempts to discern singular predictors[26]. Indeed, the well-documented principles of multifinality and equifinality cast doubt about monolithic explanations. Second, further research is warranted to explain why the symptoms may vary and persist over long periods. Data collected in previous studies proliferate an understanding of the antecedents but reveal little about the mechanisms underlying the diverse trajectories and their unique phenomenology. Research suggests heterogeneity not just in risk factors but also on the course and presentation of PTSD symptoms, as evidenced by different trajectory types. As various parameters contribute to PTSD, the expression of symptoms and the trajectories differ considerably within and between individuals[26]. Detecting the factors that are implicated in different trajectories is paramount for advancing screening and intervention efforts. Indeed, the mechanisms associated with resilient or recovered trajectories remain to be specified. Not only the types but also the quantity of risks and resilience factors that precede different PTSD trajectories should be elaborated in further study. It is not without theoretical rationale to associate PTSD risk and severity with the number of risks that an individual is exposed to. Such cumulative models are certainly not new, but merit further investigation.

There is consistent evidence for the predictive and protective function of social support and relationship quality. By implication, the dyadic coping in couples where one partner has been exposed to traumatic experiences constitutes a promising area for further investigation. Future work on predisposing and protective factors can inform intervention providers and facilitate targeted treatment. However, evidence on the predisposing conditions is not yet fully conclusive needs to be substantiated further. A mega-analysis that encompasses meta-analytic data might be a promising strategy for synthesizing the evidence and deriving practical implications.

Footnotes

1. National Institute for Health and Clinical Excellence (2005) Post- Traumatic Stress Disorder (PTSD): The Management of PTSD in Adults and Children in Primary and Secondary Care. National Institute for Health and Clinical Excellence, London.
2. Marshall GN, Schell TL, Miles JN (2013) A multi-sample confirmatory factor analysis of PTSD symptoms: What exactly is wrong with the DSM- IV structure?. Clin Psychol Rev 33: 54-66.

3.   Elhai JD, Miller ME, Ford JD, Biehn TL, Palmieri PA, et al. (2012) Posttraumatic stress disorder in DSM-5: Estimates of prevalence and symptom structure in a nonclinical sample of college students. J Anxiety Disord 26: 58-64.
4.   Andrews B, Brewin CR, Philpott R, Stewart L (2007) Delayed-onset Posttraumatic Stress Disorder: A Systematic Review of the Evidence. Am J Psychiatry 164: 1319-1326.
5.   DiGangi JA, Gomez D, Mendoza L, Jason LA, Keys CB, et al. (2013) Pretrauma risk factors for posttraumatic stress disorder: A systematic review of the literature. Clin Psychol Rev 33: 728-744.
6.   Bering R (2012) Verlauf der Posttraumatischen Belastungsstörung.
7.   Xue C, Ge Y, Tang B, Liu Y, Kang P, et al. (2015) A meta-analysis of risk factors for combat-related PTSD among military personnel and veterans. PloS one 10: e0120270.
8.   Breslau N (2009) The Epidemiology of Trauma, PTSD, and Other Posttrauma Disorders. Trauma Violence Abuse 10: 198-210.
9.   Shalev AY, Segman RH (2007) Stress Hormones and Post Traumatic Stress Disorder. Basic Studies and Clinical Perspectives.
10.   Cicchetti D, Rogosch FA (1996) Equifinality and multifinality in developmental psychopathology. Development and Psychopathology 8: 597-600.
11.   Reuben JD, Shaw DS (2015) Resilience in the Offspring of Depressed Mothers: Variation Across Risk, Domains, and Time. Clin Child Fam Psychol Rev 18: 300-327.
12.   Sayed S, Iacoviello BM, Charney DS (2015) Risk factors for the development of psychopathology following trauma. Current psychiatry reports 17: 1-7.
13.   Maercker A, Gäbler I, O'Neil J, Schützwohl M, Müller M (2013) Long-term trajectories of PTSD or resilience in former East German political prisoners. Torture 23: 15-27.
14.   Abresch K, Bering R (2009) PTSD following a terrorist attack – a meta-analysis on possible risk factors. Poster zur XI European Conference on Traumatic Stress.
15.   Iversen AC, Fear NT, Ehlers A, Hacker H, Hull JH, et al. (2008) Risk factors for post-traumatic stress disorder among UK Armed Forces personnel. Psychol Med 38: 511-522.
16.   Rona RJ, Hooper R, Jones M, Iversen AC, Hull L, et al. (2009) The contribution of prior psychological symptoms and combat exposure to post Iraq deployment mental health in the UK military. J Trauma Stress 22: 11-19.
17.   Breslau N, Peterson EL, Schultz LR (2008) A second look at prior trauma and the posttraumatic stress disorder effects of subsequent trauma: a prospective epidemiological study. Arch Gen Psychiatry 65: 431-437.
18.   Sareen J (2014) Posttraumatic stress disorder in adults: impact, comorbidity, risk factors, and treatment. Can J Psychiatry 59: 460-467.
19.   Tolin DF, Foa EB (2006) Sex differences in trauma and posttraumatic stress disorder: a quantitative review of 25 years of research. Psychological bulletin 132: 959-992.
20.   Spindler H, Elklit A, Christiansen D (2010) Risk factors for posttraumatic stress disorder following an industrial disaster in a residential area: a note on the origin of observed gender differences. Gend Med 7: 156-165.
21.   Hourani L, Williams J, Bray R, Kandel D (2015) Gender differences in the expression of PTSD symptoms among active duty military personnel. J Anxiety Disord 29: 101-108.
22.   Crum-Cianflone NF, Jacobson I (2013) Gender differences of postdeployment post-traumatic stress disorder among service members and veterans of the Iraq and Afghanistan conflicts. Epidemiol Rev 36: 5-18.

23. Riddle JR, Smith TC, Smith B, Corbeiln TE, Engel CC, et al. (2007) Millennium Cohort: the 2001–2003 baseline prevalence of mental disorders in the US military. J Clin Epidemiol 60: 192-201.

24. Rona RJ, Fear NT, Hull L, Wessely S (2006) Women in novel occupational roles: mental health trends in the UK Armed Forces. Int J Epidemiol 36: 319-326.

25. Spitzer C, Barnow S, Völzke H, John U, Freyberger HJ, et al. (2008) Trauma and posttraumatic stress disorder in the elderly: findings from a German community study. J Clin Psychiatry 69: 693-700.

26. Zhou X, Kang L, Sun X, Song H, Mao W, et al. (2013) Prevalence and risk factors of post-traumatic stress disorder among adult survivors six months a er the Wenchuan earthquake. Compr Psychiatry 54: 493-499.

27. Naeem F, Ayub M, Masood K, Gul H, Khalid M, et al. (2011) Prevalence and psychosocial risk factors of PTSD: 18 months after Kashmir earthquake in Pakistan. J Affect Disord 130: 268-274.

28. Zoladz PR, Diamond DM (2013) Current status on behavioral and biological markers of PTSD: a search for clarity in a conflicting literature. Neurosci Biobehav Rev 37: 860-895.

29. Kremen WS, Koenen KC, Afari N, Lyons MJ (2012) Twin studies of posttraumatic stress disorder: Differentiating vulnerability factors from sequelae. Neuropharmacology 62: 647-653.

30. Trickey D, Siddaway AP, Meiser-Stedman R, Serpell L, Field AP (2012) A meta-analysis of risk factors for post-traumatic stress disorder in children and adolescents. Clin Psychol Rev 32: 122-138.

31. Cox CM, Kenardy JA, Hendrikz JK (2008) A Meta-Analysis of Risk Factors That Predict Psychopathology Following Accidental Trauma. J Spec Pediatr Nurs 13: 98-110.

32. Dohrenwend BP, Turner JB, Turse NA, Adams BG, Marshall R, et al. (2006) The psychological risks of Vietnam for US veterans: a revisit with new data and methods. Science 313: 979-982.

33. Johnson H, Thompson A (2008) The development and maintenance of post-traumatic stress disorder (PTSD) in civilian adult survivors of war trauma and torture: A review. Clin Psychol Rev 28: 36-47.

34. Kaysen D, Rosen G, Bowman M, Resick PA (2009) Duration of exposure and the dose-response model of PTSD. J Interpers Violence 25: 63-74.

35. Rosen GM, Lilienfeld SO (2008) Posttraumatic stress disorder: An empirical evaluation of core assumptions. Clin Psychol Rev 28: 837-868.

36. Brailey K, Vasterling JJ, Proctor SP, Constans JI, Friedman MJ (2007) PTSD symptoms, life events, and unit cohesion in US soldiers: baseline findings from the neurocognition deployment health study. J Trauma Stress 20: 495-503.

37. Santiago PN, Ursano RJ, Gray CL, Pynoos RS, Spiegel D, et al. (2013) A systematic review of PTSD prevalence and trajectories in DSM-5 defined trauma exposed populations: intentional and non-intentional traumatic events. PloS one 8: e59236.

38. Lanius RA, Vermetten E, Loewenstein RJ, Brand B, Schmahl C, et al. (2010) Emotion modulation in PTSD: clinical and neuro biological evidence for a dissociative subtype. Am J Psychiatry 167: 640-647.

39. Wolf EJ, Miller MW, Reardon AF, Ryabchenko KA, Castillo D, et al. 52. (2012) A latent class analysis of dissociation and posttraumatic stress disorder: evidence for a dissociative subtype latent class analysis of dissociation and PTSD. Arch Gen Psychiatry 69: 698-705.

40. Bryant RA (2007) Does dissociation further our understanding of PTSD?. J Anxiety Disord 21: 183-191.

41. Gil S, Weinberg M, Or-Chen K, Harel H (2015) Risk factors for DSM 5 PTSD symptoms in Israeli civilians during the Gaza war. Brain and behaviour.

42. Finklestein M, Solomon Z (2009) Cumulative trauma, PTSD and dissociation among Ethiopian refugees in Israel. J Trauma Dissociation 10: 38-56.

43. Van der Velden PG, Wittmann L (2008) The independent predictive value

44. of peritraumatic dissociation for PTSD symptomatology after type I trauma: A systematic review of prospective studies. Clin Psychol Rev 28: 1009-1020.

45. Lensvelt-Mulders G, van Der Hart O, van Ochten JM, van Son MJ, Steele K, et al. (2008) Relations among peritraumatic dissociation and posttraumatic stress: A meta-analysis. Clinical Psychology Review 28: 1138-1151.

46. Maercker A, Mohiyeddini C, Müller M, Xie W, Yang ZH, et al. (2009) Traditional versus modern values, self-perceived interpersonal factors, and posttraumatic stress in Chinese and German crime victims. Psychol Psychother 82: 219-232.

47. Pietrzak RH, Southwick SM (2011) Psychological resilience in OEF–OIF veterans: application of a novel classification approach and examination of demographic and psychosocial correlates. J Affect Disord 133: 560-568.

48. Pietrzak R, Johnson D, Goldstein M, Malley J, Rivers A, et al. (2010) Psychosocial buffers of traumatic stress, depressive symptoms, and psychosocial difficulties in veterans of Operations Enduring Freedom and Iraqi Freedom: The role of resilience, unit support, and post deployment social support. J Affect Disord 120: 188-192.

49. Polusny MA, Erbes CR, Murdoch M, Arbisi PA, Thuras P, et al. (2011) Prospective risk factors for new-onset post-traumatic stress disorder in National Guard soldiers deployed to Iraq. Psychol Med 41: 687–698.

50. Elsesser K, Sartory G (2007) Memory performance and dysfunctional cognitions in recent trauma victims and patients with Posttraumatic Stress Disorder. Clinical Psychology and Psychotherapy 14: 464-474.

51. Stander VA, Thomsen CJ, High ll-McRoy RM (2014) Etiology of depression comorbidity in combatrelated PTSD: A review of the literature. Clinical psychology review 34: 87-98.

52. Jovanovic T, Ressler KJ (2010) How the Neurocircuitry and Genetics of Fear Inhibition May Inform Our Understanding of PTSD. Am J Psychiatry 167: 648-662.

PTSD Is Really Just a Political Ploy

John Grant

John Grant writes for This Can't Be Happening!, an independent online alternative newspaper.

"If our wars were to make killers of all combat soldiers, rather than men who have killed, civilian life would be endangered for generations or, in fact, made impossible."
-J. Glenn Gray, from The Warriors: Reflections on Men in Battle (1959)

"I lost myself when we busted down that door. I lost myself. Please don't make me tell any more."
-Tom Mullian, from "Private Charlie Mac"

"Why can't we all just get along?"
-Rodney King

According to a *New York Times* report on Memorial Day, psychologists are re-thinking Post Traumatic Stress and other combat-related issues applied to multi-tour combat soldiers. According to *Times* writer Benedict Carey, the challenge these days is less emotional healing than how to unlearn the hyper-vigilance and shoot-first, ask-questions-later violence necessary for survival in a combat zone. That is, using the current vogue term, can

"Barbarism, Civilization and Modern Politics: PTSD as A Political Football in a Hobbesian Age," by John Grant, CounterPunch, June 22, 2016. Reprinted by permission. http://www. counterpunch.org/2016/06/22/barbarism-civilization-and-modern-politics-ptsd-as-a-political-football-in-a-hobbesian-age/. First appeared on counter punch.org.

experienced warriors be adjusted from a wild, adrenaline-fueled state of barbarism to one emphasizing community and civilization?

This is a politically tricky matter, since this sort of question inevitably leads to areas critical of US war policy. It's notable that the research cited by the May 30 *Times* story is being conducted in civilian universities (Harvard, the University of Texas, the University of New Haven, the University of North Carolina) and other civilian research sites — not by the military or the Veterans Administration, federal government agencies naturally reluctant to wade into anything that might be critical of US war policy. The veteran at the center of the *Times* story is an ex-Ranger whose unit specialized in what the *Times* reported is sometimes known as "vampire work," quick raids, often late at night, on high-profile insurgent targets for capture or killing. Just the term "vampire work" suggests the experience being considered is morally ambivalent.

A *New York Times Magazine* article on June 12th titled "Aftershock" took a different tack. Writer Robert F. Worth reported on new studies by military-connected researchers that suggested to him what we think of as PTSD might be less "emotional" and more "organic." The story's promo line asks: "Could PTSD turn out to be more physical than psychological?" The story treats new research on traumatic brain injury as some kind of watershed discovery questioning the psychological focus of PTSD on issues like bad memories that don't sit right in a veteran's mind and what is known as the "moral wound." On one hand, the article says the matter is complex, while the writing and headlines heavily emphasize the focus on physical damage as a major cause of PTSD.

Worth is an experienced Middle East correspondent with a new book on that region called *A Rage For Order* that has received glowing reviews. Two of these reviewers said the book described a "Hobbesian" world descended into ethnic and religious factionalism, a world that the US military has been inserted into for decades, often in a very destructive and even contradictory manner that exacerbates these Hobbesian conditions. Add to this the often hysterical follow-up to the Orlando massacre and the mix becomes extremely volatile. A well-armed, mentally-unbalanced Afghan/American kills 49 bar goers and tells a 911 operator he's working for ISIS; he also says he's loyal to al-Qaeda and Hezbollah, Sunni and Shia organizations at odds with each other. The militarist right see this as evidence of a new Cold War. They beat the drums for more military action and bombing against ISIS in Iraq's Anbar Province and Syria. President Obama is blamed for ISIS, and the right argues the occupation of Iraq should be permanent. The fact ISIS was created as a direct reaction to the US invasion and occupation of Iraq is lost in the Hobbesian madness.

Thomas Hobbes was a 17th century English political philosopher who believed in a brute basis for life and the need for a social contract necessarily enforced by violence. Here's a famous passage from *The Leviathan*:

> "In such condition, there is no place for industry; because the fruit thereof is uncertain: and consequently no culture of the earth; no navigation, nor use of the commodities that may be imported by sea; no commodious building; no instruments of moving, and removing, such things as require much force; no knowledge of the face of the earth; no account of time; no arts; no letters; no society; and which is worst of all, continual fear, and danger of violent death; and the life of man, solitary, poor, nasty, brutish, and short."

The conservative African American philosopher Thomas Sowell in *A Conflict of Visions* very neatly breaks down the political struggles in America. He sees it as a struggle between two basic visions: the constrained and unconstrained: The constrained visionaries include those like Hobbes who see life as brutish and those like Adam Smith who see moral values as a trade-off from the rule of self-interest and a free market. The un-constrained vision is rooted in the likes of Jean-Jacques Rousseau and William Godwin; they see humanity as perfectable — or in the spirit of the current term, "progressive." Progress is possible; in other words, a moral, decent society is not a matter of "trade-offs" from self-interest, but a matter of determined decisions and actions. Sowell sees the struggle between these two political visions as a continuum: "[I]n the real world there are often elements of each inconsistently grafted on the other, and innumerable combinations and permutations."

We see this left-right political struggle played out every night between MSNBC and Fox News. The two *Times* stories on PTSD suggest such a vision-based struggle is being opened with PTSD in this election season. As is said of the writing of history — that it's written by the winners — what war-trauma means is necessarily wrapped up with politics and whose stories defining it will prevail. If endless Hobbesian wars of factionalist violence is seen as our current reality — even seen by some seeping into the continental United States in Muslim garb — the military's motive for avoiding discussion of moral and psychological consequences from war is clear. The military's policy of resilience as a counter to trauma makes sense in this view. In a brutish, Hobbesian world, survival and military success revolve around power and violence, and the idea of a moral wound becomes a frivolous indulgence — a weakness. It's not surprising military researchers might emphasizes the physical, while civilian researchers might focus on a more optimistic, cooperative basis for humanity. On one side, the consequences of brute violence to morally-fragile human beings is a matter of effectiveness, while on the other, the same consequences are a hurdle to encouraging productive, civilized communities.

Veteran Runs Amok 2400 Years Ago

Post Traumatic Stress Disorder and the difficulties of war-fighters re-adjusting to community life back home is not a problem unique to an American culture faced with returning combat veterans from places like Vietnam, Iraq and Afghanistan. In fact, it's an ancient issue. Wars deemed necessary by political leaders have always had repercussions on the individuals sent to fight them.

The Greek playwright Euripides was a military veteran of the Peloponnesian Wars between Athens and Sparta when he wrote the play titled Herakles around 421 BCE. Robert Emmet Meagher has translated the play and written commentary on it in a book titled *Herakles Gone Mad: Rethinking Heroism In an Age of Endless War*. Meagher has a polemic purpose and suggests the city-state culture in Athens was suffering a form of societal trauma our modern culture would benefit from thinking about. When plays like this were performed in public, Meagher says, most of the men in the audience had, like Euripides, fought in terribly bloody battles against the rival city-state of Sparta. Meagher cites Judith Herman's book Trauma and Recovery and her "three stages of recovery." He says the mythic nature of the Athenian theater provided veterans and their families a public context of 1) safety, 2) remembrance and mourning and, 3) re-connection in which to consider larger questions of barbarism and civilization or community. Freud might have framed this as a struggle between Eros and Thanatos, the social forces of life and death he wrote about in the years after WWI.

Meagher's effort is a response to writers like Victor Davis Hanson, an authority on the Greek war culture of the time. In 2002, Hanson published *Carnage and Culture: Landmark Battles in the Rise of Western Power* and, in 2004, *Between War and Peace: Lessons From Afghanistan and Iraq*. "What I find particularly alarming," Meagher writes, referring to Hanson's work, "are the violent mantras that he claims to have derived from his studies and his involving of them over the past several years to help plunge America into two wars." Hanson is instrumental in the establishment of a historic and mythic framework for the post-911 warrior ethos that now pervades our culture from special ops to local militarized police departments.

Herakles is not an easy drama to stomach today; it was likely so even in 421 BCE. Meagher says it's often overlooked as "a wreck . . . rarely if ever produced and seldom studied." Meagher sees it as "the voice of a weary and wise warrior, who may have fought his last battle but whose labors have only begun." Meagher points out that Euripides received fewer civic prizes than other Greek playwrights. "He hated war, but loved the warrior. ... He loved

Athens, but hated her politics. … He reconciled his patriotism with fierce and loyal dissent and paid the price." He died in exile.

Herakles, of course, is a mythic hero, the son of Alkmene from a rape by Zeus. The play is fiction. Herakles is returning from war and the underworld where he rescued his warrior friend Theseus. His homecoming is complicated by a bloody intrigue from Lykos, a usurper who has killed Kreon, the ruler of Thebes, and his family. Lykos plans to kill the rest of the royal family, including Kreon's daughter, Megara, who is Herakles' wife. With so many men off to war, Herakles finds "a curious dearth of able-bodied men" in the city. He, thus, assumes the labor of killing Lykos, an action he undertakes soon enough. Here's how Meagher describes what happens:

> "Then something goes wrong. In fact everything goes wrong. Herakles suddenly turns on his own family and savagely slaughters them; and the only explanation given is that Lyssa, insanity personified, has descended on the house and loosened Herakles from his wits, driven him clear out of his mind."

Critics of the play say, at this point, "it snaps in two with the appearance of Madness (Lyssa). From that moment, we are arguably left with two unrelated dramas: one a triumphant homecoming, and the other a domestic disaster." Meagher says, on the contrary, the two parts do work together and Euripides is in fact up to something quite serious — maybe something considered by some a bit subversive.

"All the principle risk factors for posttraumatic stress, indicated by today's psychiatric specialists," Meagher writes, "were present, even rampant, in the war between the coalitions led by Athens and Sparta: morally suspect mandate, unclear mission, civilian slaughter, torture and murder of prisoners, rape and atrocity, massacres driven by rage and revenge."

At Herakles' homecoming, Euripides has a chorus of old veterans sing Herakles' praises: "Your life-exhausting labors, ridding the world of our most feral fears and demons, have given to the rest of us a less troubled life." This, of course, is the core idea behind our current warrior ethos.

Iris, a messenger from a jealous Hera, wife of Zeus, enters the stage with Lyssa, the embodiment of madness. Iris orders Lyssa to "Madly churn [Herakles'] soul until it swirls in confusion and seethes with child-slaughtering fantasies." Lyssa reluctantly does the deed, and Herakles, in a berserk rage focused on the usurper Lykos, then proceeds to kill his wife and children. An observer/ messenger tells the tale: "He was no longer himself." "Herakles stalked the halls of his own house." "[H]e wrestled furiously with an unseen opponent." "[H]e mounted a chariot that wasn't there."

The messenger's account ends with, "If there is a more miserable man anywhere I don't know who he could be." Herakles goes into a suicidal depression. "How short of death can I outrun the shame and infamy that awaits me?" he cries.

At this point, brother-in-arms Theseus shows up and tells Herakles, "Men of your blood and stature stand and hold their ground in whatever winds the gods send against them. They don't quit." In other words, though your dark, delusional actions have caused ruin to that which you love, your life is not over: You still have much to contribute to your society.

The play ends with the two men retreating to Theseus' home, where we are led to believe Herakles will over time be healed. It's an ancient Greek play, so there's no media blame culture or criminal justice system to deal with. Jealous Hera conveniently gets the rap for causing Herakles' madness. Again, this is a safe, public space of myth and ideas where very difficult issues can be dealt with. Meagher opens his commentary by quoting the ancient Greek philosopher Heraklitos: " 'The unfolding nature of things is wont to conceal itself.' Truth likes to hide. And, alas, we like to hide from it." Euripides' play is, thus, a device to ferret out the hidden "nature of things" inside the minds of the audience.

This type of theme plays out in modern drama, as well. The other night, I watched the 1971 film *The French Connection,* a gritty portrait of an obsessed New York narcotics cop in the early days of the Drug War. Gene Hackman as Popeye Doyle is not a military man, but he's a classic warrior character; his intense focus on mission would transfer nicely to a post-911, anti-terrorism police and military mindset focused on al Qaeda and ISIS lone wolves. Unlike Herakles, Popeye has no literal family; he has a professional family. The adrenaline excitement of hunting "dirty" guys is what his life is about, no matter the cost in destroyed cars "borrowed" from passers-by, near-misses on mothers-with-baby-carriages or, in the end, the fatal shooting of a police partner — albeit a cop who disliked him and taunted him about his intense, reckless nature that resulted in an earlier death of another detective.

An ancient Norse warrior fighting in a frenzy was known as a berserker. Both Herakles and Popeye Doyle kill unintended people close to them in a berserker frenzy. Friendly fire and collateral damage are the euphemisms we use these days for these kinds of unintended victims of violence. Sometimes it can strike very close to home. Due to a friend's understanding and intervention, Herakles will be healed and become part of the community. Though his French drug-supplier target gets away scot-free, due to the institutional understanding of the NYPD, Popeye is taken off the narcotics squad and moved to another assignment. Neither faces formal consequences for his actions; any and all consequences are internal and psychological.

From the Wild Zone to Community

Besides any potential critique of US war policy, the *Times* story on multi-tour combat soldiers adjusting to life back home gets close to touching the third-rail of anti-war movement political etiquette — the rule that says it's OK to criticize the war but not the warrior. Much of this etiquette question depends on who's talking about the problem: Are they friendly to US war policy or are they critical. In his play, was Euripides critical of Herakles or was he critical of the wars that had contributed to making Herakles run amok? Or was he just representing reality as he saw it in a courageous artistic fashion?

"The military is very good at identifying and amplifying the psychological factors that make a high-performance fighter," Benedict Carey writes. "The Pentagon has spent hundreds of millions of dollars on testing and analyzing these elements, but its researchers publish very few of their findings and refuse to speak in specifics on the record." The rigid regime of secrecy that controls information on military and intelligence agency activities also means these institutions are tight-lipped about their research into the act of killing. The military has a clear incentive to make killing more efficient and effective.

Starting in 2003 with *On Killing: The Psychological Cost of Learning to Kill in War and Society* by Lt. Col. Dave Grossman, all sorts of research has been undertaken on how to better get a man or woman to kill another human being. Grossman examined the record and history and found that the average person is reluctant to kill. How to overcome that natural reluctance and what kind of person is best suited for the task has become a field of knowledge, which Grossman has called killology. The Pentagon is in the leading edge of this kind of research.

This encouragement of an effective killer mentality works both ways in our "Hobbesian" wars. The much less sophisticated but, nevertheless, equally hyper-vigilant and hyper-masculine mindsets of trained fighters in organizations like al Qaeda and ISIS no doubt, like our military, work at improving their capacity for killing, since grotesque ruthlessness has become one of their strong suits. In light of Martin Luther King's idea of a widening gyre of vengeance and violence, this becomes a formula for self-generating, endless war. If you consider the misogynous elements of our Middle Eastern enemies and add the notion that in intense mortal combat one necessarily must assume some of one's adversaries' ruthless qualities in order to prevail over them — you've got the recipe for serious problems when experienced veterans of this kind of combat try to adjust to the social contracts of community at home.

Another tricky political implication of the *Times* story is how it relates to members of local, state and federal law enforcement agencies. Many multi-tour combat veterans end up in these jobs. Arguably this revolving-door reality contributes to the further militarization of our police forces and the tight relationships connecting federal military and police institutions with their local counterparts through the many regional and urban fusion centers. Language matters. What, for example, are the implications of the fact the police unit covering the African American community in Cleveland where 12-year-old Tamir Rice was shot and killed was called a Forward Operations Base (a FOB), the term of art for bases in Iraq and Afghanistan?

Mass incarceration and police killings of African Americans like young Rice led to the Black Lives Matter movement, which has become a left/right political flashpoint that has spawned a reaction among police known as the Blue Lives Matter movement. Huge blue billboards outside areas like Philadelphia and Chattanooga, Tennessee, feature a gold badge and the words BLUE LIVES MATTER. Cops are encouraged by the political right to feel cornered and to close ranks. Last month, Louisiana's governor signed a "Blue Lives Matter" bill that made police officers a protected class under hate-crime law. The irony is that hate crime laws were designed to help powerless, abused minorities, not one of the most powerful lobbies in America whose members consistently seem untouchable by the law. Add to this beleaguered sense among cops the cancerous problem of secrecy among the federal-to-local institutions of military and police and it's easy to see how the concept of "community" policing itself is considered by many to be on the ropes.

Dr. Charles A. Morgan III, a psychiatrist at the University of New Haven who has worked with special operations veterans, told the *Times* that the well-adjusted, civilized person "takes in information and then retreats into their head and wants to think about it, then maybe checks the environment again and thinks some more." Not so, he says, with a well-trained, multi-tour combat soldier in today's military. He or she is trained to "make a quick decision — then act and adjust as they go." It's not very flattering, but that smacks a lot of "Shoot first, ask questions later." One of the vets the *Times* writes about is frank about this. He's described as a tough man, always driven to be out in front ready to make things right. He rages at bad drivers and litterers — people who upset him by doing, or not doing, something. He wants to confront them and straighten them out. "You react — and next thing you know, the police are there," he says. This veteran is lucky; he has a supportive family and friends who have helped him "see the humanity of the people I was confronting." Others are not so lucky; and some of them are wearing police uniforms.

The question is an ancient one: What's "normal" and who decides? Is the dangerous, Hobbesian context of war requiring hyper-vigilance, quick thinking and very violent reactions normal? Or is normal more progressive and about family and job and cooperation with a diversity of people in pursuit of community and a civilized social contract? The struggle will go on.

In *The Hurt Locker,* the protagonist is a de-fuser of bombs in Iraq; he's incredibly brave, very good at the job and highly respected. When he goes home, he's lost, a fish out of water. At the end, following a scene of alienation in a grocery store, he's back in a cumbersome bomb suit in a dusty street in Iraq — "at home" again. How does society get a character like this to want to be with family members and non-veteran friends? To want to work at a job that doesn't trigger adrenaline but satisfies something else less violent but equally as rewarding. And, finally, how do we get our hypothetical multi-tour veteran to accept others unlike himself — not because he's ordered to but because diversity, difference and complexity are good — the secret to living in a community with others.

In "The Women of Trachis," the Greek playwright Sophocles has Herakles returning to a wife named Deianeira. In his commentary, Meagher says that "Warriors . . . live on the edge of the human circle. . . . And when the warrior returns, he all too often brings the wild back with him." Deianeira is torn: "Which is worse, having a husband at war or having a warrior at home?"

In the Euripides play, Theseus stops Herakles from killing himself and opens a healing path. Meagher puts it this way: "[T]he full narrative of Herakles' trauma must and will be reconstructed . . . [It] is an essential therapeutic element in the healing of trauma." The horrific facts can't be changed, but what they mean for the future can be "reconstructed." Theseus tells his comrade-in-arms acceptance and courage are what's required. "Compassion is the oxygen of any community worthy of the name," Meagher writes. "War is undoubtedly hell, but the peace that follows can be an even greater hell for the warrior."

There is only one place to end this story and that's in the arena of politics, where the real sorting out of these narrative struggles are undertaken. Meagher subtitles his book *Rethinking Heroism in an Age of Endless War*. The new, re-thought hero that would help open a path to healing for this torn nation is the hero who stops trying to argue that our debacles of war were patriotic necessities rather than tragic stepping-stones for further cycles of vengeance and violence. It's true, we need to better respect and honor our wounded veterans; but we also need to understand that "the wild" brought back by multi-tour combat vets from the "edge of the human circle" is not constructive for community or for civilization itself.

CHAPTER 4

Do Returning Soldiers with PTSD Get the Treatment They Need?

Overview: The VA Faces Challenges with Returning Soldiers' Mental Health Claims

Leighton Walter Kille

Leighton Walter Kille is editor in chief at The Conversation. He previously worked at Harvard Kennedy School Shorenstein Center on Media, Politics and Public Policy. He frequently writes about public healthcare and about the military.

In September 2015, a third-party report prepared for the U.S. Department of Veterans Affairs was released detailing a "leadership crisis" within the health care delivery system that serves over 9.1 million veterans. This report was mandated by the Veterans Access, Choice, and Accountability Act of 2014, which was passed by Congress amidst accusations that these healthcare facilities were underserving its patients. In some cases, delayed care was blamed for the death of veterans, some of whom were put on "secret lists" meant to falsify the documented patient wait times at V.A. facilities.

The report came on the heels of a tumultuous year and a half for the V.A. In May 2014, the department's Inspector General launched an investigation after managers of a V.A. hospital in Phoenix, AZ were accused of concealing months-long wait times; the probe eventually widened to include 26 medical facilities. Dr. Robert Petzel, the V.A. Undersecretary for Health quickly resigned, followed by Secretary Eric Shinseki. Two-months later, Robert McDonald was appointed to the position with a mandate to address long-standing problems at the agency. He soon faced criticism that he wasn't moving fast enough. In July 2015, McDonald appeared at a hearing of the House Veteran Affairs Committee, in which he asked for funds to close the $2.5 billion gap for his department's

"The U.S. Veterans Affairs Department and Challenges to Providing Care for Service Members: Research Roundup," by Leighton Walter Kille, Journalist's Resource, 11/10/2015. http://journalistsresource.org/studies/government/health-care/veterans-affairs-department-health-care-hospitals. Licensed Under CC BY 3.0 Unported.

2015 budget. During the hearing, McDonald was questioned by representatives on why these concerns were not brought up sooner and on his department's lack of accountability.

The intense pressure on V.A. facilities is the consequence of a number of interlinked factors. Thanks to improved medical care, more service members survive battle — currently, 16 are wounded for every one killed, compared to 2.6 soldiers wounded for every one killed in Vietnam. When soldiers do come home, their injuries can be more profound and the care required more involved. Thousands suffer from post-traumatic stress disorder (PTSD), many have lost one or more limbs, and even injuries that seem to leave no external sign can have a severe impact, including traumatic brain injury (TBI). Meanwhile, many of the V.A.'s technical patient management systems are out of date, leading to considerable duplication, delays and errors.

The proposed budget for the V.A. — which enrolls 9.1 million veterans of the estimated 21.9 million living U.S. veterans — in fiscal year 2015 is $158.6 billion, according to a May 2014 Congressional Research Service (CRS) report, which also notes that in 2015 the V.A. "anticipates treating more than 757,000 Operation Enduring Freedom (OEF), Operation Iraqi Freedom (OIF), and Operation New Dawn (OND) veterans." Between fiscal years 2011 and 2014, the number of V.A. enrollees increased 6.3%.

The Department of Defense estimates that more than 50,000 service members have been wounded in action during the Global War on Terror conflicts, but that figure does not fully capture mental health needs or still-emerging disabilities. A 2013 CRS report provides a detailed look at all casualty statistics and spells out the extent of the mental health injuries. A 2014 survey by the *Washington Post* and Kaiser Family Foundation of Iraq and Afghanistan veterans found deep dissatisfaction with current levels of government care. The Iraq and Afghanistan Veterans of America (IAVA) issued a 2014 report exploring the troubles with the V.A. claims backlog and detailing the experiences of service members.

A 2013 report from the Harvard Kennedy School estimates that spent or accrued costs for post-9/11 veterans' medical and disability care are already $134.3 billion, and may run as high as $970.4 billion by 2053. For more, see Brown University's "Costs of War" project which states as one of its goals "to identify less costly and more effective ways to prevent further terror attacks."

As *The New Republic* noted in a May 21 2014 article, the V.A.'s problems are anything but new: A 2001 report from the Government Accounting Office warned that wait times were often excessive even then. In 2007 the Army general in charge of the Walter Reed medical center was fired after the *Washington Post* revealed poor living conditions and excessive red tape at the facility. A presidential commission recommended "fundamental changes" to the V.A. system, but change has been slow to come. In 2013, a whistleblower revealed chronic understaffing and life-threatening medical mistakes at a Mississippi V.A. hospital and in July of that year, the Department of Veterans Affairs released a "strategic plan" to eliminate the claims backlog.

Below is a roundup of other background research on the Veterans Affairs Department and the challenges it faces in providing care to former soldiers, now and in the future. For journalists covering veterans issues, the *American Journal of Public Health* publishes a wide range of studies, including new research on suicide risks, gender disparities and the challenges of providing care to homeless veterans.

"Access to the U.S. Department of Veterans Affairs Health System: Self-reported Barriers to Care Among Returnees of Operations Enduring Freedom and Iraqi Freedom."

Elnitsky, Christine A.; et al. BMC Health Services Research, December 2013, 13:498. doi: 10.1186/1472-6963-13-498.

Abstract: "The U.S. Department of Veterans Affairs (VA) implemented the Polytrauma System of Care to meet the health care needs of military and veterans with multiple injuries returning from combat operations in Afghanistan and Iraq…. We studied combat veterans (n = 359) from two polytrauma rehabilitation centers using structured clinical interviews and qualitative open-ended questions, augmented with data collected from electronic health records. Our outcomes included several measures of exclusive utilization of VA care with our primary exposure as reported access barriers to care. Results: Nearly two thirds of the veterans reported one or more barriers to their exclusive use of VA healthcare services. These barriers predicted differences in exclusive use of VA healthcare services. Experiencing any barriers doubled the returnees' odds of not using VA exclusively, the geographic distance to VA barrier resulted in a seven-fold increase in the returnees' odds of not using VA, and reporting a wait time barrier doubled the returnee's odds of not using VA. There were no striking differences in access barriers for veterans with polytrauma compared to other returning veterans, suggesting the barriers may be uniform barriers that predict differences in using the VA exclusively for health care."

"Health Care Spending and Efficiency in the U.S. Department of Veterans Affairs."

Auerbach, David I.; Weeks, William B.; Brantley, Ian. RAND
Corporation, 2013.

Abstract: "In its 2013 budget request, the Obama administration sought $140 billion for the U.S. Department of Veterans Affairs (VA), 54% of which would provide mandatory benefits, such as direct compensation and pensions, and 40% of which is discretionary spending, earmarked for medical benefits under the Veterans Health Administration (VHA). Unlike Medicare, which provides financing for care when its beneficiaries use providers throughout the U.S. health care system, the VHA is a government-run, parallel system that is primarily intended for care provision of veterans. The VHA hires its own doctors and has its own hospital network infrastructure. Although the VHA provides quality services to veterans, it does not preclude veterans from utilizing other forms of care outside of the VHA network — in fact, the majority of veterans' care is received external to the VHA because of location and other system limitations. Veterans typically use other private and public health insurance coverage (for example, Medicare, Medicaid) for external care, and many use both systems in a given year (dual use). Overlapping system use creates the potential for duplicative, uncoordinated, and inefficient use. The authors find some suggestive evidence of such inefficient use, particularly in the area of inpatient care. Coordination management and quality of care received by veterans across both VHA and private sector systems can be optimized (for example, in the area of mental illness, which benefits from an integrated approach across multiple providers and sectors), capitalizing on the best that each system has to offer, without increasing costs."

"Recovering Servicemembers and Veterans: Sustained Leadership Attention and Systematic Oversight Needed to Resolve Persistent Problems Affecting Care and Benefits."

Government Accountability Office, November 2012, GAO-13-5.

Findings: "Deficiencies exposed at Walter Reed Army Medical Center in 2007 served as a catalyst compelling the Departments of Defense (DOD) and Veterans Affairs (VA) to address a host of problems for wounded, ill, and injured servicemembers and veterans as they navigate through the recovery care continuum. This continuum extends from acute medical treatment and stabilization, through rehabilitation to reintegration, either back to active duty or to the civilian community as a veteran. In spite of 5 years of departmental efforts, recovering servicemembers and veterans are still facing problems with this process and may not be getting the services they need. Key departmental efforts included the creation or modification of various care coordination and case management programs, including the military services' wounded warrior programs. However, these programs are not always accessible to those who need them due to the inconsistent methods, such as referrals, used to identify potentially eligible servicemembers, as well as inconsistent eligibility criteria across the military services' wounded warrior programs. The departments also jointly established an integrated disability evaluation system to expedite the delivery of benefits to servicemembers. However, processing times for disability determinations under the new system have increased since 2007, resulting in lengthy wait times that limit servicemembers' ability to plan for their future. Finally, despite years of incremental efforts, DOD and VA have yet to develop sufficient capabilities for electronically sharing complete health records, which potentially delays servicemembers' receipt of coordinated care and benefits as they transition from DOD's to VA's health care system."

"Department of Veterans Affairs: Strategic Plan to Eliminate the Compensation Claims Backlog."

Department of Veterans Affairs, January 2013

Introduction: "The VBA completed a record-breaking 1 million claims per year in fiscal years 2010, 2011, and 2012. Yet the number of claims received continues to exceed the number processed. In 2010 VBA received 1.2M claims. In 2011, VBA received another 1.3M claims, including claims from veterans made eligible for benefits as a result of the Secretary's decision to add three new presumptive conditions for Veterans exposed to Agent Orange. In 2012, VBA received 1.08M claims. Over the last three years, the claims backlog has grown from 180 thousand to 594 thousand claims.... But too many veterans have to wait too long to get the benefits they have earned and deserve. These delays are unacceptable. This report outlines VA's robust plan to tackle this problem and build a paperless, digital disability claims system — a lasting solution that will transform how we operate and ensure we achieve the Secretary's goal of eliminating the claims backlog and improving decision accuracy to 98 percent in 2015."

"Departments of Defense and Veterans Affairs: Status of the Integrated Electronic Health Record (iEHR)."

Panangala, Sidath Viranga; Jansen, Don J. Congressional Research Service, 2013.

Introduction: "In December 2010, the Deputy Secretaries of [the Department of Defense and the Veterans Administration] directed the development of an integrated Electronic Health Record (iEHR) , which would provide both Departments an opportunity to reduce costs and improve interoperability and connectivity. On March 17, 2011, the Secretaries of DOD and VA reached an agreement to work cooperatively on the development of a common electronic health record and to transition to the new iEHR by 2017. On February 5, 2013, the Secretary of Defense and the Secretary of Veterans Affairs announced that instead of building a single integrated electronic health record (iEHR), both DOD and VA will concentrate on integrating VA and DOD health data by focusing on interoperability and using existing technological solutions. This announcement was a departure from the previous commitments that both Departments had made to design and build a new single iEHR, rather than upgrading their current electronic health records and trying to develop interoperability solutions…. It is unclear at this time what the long-term implications of the most recent change in the program strategy will be."

"Uninsured Veterans and Family Members: Who Are They and Where Do They Live?"

Haley, Jennifer; Kenney, Genevieve M. Urban Institute, May 2012.

Findings: Approximately 1 in 10 — 1.3 million — of the country's 12.5 million nonelderly veterans did not have health insurance coverage or access to Veterans Affairs (VA) health care as of 2010.

When family members of veterans are included, the uninsured total rises to 2.3 million. An additional 900,000 veterans use VA health care but have no other coverage. Nearly 50% of uninsured veterans have incomes at or below 138% of the Federal Poverty Line ($30,429 for a family of four in 2010). Under the Affordable Care Act (ACA), these would qualify for coverage as of January 2014. Another 40.1% of veterans and 49% of their families have incomes that qualify for new subsidies through health insurance exchanges with the ACA. The uninsured rate is 12.3% in states with the least progress on exchange implementation, compared with 9.6% to 9.8% for veterans in states with most progress to health insurance exchange implementation.

"Improving Trends in Gender Disparities in the Department of Veterans Affairs: 2008–2013."

Whitehead, Alison M.; et al. American Journal of Public Health, September 2014, Vol. 104, No. S4, S529-S531, doi: 10.2105/ AJPH.2014.302141.

Abstract: "Increasing numbers of women veterans using Department of Veterans Affairs (VA) services has contributed to the need for equitable, high-quality care for women. The VA has evaluated performance measure data by gender since 2006. In 2008, the VA launched a 5-year women's health redesign, and, in 2011, gender disparity improvement was included on leadership performance plans. We examined data from VA Office of Analytics and Business Intelligence quarterly gender reports for trends in gender disparities in gender-neutral performance measures from 2008 to 2013. Through reporting of data by gender, leadership involvement, electronic reminders, and population management dashboards, VA has seen a decreasing trend in gender inequities on most Health Effectiveness Data and Information Set performance measures."

"Racial Disparities in Cancer Care in the Veterans Affairs Health Care System and the Role of Site of Care."

Samuel, Cleo A.; et al. American Journal of Public Health, September 2014, Vol. 104, No. S4, S562-S571. doi: 10.2105/ AJPH.2014.302079

Abstract: "We assessed cancer care disparities within the Veterans Affairs (VA) health care system and whether between-hospital differences explained disparities…. Compared with Whites, Blacks had lower rates of early-stage colon cancer diagnosis; curative surgery for stage I, II, or III rectal cancer; 3-year survival for colon cancer; curative surgery for early-stage lung cancer; 3-dimensional conformal or intensity-modulated radiation; and potent antiemetics for highly emetogenic chemotherapy…. Conclusions: Disparities in VA cancer care were observed for 7 of 20 measures and were primarily attributable to within-hospital differences."

"Retaining Homeless Veterans in Outpatient Care: A Pilot Study of Mobile Phone Text Message Appointment Reminders."

McInnes, D. Keith; et al. American Journal of Public Health, September 2014, Vol. 104, No. S4, S588-S594. doi: 10.2105/ AJPH.2014.302061.

Abstract: "We examined the feasibility of using mobile phone text messaging with homeless veterans to increase their engagement in care and reduce appointment no-shows… Results: Participants were satisfied with the text-messaging intervention, had very few technical difficulties, and were interested in continuing. Patient-cancelled visits and no-shows trended downward from 53 to 37 and from 31 to 25, respectively. Participants also experienced a statistically significant reduction in emergency department visits, from 15 to 5 and a borderline significant reduction in hospitalizations, from 3 to 0. Conclusions: Text message reminders are a feasible means of reaching homeless veterans, and users consider it acceptable and useful. Implementation may reduce missed visits and emergency department use, and thus produce substantial cost savings."

A Carolina Community Provides Resources for Treatment

Charlotte Bridge Home, Foundation for the Carolinas

Charlotte Bridge Home in Charlotte, North Carolina, organized in 2011 to provide veterans and their loved ones access to national and community resources. The Foundation for the Carolinas supports the home with funding and consulting services.

Message From Tommy Norman, Founder and Chair of Charlotte Bridge Home

Charlotte Bridge Home urges our community to join together in support of our service men and women.

Charlotte North Carolina and its surrounding communities are receiving a significant number of post-9/11veterans who are choosing this region as their civilian home. Their numbers are rising and will increase substantially over the next five years.

We are fortunate to have these capable men and women among us. However, many are dealing with significant challenges as they recover from wounds, pursue further education, and healthcare resources and seek employment in a difficult economy. In addition to the challenges experienced by previous generations of veterans, post-9/11 veterans (including an unprecedented number of National Guard and Reserve men and women) face other issues due to multiple deployments, bomb blasts, surviving severe injuries due to advanced medicine and navigating an overloaded VA system.

Charlotte Bridge Home was organized in 2011 to holistically connect veterans and their families to available national and community resources and advocate for system and community change around the critical issues impacting these veterans. We are not duplicating existing efforts, but rather are helping to

"Support for Returning Veterans in Charlotte-Mecklenburg," by Tommy Norman, Charlotte Bridge Home, May 2012. Reprinted by permission.

connect the "dots" and lift up the entire network of support for our veteran population.

As one of our initial steps, Charlotte Bridge Home enlisted the support of Foundation For The Carolinas to help launch the organization and, in partnership with the Foundation's Center for Civic Leadership, fund this study and provide consulting support. One of the first of its kind in the country, this report – with its superb detail and analysis – dramatically points out significant issues our service men and women are facing as they transition to civilian life in our community. Their challenges can be overwhelming. It also describes the current network of support available to veterans and identifies some possible steps Charlotte Bridge Home and the larger Charlotte community should consider in helping our veterans and their families successfully reintegrate.

In addition to this study, the Foundation funded development of a comprehensive resource guide that provides detailed information on the services and support currently available to veterans in our community. Charlotte Bridge Home will maintain and update this guide over time.

Our ultimate hope is that — in addition to providing valuable information about veterans – this assessment will be used to ignite a community conversation about the needs and challenges of our returning veterans and how the Charlotte community can come together to build a stronger network of support for these veterans and their families. We should remain mindful that these veterans are not coming home to agencies; they are coming home to communities! No template exists for us to follow. National leaders and advocates on this subject are looking to Charlotte as a community that can help write the script for how returning veterans can be better served at the local level. Charlotte Bridge Home is honored and excited to be a part of this effort.

Executive Summary

Over 6,000 veterans of the Gulf War II era—those who have served since 9/11—are already living in Charlotte-Mecklenburg. Due to the end of the war in Iraq and future scale-down in the war in Afghanistan, the number of returning veterans will steadily increase over the next several years. Charlotte is expected to remain a "hotspot" for their relocation upon leaving the military. Some of these men and women are quickly adjusting to civilian life, using their many skills, talents and leadership qualities to make the successful transition home. However, others—including some with significant service-connected disabilities—face a range of challenges that are hindering their ability to "hit the ground running" in their new life in Charlotte. Veterans identified the following as the most prevalent challenges they face:

Although the federal government is working on many fronts to expand its capacity to address the growing needs of returning veterans, realistically, it will never be able to meet the full demand for support. Consequently, local communities are being urged to take a greater role in helping veterans and their families reintegrate. The Charlotte community could help develop a stronger network of support for our returning veteran population by focusing on the following seven key strategies. These strategies are suggested as a starting point for community conversations, planning and decision making. No doubt, additional strategies and opportunities will emerge and should be considered.

Strategies for building a stronger network of support
for veterans in Charlotte-Mecklenburg

1. More aggressively reach out to and engage veterans by:

A. Using various channels of communication—e.g. television, social media, brochures, etc.;

B. Having social service and other community organizations identify military or veteran status as part of their intake processes and increasing the knowledge of their staff about working more effectively with veterans;

Key Challenges returning Veterans Face

- Finding employment (the challenge most often identified by veterans)
- Dealing with a loss of purpose and isolation after leaving the military
- Navigating the complex and confusing network of benefits, services and support that is available to veterans
- Having long waits to obtain disability and other benefits from the U.S. Department of Veteran Affairs (VA) as a result of significant backlogs in processing claims
- Getting ready access to healthcare, including behavioral health services
- Coping with Post Traumatic Stress Disorder (PTSD), Traumatic Brain Injury (TBI) and/or major depression that are prevalent among veterans who have served in the wars in Iraq and Afghanistan
- Accessing and having success with postsecondary education
- Dealing with housing and financial instability that could ultimately lead to homelessness for some
- Accessing resources that uniquely address the needs and challenges of female veterans
- Finding support for family members of veterans—spouses, children, siblings—who may be dealing with caretaking and other reintegration issues, including relationship issues with the veteran

C. Engaging spiritual leaders to help identify and support veterans in their congregations;

D. Continuing to connect with veterans during sporting, social and other community events; and

E. Encouraging community and human service organizations to hire more veterans to facilitate more peer-to-peer connections between veterans.

2. **Help returning veterans learn about and gain easier access to the myriad of benefits and resources that may be available to them by:**

A. Establishing a local, well-publicized portal or clearinghouse where veterans can connect to resources through one-on-one support; (This is Charlotte Bridge Home's primary role.)

B. Maintaining an up-to-date local guide to resources available to veterans and their families; (The Charlotte Bridge Home Resource Guide has been developed and the organization will maintain and update it over time.)

C. Developing a robust network of peer volunteers to provide one-on-one support to veterans;

D. Supporting /lifting up the ongoing (and all voluntary) efforts of the Charlotte Area Response Team (C.A.R.T.) that was established to help coordinate and share information among the network of local providers working with veterans; and

E. Exploring additional transportation options for disabled and low-income veterans to physically connect them to critical services.

3. **Help veterans better prepare for, connect with and sustain successful employment in living-wage jobs and careers by pursuing a holistic strategy that focuses on four interrelated fronts:**

A. Engaging the business community to recruit and provide job opportunities for returning veterans and spouses of disabled veterans, as well as using HR practices that promote retention and advancement of veterans after hiring;

B. Growing the capacity of our local workforce development sector to provide more veteran-centered pre-employment and soft skills training, resume development and job coaching, career planning that helps veterans build on and translate their military skills, job placement and retention support and connections to entrepreneurship training and opportunities;

C. Raising the level of support for veterans at out postsecondary education institutions to help veterans achieve success and ultimately gain sustainable employment; and

D. Increasing veterans' access to healthcare, behavioral health and other resources to promote their well-being and support their employment goals.

4. Ensure that veterans have greater access to healthcare and behavioral health resources by:

A. Encouraging more returning veterans to enroll in the VA healthcare system;

B. Exploring partnerships between private sector healthcare providers and theVA to identify opportunities for collaboration;

C. Increasing the awareness and education of local health, mental health and human service providers in identifying and understanding issues related to PTSD, TBI and other behavioral health issues that veterans often face;

D. Encouraging and supporting efforts of local mental health organizations to provide peer-to-peer mentoring, support groups and/or pro bono counseling for veterans and their families; and

E. Exploring non-traditional healing options such as yoga, medication and recreation activities to support veterans trying to cope with the stresses and emotional challenges of reintegration.

5. Increase options for affordable housing, shelter and temporary financial assistance for veterans who are already homeless or at risk of becoming homeless by:

A. Developing/supporting initiatives to provide transitional and/or supportive housing for homeless veterans;

B. Providing more foreclosure assistance;

C. Bringing together non-profits that have recently begun focusing on the housing needs of veterans to coordinate and leverage their resources;

D. Creating a revolving fund or other tool through which veterans can gain access to emergency low/no-interest and short-term loans or grants to help them maintain their housing while awaiting benefit decisions or payments;

E. Providing financial management and budget counseling; and

F. Providing no/low-cost legal services for veterans to help with benefits claims appeals and/or other legal issues that may be adversely affecting their financial stability.

6. Give greater attention to the unique needs and challenges of female veterans by:

A. Tailoring outreach and engagement specifically to female veterans;

B. Providing a safe, welcoming environment for female veterans to share their unique needs and experiences and connect with appropriate resources;

C. Offering counseling and support groups for females dealing with MST, PTSD and other issues related to reintegration; and

D. Providing transitional and/or supportive housing for female veterans with and without children.

7. Expand resources and connections for veteran families by:

A. Providing more opportunities for family support groups, peer-to-peer (family-to-family) mentoring and professional counseling;

B. Exploring using the Community Circles of Support or model (or similar model) for veteran families;

C. Offering greater support and respite for family caregivers of severely disabled veterans; and

D. Providing/supporting recreational or other types of planned activities for veteran families to enhance family relationships.

No one individual or organization can carry the load of building a stronger network of support for veterans.
It will require the collective commitment of diverse stakeholders working together to:

- **Educate community leaders, employers, philanthropists, service providers, congregations and others about our veteran population**, the skills and talent they bring and the challenges they and their families often face in making the transition from military to civilian life;
- **Develop a clear vision, theory of change and expectations** for how the community could/should come together to address the holistic needs of veterans and their families;
- **Set priorities** for taking action. Far too many needs exist to take them on all at once;
- **Coordinate, communicate and build partnerships** among local organizations and volunteers and forging stronger and more innovative partnerships with the VA and other state and local agencies who routinely serve veterans;
- **Help community philanthropists and other funders understand the highest priorities for building a network of support for veterans and their families**, and encouraging

them to make funding decisions that will have the greatest collective impact; and

- **Continuously capture and analyze data about returning veterans in Mecklenburg County** to help inform community efforts and use in developing metrics to measure and understand the collective impacts of programs and practices serving the veteran community.

Creative Expression Is Effective in Treating PTSD

Joshua Smyth and Jeremy Nobel

Joshua Smyth, PhD, is distinguished professor of bio-behavioral health and medicine at Pennsylvania State University. His research interests focus on the psychological and physical effects of stress. Co-author Jeremy Nobel, MD, MPH, is an adjunct lecturer at the Harvard School of Public Health and President, Foundation for Art and Healing.

Successful treatment of post-traumatic psychological symptoms, including Post-Traumatic Stress Disorder (PTSD), is difficult. Individuals suffering with PTSD re-experience the traumatic event(s) years and even decades later, reliving their helplessness, fear, and horror (e.g., through flashbacks or nightmares) associated with the traumatic event. Such strong, negative reactions can create a motivation to avoid any environment in which re-living the anxiety of the trauma could be triggered. Although avoidance may prevent the onset of intense anxiety, it also results in social isolation and withdrawal from experiences that were previously enjoyed. For example, many individuals with PTSD describe years of declining invitations to social and family events to avoid anxiety and anger. In extreme cases, individuals endorse fear and discomfort about leaving the house at all, which they characterize as shameful and demoralizing. Thus, many individuals with PTSD perceive themselves as trapped in a cycle that reinforces avoidance of situations that may trigger anxiety, without a way out.

Fortunately, there are effective behavioral treatments for PTSD. But the most successful ways to treat PTSD, including exposure-based therapies, typically require individuals to gradually confront the anxiety associated with their traumas. In other words, exposure-based therapies operate in stark contrast to patients' motivation to avoid any environment that could trigger anxiety. For instance, a patient currently experiencing distress, such as from an abusive relationship, may not engage in such therapy, or respond poorly to exposure. Patients frequently begin these treatments and terminate them before they experience benefits, leaving some patients even more hopeless than they were when they began. More generally, a variety of social processes, including the stigma of mental illness, also can keep individuals from seeking traditional treatment. Thus, over the last two decades, researchers and clinicians have explored the effectiveness of a series of alternative or supplemental therapies for individuals with PTSD that do not necessitate exposure to the facts of the trauma, and/or may avoid the stigma of receiving mental health treatment. Such therapeutic approaches include expressive writing and expressive group therapy, a range of creative therapies (e.g., art, music, body-oriented), and mindfulness training.

Although these alternative therapies differ in their exact execution, they share an underlying set of assumptions. Each of these approaches allows individuals with PTSD to experience and/or express their thoughts and feelings without necessarily having to verbalize the trauma, share this verbalizing with others, or directly confront the trauma, if they are not ready. Alternative therapies, in general, also focus on creating an environment in which the patient feels safe, and then providing an expressive medium that does not threaten that feeling of safety.

The Current State of Research

A number of non-traditional creative/expressive therapies has demonstrated at least preliminary effectiveness in reducing PTSD symptoms, reducing the severity of depression (which often accompanies PTSD), and/or improving quality of life. This evidence ranges from the results of full-scale clinical trials where a treatment group is compared to a control condition, to descriptive case studies where results from the treatment of one or a few individuals are presented in great detail.

Expressive Writing (EW) is a brief intervention that instructs individuals to write about their deepest thoughts and feelings about a stressful event without regard to the structure of the writing (see Box 1). Writing is typically done in 3-5 sessions of 15-20 minutes over the course of hours, days, or weeks. This approach is thus highly personal, emotional, and based on the individual being willing and able to express themselves through language and writing. A number of clinical trials examining the effectiveness of alternative therapies on PTSD have been conducted with expressive writing, and several of these trials have demonstrated some beneficial effects of EW. These successful trials demonstrate that EW can reduce the distress that accompanies one's thoughts and feelings over time. A set of trials that failed to find positive effects suggests that EW may be more beneficial when writing about the trauma privately, without verbally sharing the trauma with others. More generally, these trials suggest that EW is most effective for individuals currently experiencing strong negative emotions related to the trauma.

Additional research has shown that EW offers the opportunity for exposure, in that individuals habituate to the anxiety aroused by writing about their experiences across sessions. Like exposure-based therapies, EW thus carries the risk of increasing immediate anxiety, but can reduce anxiety over time. This brief treatment may be particularly suitable for individuals who are comfortable with verbal expression but have concerns about potential reactions from loved ones or therapists. EW also may be used as an adjunct to traditional psychotherapy. Qualitative data from case reports and clinical trials show that patients often perceive EW as a meaningful, positive experience (see Box 1).

Creative Therapies, including art, music, drama, and body-oriented approaches, are a diverse set of techniques that hold in common that thoughts and feelings about a trauma are represented without verbal descriptions of the event(s). Visual and auditory stimuli are used to symbolize the pain and suffering that result from trauma (such as fear, horror, loneliness, and distrust), and

> ## Box 1: Expressive Writing Instructions.
>
> For the next (three) days, I would like for you to write about your very deepest thoughts and feelings about an extremely important emotional issue that has affected you and your life. In your writing, I'd like you to really let go and explore your very deepest emotions and thoughts. You might tie your topic to your relationships with others, including parents, lovers, friends, or relatives. You might tie your writing to your past, your present, or your future, or to who you have been, who you would like to be, or who you are now. You may write about the same general issues or experiences on all days of writing, or write about different topics each day. All of your writing is completely confidential. Don't worry about spelling, sentence structure, or grammar. The only rule is that you once you begin writing, you continue until time is up.
>
> From **Smyth, J.M., Pennebaker, J.W., & Arigo, D. (in press). What are the health effects of disclosure? In A. Baum & T. Revenson (Eds.), Handbook of Health Psychology (2nd ed.) New York, NY: Taylor & Francis.**

the process of expressing oneself is often more important than the finished product. Although the literature on these methods is largely limited to case studies of successful implementations of the specific therapy without comparison groups, the long history of their use in residential and inpatient treatments for PTSD speaks to the impression that they are effective.

Also noteworthy is that studies directly comparing language-based and artistic expression of trauma-related thoughts and emotions tend to demonstrate some participant preference for drawing, sculpting, and painting over writing. This preference is perhaps due to artistic methods often inducing less anxiety than language-based methods (see Box 3). Many of the creative therapies studies have not used control conditions or long-term follow-up assessments of PTSD symptoms, and each study typically includes only a small number of individuals. Consequently, it is as of yet unclear whether (and for whom) creative expression is most beneficial for PTSD symptoms. Some preliminary conclusions suggest that the creative therapies might be particularly effective with patients who struggle with language (either due to age, developmental deficiency, or other co-morbid disorder). Specifics about each type of creative therapy are presented below.

Art Therapies involve patients using some medium (e.g., painting, drawing, collage) to represent their feelings or emotions related to their trauma; the creative product also may be used as a starting point to disclose a patient's traumatic experiences to a therapist or group. A set of randomized controlled trials that employed the use of drawings and collages with adults experiencing PTSD- symptoms demonstrated that art therapy lowered PTSD symptom severity more than control groups, but that these reductions did not extend to depression or other physical symptoms reported at a follow-up period at least a month away. Deriving firm conclusions about art therapy is difficult because these programs often employ both creative and cognitive processing of trauma.

The success of these multi-modal programs suggests that art therapy is useful as accompaniment to verbal therapies, but more research is needed to understand how and when art therapies should be used with patients (particularly in the absence of other therapeutic approaches).

Music Therapies engage patients to use music in a variety of ways (e.g., playing music, beating a drum, listening to and sharing songs) to encourage emotional expression in a non-threatening environment. Through the playing of music patients are able to learn how to self-regulate emotions and can form interpersonal connections when playing with others. The majority of evidence for the positive benefit of creating and playing music comes in the form of case studies with children, suggesting music as a way to create bonds with a caregiver or therapist when language use is difficult.

Box 2: Feedback from patients with PTSD who have participated in Expressive Writing.

"I thought a lot about what I wrote in between the writing sessions, and each one was easier to get through than the last. Before the writing, I held back from telling others about (the trauma). I never told anyone about it. But afterward, I opened up to close friends about it, and I think that it made our relationships better."

"Thank you for giving me the opportunity to write about (my traumas). I was really down before I did this, but now I feel a lot better. It's as if a huge burden has been lifted."

Adapted from Sloan, D.M, & Marx, B.P. (2006). Exposure through written emotional disclosure: Two case examples. Cognitive and Behavioral Practice, 13, 227-234.

Alternatively, music therapies that involved listening to songs that represented oneself or a stressful event/trigger of PTSD has been used with both survivors of childhood abuse and combat veterans. In these studies, the music offers a starting point for the therapist or group to lead a discussion where the patient describes what thoughts are coming to mind while listening.

Thus far, evidence for music therapy largely comes from case studies lacking control groups; as a result, it is unknown whether the music therapy itself is effective or whether benefits are due to other factors, such as patients discussing emotions with a therapist or group, social contact, etc. Furthermore, although some salutary effects of music therapy on PTSD have been observed (e.g., increasing disclosure, reducing behavioral problems due to the trauma in children), more long-term follow-ups are needed that explicitly examine reductions in PTSD symptom severity and other co-morbid disorders. This addition to the literature would allow examination of the extent to which music therapy is effective on its own, or is best served when partnered with other types of cognitive-based therapies.

Drama Therapies create safe, playful environments where patients are able to act out anxieties or conflicts due to their trauma. The goal is to evoke a patient's emotions and provide a platform on which one's anxiety can be expressed and the stigma of those emotions can be expelled. Drama therapy has been used with a group of Vietnam veterans, for example, where patients acted out confrontations with enemy fighters or personal events, such as punishment scenes where the patients or others are chastised for weakness. These scenes enabled the veterans to see that they were not alone in their anger and grief, and also demonstrated that they could tolerate the emotions associated with their memories. Unfortunately, there is little self-report or objective evidence that this method reduces symptoms of PTSD, and it has yet to be directly contrasted with other approaches.

Dance and Body Movement Therapies propose that one's negative, emotion-laden experiences are represented in the body in the form of tension and pain. Thus, dealing with a patient's trauma must involve physical processing so that unconscious conflicts can be brought into one's awareness. Dance and body movement therapies often begin with teaching the patient how to relax and then slowly increasing movement and contact with others. Other forms of body movement therapies uses procedures akin to acupuncture, where negative memories associated with various locations in the body are tapped so as to relieve stress and create balance in one's life. Little peer-reviewed empirical evidence has been published in support of dance and body movement therapies, and the results that have been published remain controversial as they lacked effective baseline and follow-up analyses.

Nature Therapies involve a set of related activities that utilize a mix of relaxation and creative approaches involving nature. Nature-assisted therapies include both horticultural therapy (i.e., the use of plants and gardening techniques to induce clinical change) and

Box 3: Feedback from patients with PTSD who have participated in Creative Interventions.

Artwork: "The drawings were an excellent way of subconsciously getting down to the real feelings that so many of us have tried to build a wall around. Sometimes these walls need to come down so real healing can begin...thank you."

Quoted in Henderson, P., Rosen, D., & Mascaro, N. (2007). Empirical study on the healing nature of mandalas. Psychology of Aesthetics, Creativity, and the Arts, 1, 148-154.

"It was more annoying to write...I couldn't write fast enough...the words just didn't do it right. (With drawing), I'm not sweaty or jumpy when I wake up (from a nightmare)...I'm calmer. More relaxed. I can go back to bed and go to sleep. (Also), the nightmare starts sooner than it used to...I wake up before I get to the ambush."

Quoted in Morgan, C.A., & Johnson, D.R. (1994). Use of a drawing task in the treatment of nightmares in combat-related Post-Traumatic Stress Disorder. Art Therapy, 12, 244-247.

"(Artwork) has provided me with a lot of relief, and helped me to feel more comfortable and calmer."

American Art Therapy Association (2010). Art therapy for the treatment of PTSD. Mundelein, IL: Stadler, J.

Expressive Group Therapy: "I really benefitted from participating. This group was one of the most useful pieces of my treatment."

Adapted from Zaidi, L.Y. (1994). Group treatment of adult male inpatients abused as children. Journal of Traumatic Stress, 7, 719-727.

Group Drumming: "...it gives a feeling of togetherness which makes it possible for you to share everything with the group...it's as if they saw everything, so I can tell them about myself. If I spoke about personal issues it's only due to the group drumming which enabled us to open up."

Quoted in Bensimon, M., Amir, D., & Wolf, Y. (2008). Drumming through trauma: Music therapy with post-traumatic soldiers. The Arts in Psychotherapy, 35, 34-48.

Body Movement Therapy: "She described her wounded heart as full of 'poisonous pus,' and that she wanted to be rid of it. As she shared this image with me, she also shared that she had recently spoken with her children for the first time since leaving them. In previous phone calls, she had been unable to speak because of her intense grief. Expressing a desire to 'push the pus away,' she named it 'shame,' and through visualization and movement, we created a movement sequence to 'push' it out of her heart. At the end of this session, she expressed gratitude for her exercises, saying, 'they allow me to touch the pain in my heart.'"

Adapted from Gray, A. E. L. (2001). The body remembers: Dance/movement therapy with an adult survivor of torture. American Journal of Dance Therapy, 23, 29-43.

Horticultural Therapy: "One of the things that fueled my (alcohol) addiction was the pain I felt as a survivor of severe sadistic childhood physical and sexual abuse, at the hands of my father and other relatives. Working with you and your staff in the greenhouse, or on the grounds, was just what I needed at the end of a long hard day of spiritual, mental, and emotional work. Sometimes, not often, I would come to you feeling completely overwhelmed, disoriented and panicky and your quiet supportive manner and the work with God's earth soothed me tremendously."

Quoted in Hewson, M. (2001). Horticultural therapy and post-traumatic stress recovery. Journal of Therapeutic Horticulture, 12, 1-9.

natural-environments therapies (i.e., experiential group processes that involve adventure and/or wilderness expeditions). As in several of the creative therapy literatures, much of the existing evidence comes from case reports and qualitative studies, with a few uncontrolled (pre/post) and randomized controlled trials. This literature generally supports the use of these techniques for patients with a range of cognitive and behavioral symptoms, such as Alzheimer's disease, depression, substance abuse, and chronic illness. When applied to PTSD, the inclusion of a wilderness expedition did not enhance the effect of inpatient treatment in a nonrandomized trial. The addition of horticultural therapy to residential and inpatient programs are received well by patients (mainly combat veterans), treatment providers, and other staff, and users often anecdotally report benefit. These methods require further investigation using randomized, controlled trials, but they may have potential for reducing distress among patients with PTSD.

Mindfulness Therapies focus primarily on observing one's internal and external states and accepting one's past experiences, so as to better tolerate the distress associated with trauma reminders (see Box 4). Mindfulness has been tested using experimental methods but with small samples, often without control conditions, primarily among veterans, and typically in group settings. These studies suggest that mindfulness therapies may be effective in the short-term for reducing PTSD symptom severity, but that the effectiveness of these therapies do not persist over time (although it remains to be seen if ongoing practice will maintain benefits).

It is also important to again note that group based treatments in and of themselves (regardless of specific approach) may be beneficial for individuals with PTSD who often avoid social interaction to prevent triggering trauma-related anxiety (by way of fostering safe and supportive social interactions, etc.). The short-term effectiveness of mindfulness-based therapies shows potential for using such approaches as first-line treatments for PTSD (which may be useful for stabilization and establishing a sense of safety), but indicates the need for additional and/or ongoing intervention. Clinical observation and case reports document the relief experienced by individuals who are able to increase their distress tolerance. This improvement is associated with greater self-efficacy and readiness for exposure-based work, suggesting that this approach may be useful as an initial intervention in sequenced or stepped care models.

> ## Box 4. Principles of
> ## Mindfulness Training.
>
> (1) Effortful focus on environment and internal states (awareness of the present moment)
>
> (2) Nonjudgmental observance and acceptance of emotions, thoughts, and physical sensations
>
> (*) Relevant to PTSD, mindfulness practice may provide the skills necessary to:
>
> - Increase tolerance of distress associated with negative experiences (i.e., "surfing the wave" of negative emotion) to reduce avoidance
> - Enable attention to immediate emotions during psychotherapy
> - Engage more fully in life as it occurs, rather than focusing on the past or future, which may improve relationships and quality of life
>
> Adapted from Vujanovic, A.A., Niles, B., Pietrefesa, A., Schmertz, S.K., & Potter, C.M. (2011). Mindfulness in the treatment of posttraumatic stress disorder among military veterans. Professional Psychology: Research and Practice, 42, 24-31.

What We Do Not Currently Know

Although there is promise to these creative/expressive therapies for the treatment of PTSD, the lack of high quality controlled trials leaves many questions unanswered. First and foremost, it is unclear which type of PTSD patient would be most benefitted by which therapy. Characteristics of the patient, the nature of the cause of PTSD, and the degree to which the patient can trust a mental health provider, and many other factors will influence which treatment will be preferred and which most successful. Notably, there has been little consistency across research with respect to the severity of PTSD in patients, the co-morbidity of PTSD with depression and other conditions, and the extent to which a patient is currently experiencing trauma-related symptoms or not.

Another issue concerns the extent to which the therapy itself is effective or whether many of the salutary effects for patients are due to the engaging in (safe and supportive) interpersonal interactions. Due to the avoidance tendencies of individuals suffering with PTSD, many patients withdraw themselves from others, including from close friends and family members. Many studies conducted lack control conditions and, further, even in the studies that did, many of the patients in the control group still improved. Although the results of the controlled clinical trials examining the salutary effects of EW on PTSD, for example, cannot be fully explained by referencing the opportunity for positive social interaction, nevertheless the opportunity to experience and express emotion in a safe and controlled interaction for PTSD sufferers appears to be important. Any study that lacked an appropriate control condition is limited in its interpretation as a patient's positive gains can be attributed to the opportunity to interact with others (e.g., therapist, other patients), or other nonspecific factors, rather than the specific therapy.

Related to the above, it is often not clear precisely what components of a therapy are necessary, and which component(s) leads to treatment success. The studies described above were grouped according to their general modes of intervention, but there is often great variability both within and between therapies. For example, music therapy might consist of having patients physically create music using a drum, or having patients present songs they feel de ne their stressful event which are then played to a group and discussed. Furthermore, the creative therapies often employ multi-modal designs (e.g., patients both play music and create art sculptures, or patients both engage in both creative and cognitive components), making it difficult to ascertain what specifically caused the positive effects. Even expressive writing, which has been tested most widely based on an established protocol, varies widely in its execution of instructions (e.g., what patients are told to write about, whether patients are asked to talk to others about their writing). These variations likely have an influence on whether the therapy will be successful or not.

Finally, the number of treatment sessions ranges from 3 (for tests of expressive writing) to upward of 100 (for descriptions of some art and multi-modal therapies), and follow-up intervals range from immediately post-treatment to 24 months after treatment concludes. As a result, it is not clear how much of each treatment is necessary for symptom reduction or how long the effects of a given treatment may last. It will be necessary to determine these aspects of expressive, creative, and mindfulness approaches before clinical recommendations or best-practice guidelines are warranted.

What We Need to Do Next

Expressive, creative, and mindfulness-based approaches appear acceptable to patients, and show some promise for treating PTSD – especially for patients currently experiencing trauma-related symptoms and for those unable to articulate their symptoms and memories in words. Yet much work remains to be done before it is possible to conclusively state the effectiveness of expressive, creative, and mindfulness therapies and bring these healing approaches to patients.

The most immediate action item is to conduct more high quality research, ideally including appropriate control conditions, careful measurement, and long-term assessments. Research should also assess patient characteristics and how they relate to treatment preference and response, so as to learn how best to match individuals with an appropriate therapy.

A number of more specific questions also remain unanswered, including the importance of interpersonal interactions to the therapy, the importance of co-morbidity to the expected benefits of the specific therapy, and the importance of the nature of the trauma that caused the PTSD. Just as exposure-based therapy is not appropriate for all patients, neither will any non-traditional creative/expressive therapy be universally suitable. The direction of future research must be aimed at understanding which specific

Box 5. Feedback from patients with PTSD or trauma histories who have participated in mindfulness training.

"Don't ask me, what I was expecting the other people to be? Raving lunatics, people with axes in their hands, I haven't a clue – but they were not....it was you, it was my next door neighbour. They weren't giggling half wits. I know that is rather narrow minded but they were ordinary everyday run of the mill people which reinforces the fact that that is what I am as well. I'm not a nut...I'm just an ordinary, everyday run of the mill person who ended up in the crap for whatever reason, and so are they. So that was another thing that was a great plus."

"...I felt the meditation was going inside the body.... as if I've got into the root, is probably the best way to describe it. And I can get right to the nucleus of it and I can feel it."

Quoted in Finucane, A., & Mercer, S.W. (2006). An exploratory mixed methods study of the acceptability and effectiveness of mindfulness-based cognitive therapy for patients with active depression and anxiety in primary care. BMC Psychiatry, 6, 1-14.

"I am feeling things the pain has been masking. It [the pain] took up all my energy. I have a lot of things to talk [about] to my therapist now—that I had not thought of before."

Quoted in Price, C.J., McBride, B., Hyerle, L., & Kivlahan (2007). Mindful awareness in body-oriented therapy for female veterans with post-traumatic stress disorder taking prescription analgesics for chronic pain: A feasibility study. Alternative Therapies in Health and Medicine, 13, 32-40.

type of therapy will have the most positive effects for a particular patient. Furthermore, as part of the need for more research, cost analyses should be considered. Although exposure based therapies have proven effective, they can be time- and resource- intensive. Some of the creative/expressive therapies are lower in cost to administer. In addition, the potential to use group therapy for some individuals with PTSD would significant lower the burden of cost of treating patients. With that said, many of these treatments are currently implemented in an ongoing (and often time- and labor-intensive) fashion. Determining the best "fit" to patients, and the most effective and efficient manner of delivery, remains a vital objective for ongoing work.

References

Baer, R.A., Smith, G.T., & Allen, K.B. (2004). Assessment of mindfulness by self-report: The Kentucky inventory of mindfulness skills. *Assessment*, 11, 191-206. Batten, S.V., Follette, V.M. , Rasmussen Hall , M.L. , & Palm , K.M. (2002). Physical and psychological effects of written disclosure among sexual abuse survivors . *Behavior Therapy* , 33, 107-122 .

Bensimon, M., Amir, D., & Wolf, Y. (2008). Drumming through trauma: Music therapy with post-traumatic soldiers *The Arts in Psychotherapy*, 35, 34-48.

Blake, R.L., & Bishop, S.R. (1994). The Bonny Method of guided imagery and music (GIM) in the treatment of post-traumatic stress disorder (PTSD) with adults in the psychiatric setting. *Music Therapy Perspectives*, 12, 125-129.

Bonny, H. (1978). *Facilitated guided imagery and music sessions* (GIM Monograph #1). Balitimore, MD: ICM Books.

Brown, E.J., & Heimberg, R.G. (2001). Effects of writing about rape: Evaluating Pennebaker's paradigm with severe trauma. *Journal of Traumatic Stress*, 14, 781-790.

Bugg, A., Turpin, G., Mason, S., & Scholes, C. (2009). A randomized controlled trial of the effectiveness of writing as a self-help intervention for traumatic injury patients at risk for developing Post-Traumatic Stress Disorder. *Behavior Research and Therapy*, 47, 6-12.

Callahan, R.J., & Callahan, J. (2000). Stop the nightmares of trauma: Thought Field Therapy, the power of therapy for the 21st century. Chapel Hill, NC: Professional Press.

Collie, K., Backos, A., Malchiodi, C., & Spiegel, D. (2006). Art therapy for combat-related PTSD: Recommendations for research and practice. *Art Therapy*, 23, 157-164.

Creamer, M., O'Donnell, M.L., & Pattison, P. (2004). The relationship between acute stress disorder and posttraumatic stress disorder in severely injured trauma survivors. *Behaviour Research and Therapy*, 42, 315-328.

Deaver, S. (2002). What constitutes art therapy research? *Art Therapy*, 19, 23-27.

Foa, E.B., Hembree, E.A., & Rothbaum, B.O. (2007). *Prolonged exposure therapy for PTSD: Emotional processing of traumatic experiences. Therapist guide.* New York: Oxford University Press.

Folkes, C.E. (2002). Thought field therapy and trauma recover. *International Journal of Emergency Mental Health*, 4, 99-104.

Frattaroli, J. (2006). Experimental disclosure and its moderators: A meta-analysis. *Psychological Bulletin*, 132, 823-865.

Frisina, P.G., Borod, J.C., & Lepore, S.J. (2004). A meta-analysis of the effects of written emotional disclosure on the health outcomes of clinical populations. *Journal of Nervous & Mental Disease*, 192, 629- 634.

Gidron, Y., Peri, T., Connolly, J.F., & Shalev, A.Y. (1996). Written disclosure in posttraumatic stress disorder: Is it beneficial for the patient? *Journal of Nervous and Mental Disease*, 184, 505–507.

Gordon-Cohen, N. (1987). Vietnam and reality – The story of Mr. D. *American Journal of Dance Therapy*, 10, 95-109.

Gaudiano, B.A., & Herbert, J.D. (2000). Can we really tap our problems away? A critical analysis of thought field therapy. *The Skeptical Inquirer*, 24, 29-33.

Henderson, P., Rosen, D., & Mascaro, N. (2007). Empirical study on the healing nature of mandalas. *Psychology of Aesthetics, Creativity, and the Arts*, 1, 148-154.

Hoyt, T., & Yeater, E.A. (2011). The effects of negative emotion and expressive writing on post-traumatic stress symptoms. *Journal of Social and Clinical Psychology*, 30, 549-569.

Hussey, D.L., Reed, A.M., Layman, D.L., & Pasiali, V. (2007). Music therapy and complex trauma: A protocol for developing social reciprocity. *Residential Treatment for Children & Youth*, 24, 111-129.

James, M., & Johnson, D.R. (1996). Drama therapy in the treatment of combat-related post-traumatic stress disorder. *The Arts in Psychotherapy*, 23, 383-395.

Johnson, C., Mustafe, S., Sejdijaj, X., Odell, R., & Dabishevci, J. (2001). Thought Field Therapy – Soothing the bad moments of Kosovo. *Journal of Clinical Psychology*, 57, 2137-1240.

Johnson, D.R. (1982). Developmental approaches in drama therapy. *The Arts in Psychotherapy*, 9, 183-189.

Johnson, D.R. (1986). The developmental method in drama therapy: Group treatment with the elderly. *The Arts in Psychotherapy*, 13, 17-33.

Johnson, D.R. (1991). The theory and technique of transformations in drama therapy. *The Arts in Psychotherapy*, 18, 285-300.

Kabat-Zinn, J. (2000). Indra's net at work: The mainstreaming of Dharma practice in society. In G. Watson, S. Batchelor, & G. Claxton (Eds.), *The psychology of awakening: Buddhism, science, and our day- to-day lives* (pp. 225-249). York Beach, ME: Samuel Weiser.

Kaiser, D., Dunne, M., Malchiodi, C. Feen, H., Howie, P., Cutchei, D., & Ault, R. (2005). *Call for art therapy research on PTSD*. Mundelein, IL: American Art Therapy Association, Inc.

Kimbrough, E., Magyari, T., Langenberg, P., Chesney, M., & Berman, B. (2010). Mindfulness intervention for child abuse survivors. *Journal of Clinical Psychology*, 66, 17-33.

King, L.A. (2001). The health benefits of writing about life goals. *Personality and Social Psychology Bulletin*, 27, 798-807.

King, L.A., & Miner, K.N. (2000). Writing about the perceived benefits of traumatic events: Implications for physical health. *Personality and Social Psychology Bulletin*, 26, 220-230.

Koopman, C., Ismailji, T., Holmes, D., Classen, C.C., Palesh, O., & Wales, T. (2005). The effects of expressive writing on pain, depression, and Posttraumatic Stress Disorder symptoms on survivors of intimate partner violence. *Journal of Health Psychology*, 10, 211-221.

Krakow, B., Sandoval, D., Schrader, R., Keuhne, B., Mcbride, L. Yau, C.L., & Tandberg, D. (2001). Treatment of chronic nightmares in adjudicated adolescent girls in a residential facility. *Journal of Adolescent Health*, 29, 94-100.

Johnson, D.R., Lubin, H., James, M., & Hale, K. (1997). Single session effects of treatment components within a specialized inpatient Post- Traumatic Stress Disorder program. *Journal of Traumatic Stress*, 10, 377-390.

LeLieuvre, R.B. (1998). "Goodnight Saigon": Music, fiction, poetry, and lm in readjustment group counseling. Professional Psychology: *Research and Practice*, 29, 74-78.

Lepore, S.J., & Greenberg, M.A. (2002). Mending broken hearts: Effects of expressive writing on mood, cognitive processing, social adjustment and health following a relationship breakup. *Psychology & Health*, 17, 547-560.

Lepore, S.J., Silver, R.C., Wortman, C.B., & Wayment, H.A. (1996). Social constraints, intrusive thoughts, and depressive symptoms among bereaved mothers. *Journal of Personality and Social Psychology*, 70, 271-282.

Lyshak-Stelzer, F., Singer, P., St. John, P., & Chemtob, C.M. (2007). Art therapy for adolescents with posttraumatic stress disorder symptoms: A pilot study. *Art Therapy*, 24, 163-169.

Morgan, C.A., & Johnson, D.R. (1995). Use of a drawing task in the treatment of nightmares in combat-related post-traumatic stress disorders. *Art Therapy*, 12, 244-247.

Nakamura, Y., Lipschitz, D.L., Landward, R., Kuhn, R., & West, G. (2011). Two sessions of sleep-focused mind-body bridging improves self-reported symptoms of sleep and PTSD in veterans: A pilot randomized control trial. *Journal of Psychosomatic Research*, 70, 335- 345.

Niles, B.L., Klunk-Gillis, J., Ryngala, D.J., Silberbogen, A.K., Paysnick, A., & Workl, E.J. (2011). Comparing mindfulness and psychoeducation treatments for combat-related PTSD using a telehealth approach. *Psychological Trauma: Theory, Research, Practice, and Policy*.

Nixon & Kling (in press).

Pennebaker, J.W. (1997). Writing about emotional experiences as a therapeutic process. *Psychological Science*, 8, 162-166. Pennebaker, J.W. (2000). Telling stories: The health benefits of narrative. *Literature and Medicine*, 19, 3-18.

Pennebaker, J.W., & Beall, S.K. (1986). Confronting a traumatic event: Toward an understanding of inhibition and disease. *Journal of Abnormal Psychology*, 95, 274–281.

Pennebaker, J.W., Colder, M., & Sharpe, L.K. (1990). Accelerating the coping process. *Journal of Personality and Social Psychology*, 58, 528-537.

Possemato, K., Ouimette, P., & Geller, P.A. (2010). Internet-based expressive writing for kidney transplant recipients: Effects on posttraumatic stress and quality of life. *Traumatology*, 16, 49-54.

Reichert, E. (1994). Expressive group therapy with adult survivors of sexual abuse. *Family Therapy*, 21, 99-105.

Resick, P. A., Monson, C. M., & Chard, K. M. (2007). *Cognitive processing therapy: Veteran/military version.* Washington, DC: Department of Veterans' Affairs.

Robarts, J.Z. (2000). Music therapy and adolescents with anorexia nervosa. *Nordic Journal of Music Therapy*, 9, 3-12.

Robarts, J.Z. (2003). The healing function of improvised songs in music therapy with a child survivor of early trauma and sexual abuse. In S. Hadley (Ed.), *Psychodynamic music therapy: Case studies* (pp.141-182). Gilsum, NH: Barcelona.

Robarts, J.Z. (2006). Music therapy with sexually abused children. *Clinical Child Psychology and Psychiatry*,11, 249-269.

Röhricht, F. (2009). Body oriented psychotherapy: The state of the art in empirical research and evidence-based practice: A clinical perspective. *Body, Movement, and Dance in Psychotherapy*, 4, 135-156.

Sakai, C.E., & Connolly, S.M., & Oas, P. (2010). Treatment of PTSD in Rwandan child genocide survivors using Thought Filed Therapy. *International Journal of Emergency Mental Health*, 12, 41-49.

Sloan, D.M., & Marx, B.P. (2004). A closer examination of the written emotional disclosure procedure. *Journal of Consulting and Clinical Psychology*, 72, 165-175.

Sloan, D.M., & Marx, B.P. (2006). Exposure through written emotional disclosure: Two case examples. *Cognitive and Behavioral Practice*, 13, 227-234.

Sloan, D.M., Marx, B.P., & Epstein, E.M. (2005). Further examination of the exposure model underlying the efficacy of written emotional disclosure. *Journal of Consulting and Clinical Psychology*, 73, 549-554.

Sloan, D.M., Marx, B.P., & Greenberg, E.M. (2011). A test of written emotional disclosure as an intervention for posttraumatic stress disorder. *Behaviour Research and Therapy*, 49, 299-304.

Smith, B.W., Ortiz, J.A., Steffen, L.E., Tooley, E.M., Wiggins, K.T., Yeater, E.A., Montoya, J.D., & Bernard, M.L. (2011). Mindfulness is associated with fewer PTSD symptoms, depressive symptoms, physical symptoms, and alcohol problems in urban re ghters. *Journal of Consulting and Clinical Psychology, 79,* 613-617.

Smyth, J. M. (1998). Written emotional expression: Effect sizes, outcome types, and moderating variables. *Journal of Consulting and Clinical Psychology, 66,* 174–184.

Smyth, J.M., Hockemeyer, J.R., & Tulloch, H. (2008). Expressive writing and post-traumatic stress disorder: Effects of trauma symptoms, mood states, and cortisol reactivity. *British Journal of Health Psychology, 13,* 85-93.

Smyth, J.M., Nazarian, D., & Arigo, D. (2008). Expressive writing in the clinical context. In A. Vingerhoets, I. Nyklicek, & J. Denollet (Eds.), Emotion regulation and the anxiety disorders: *Adopting a self- regulation perspective* (pp. 215-233). New York: Springer.

Stadler, J. (2010). *Art therapy for the treatment of PTSD.* Mundelein, IL: American Art Therapy Association, Inc.

Stanton, A. L., Danoff-Burg, S., Sworowski, L. A., Collins, C. A., Branstetter, A. D., Rodriguez-Hanley, A., et al. (2002). Randomized, controlled trial of written emotional expression and benefit finding in breast cancer patients. *Journal of Clinical Oncology, 20,* 4160–4168.

Tacon, A.M. (2011). Mindfulness, cancer, and pain. *Alternative Medicine Studies, 1,* 60-63.

Vujanovic, A.A., Niles, B., Pietrefesa, A., Schmertz, S.K., & Potter, C.M. (2011). Mindfulness in the treatment of posttraumatic stress disorder among military veterans. *Professional Psychology: Research and Practice, 42,* 24-31.

Zaidi, L.Y. (1994). Group treatment of adult male inpatients abused as children. *Journals of Traumatic Stress, 7,* 719-727.

Zang, Y., Hunt, N., & Cox, T. (2002). The effect of a guided narrative technique among children traumatized by the earthquake. http://www. inter-disciplinary.net/wp-content/uploads/2011/02/zangtpaper.pdf

Talking It Out Helps Veterans Deal with PTSD

Goodtherapy.org

Goodtherapy.org is an association of mental health professionals representing more than 30 countries. The association's editorial team provides useful information about mental health, psychotherapy, and wellness to a wide and growing audience.

Many military veterans experience a group of mental health conditions that tend to disproportionately affect military personnel. These conditions may include posttraumatic stress (PTSD), depression, anxiety, traumatic brain injury (TBI), and substance abuse, among other issues. Due to the traumatic environment in which active military combatants serve, veterans are at a significantly higher risk for developing these health concerns. These concerns can often be addressed and resolved with the support of a mental health professional.

PTSD in Veterans

Posttraumatic stress is an anxiety issue that may develop after an individual is exposed to a traumatic or overwhelming life experience. While the human body tends to return to baseline levels after experiencing a stressful event, people experiencing PTSD continue to release stress-related hormones and chemicals. Posttraumatic stress is characterized by four basic types of symptoms:

1. Reliving the event

- Repeatedly experiencing the event in flashbacks
- Having intrusive, repeated, and upsetting memories of the event
- Regularly having nightmares about the event

"Military and Veterans Issues," GoodTherapy.org, December 8, 2015. Reprinted by permisison.

- Having intense and discomforting reactions to objects or situations that remind you of the event

2. Avoidance

- Staying away from people, places, or even thoughts that remind you of the event
- Emotional numbness
- Feelings of detachment
- Bottom of Form
- Top of Form
- Bottom of Form
- Memory problems
- Loss of interest in everyday activities
- Being emotionally guarded
- Feelings of hopelessness

3. Hyperarousal

- Constantly scanning the surroundings for any signs of danger
- Problems concentrating
- Increased irritability
- Being easily startled
- Erratic sleep patterns

4. Negative thoughts, moods, or feelings

- Feeling guilty about the event
- Criticizing or blaming other individuals for the event
- Loss of interest in activities and people

Though traumatic incidents—such as participating in combat, experiencing sexual abuse, or having a car accident—must occur for a person to develop PTSD, not all traumatic experiences result in posttraumatic stress. Only a small percentage of people who go through trauma experience PTSD. The lifetime prevalence of PTSD among American women is 10%, while only 4% of American men will experience PTSD at some point during their life.

American combat veterans have a much higher prevalence of PTSD than American civilians. Between 11-20% of veterans from

Operations Iraqi Freedom (OIF) and Enduring Freedom (OEF) experience posttraumatic stress in a given year. Approximately 12% of Gulf War (Desert Storm) veterans and 15% of Vietnam veterans are affected by PTSD on an annual basis. The lifetime prevalence of PTSD for Vietnam veterans is 30%.

Military personnel are at higher risk for developing posttraumatic stress because service members are intimately involved in wartime incidents that may be frightening, horrifying, and at times, life-threatening. One emotionally overwhelming incident may be enough for PTSD to develop, but combat often facilitates prolonged and repeated exposure to traumatic events.

Sexual Abuse in the Military

Military sexual trauma (MST), defined by the Department of Veteran Affairs (VA) as "sexual harassment that is threatening in character or physical assault of a sexual nature that occurred while the victim was in the military, regardless of geographic location of the trauma, gender of the victim, or the relationship to the perpetrator," is a significant and pervasive concern in the military.

Some studies estimate that approximately 1% of veteran males (32,000 men) and 22% of veteran females (23,000 women) are exposed to sexual assault or repeated sexual harassment during their military service. Between 10% and 33% of servicewomen may experience attempted rape during this time period. The prevalence rates of MST may range from 4% to as high as 85% based on the method of data collection and the definition of MST used.

There are a variety of emotional, behavioral, physical, and mental health issues that have been linked to MST. Primary among these are depression, posttraumatic stress, anxiety, substance dependency, and an increased risk of suicide. Roughly 50-60% of female veterans who experience MST eventually develop posttraumatic stress. This rate is approximately three times higher than male veterans in similar circumstances. Of servicewomen who develop PTSD due to military sexual trauma, an estimated 75% develop co-morbid depression, and over 30% may develop anxiety.

Servicemen who experience posttraumatic stress due to exposure to military sexual trauma are more likely to abuse alcohol, drugs, and other substances than servicewomen who have experienced similar trauma. A study involving more than 2300 male and female military personnel who served in OEF/OIF revealed that sexual harassment was the only stressor that was independently linked to suicidal ideation among female veterans—even when accounting for depression and the misuse of alcohol.

Depression and Anxiety in Veterans

Mental health conditions that adversely affect mood, such as depression and anxiety, are also prevalent among military veterans—and veterans may experience these issues for many different reasons. Factors such as poor health (physical and mental), unemployment, and financial difficulties can contribute to negative thoughts and moods.

Upon returning home, some veterans report feeling disconnected from family members and friends. The belief that no one is able to relate to their experiences or offer meaningful emotional support can prompt service members to bottle up their feelings or even seek social isolation. Such actions though, may only serve to exacerbate the situation.

There are other factors which may also play a role in developing negative thought patterns. For example, the grief of losing one's friends during combat, coupled with feelings of survivor's guilt can lead to the development of depression and anxiety if they are not effectively treated.

Traumatic Brain Injury (TBI) and Veterans

Traumatic brain injury is currently one of the most discussed topics in the medical and mental health communities, as many veterans have returned home with the symptoms of the condition. It has even been called a "signature injury" of Operations Iraqi Freedom and Enduring Freedom. Traumatic brain injury may be caused by a blow to the head, the head striking an object, or by an explosion in close proximity.

People who experience a brain injury may become confused, disoriented, experience slow or delayed thinking, and may even slip into a coma. Memory loss of events preceding and immediately following the injury is also common. Other symptoms associated with TBI are headaches, dizziness, and difficulty paying attention. In some cases, traumatic brain injury can result in physical deficits, behavioral changes, emotional deficiencies, and loss of cognitive ability.

In the most recent conflicts in Afghanistan and Iraq, 78% of all combat injuries are caused by explosive munitions. Mild TBI or concussion is one of the most prevalent combat injuries, affecting roughly 15% of all active military combatants in Iraq and Afghanistan. Due to the devastating effect of roadside bombs in these countries, the ability to effectively treat traumatic brain injury is of great importance in veteran care.

Other Mental Health Issues Experienced by Veterans

While posttraumatic stress, depression, anxiety, and traumatic brain injury are at the forefront of most people's minds when it comes to veteran care, there are other mental health conditions that warrant attention. These include:

- Drug and alcohol abuse
- Suicidal ideation
- Anger issues
- Sleep apnea
- Dementia

An individual who serves in the military will not necessarily develop a mental health condition. Further, a mental health concern experienced by a veteran may have no relation to the veteran's military service. Mental health professionals who work with veterans will typically assess each person individually and take all symptoms and life experiences into consideration before making a diagnosis or starting treatment.

Therapy for Military and Veterans Issues

The U.S. Department of Veterans Affairs (VA) provides a wide range of mental health services and treatments to aid military veterans. Treatments may be given in a variety of settings: short-term inpatient care, outpatient care in a psychosocial rehabilitation and recovery center (PRRC), or residential care.

For veterans experiencing posttraumatic stress, antidepressant, anti-anxiety, and mood-stabilizing drugs may be prescribed by a doctor or psychiatrist. These medications can address depression and anxiety issues, reduce irritability, improve sleep patterns, and help to ease nightmares or intrusive thoughts.

While the use of mood-influencing medications is particularly common in treating depression and anxiety, talk therapies can also be very beneficial. For example, cognitive behavioral therapy, acceptance and commitment therapy (ACT), and interpersonal therapy (IPT) can help affected veterans reduce emotional pain and reestablish positive social relationships. Certain types of therapies-- such as cognitive processing therapy (CPT) or prolonged exposure therapy (PE)--may also be used to promote positive thought patterns and behaviors in veterans experiencing mental health issues. Medical guidelines strongly recommend both CBT and PE for the treatment of posttraumatic stress. Mental Health Residential Rehabilitation Treatment Programs (MH RRTPs), established by the VA, provide a 24/7 health care setting for veterans with PTSD.

Veterans with traumatic brain injury may experience a variety of mental health issues. Different therapeutic strategies may be applied, depending on which areas of a person's functioning are affected. Common treatments for TBIs include rehabilitation therapies (for example, speech-language therapy), medication, assistive devices, and learning strategies to address cognitive, emotional, and behavioral deficits.

Support and Therapy for Military Families

Military life and deployment can take a toll on each member in the family system. Children and teenagers may become irritable or rebellious, and the parent at home may have to cope with the increased burden of caring for the family alone on a daily basis. Deployment can lead family members to feel anxious, alone, or unsupported. Military families also have to face the possibility that the deployed family member may return seriously injured or may not return at all. A family who is out of touch with extended family members or the military community may be more likely to experience increased stress during this period.

While happiness and relief may often be experienced when a deployed family member returns home, initial joy might give way to feelings of frustration as issues associated with reintegration arise. The returning parent may have experienced personality changes or developed mental or physical health concerns, children may have been born or reached a different stage of development, and marital bonds may have weakened. The need to readjust to new roles within the family system may lead to increased tension between family members.

Many resources are available for military families leading up to and during deployment. Family therapy programs help parents explain the deployment process to young children, while support programs are in place to help returning veterans and their family members go through the reintegration process with as few issues as possible. At present, the VA has identified six key ways to assist military families:

- Increase behavioral health care services
- Promote awareness that psychological health is as important as physical health
- Promote housing security for veterans and military families
- Increase opportunities for federal careers
- Increase opportunities for private-sector careers
- Provide more opportunities for educational advancement

Unused Resources Available to Veterans

Though the United States Department of Veteran Affairs (VA) has expanded its mental health services and integrated supplementary programs for the benefit of veterans who are experiencing mental health issues, a significant proportion of these services remain unused. Of all army veterans who have a mental health concern, approximately 60% do not seek assistance from a mental health professional. Studies indicate that roughly 70% of veterans with posttraumatic stress or depression do not seek help.

Surveys conducted among veterans experiencing mental health challenges have highlighted a number of reasons for the under-utilization of available resources. Common responses include:

- Fear of being stigmatized within the military community
- Fear of confronting trauma
- Constrained access to care (due to location or wait time)
- Lack of expertise among available mental health care providers
- Belief that friends and family are able to provide all needed care
- Lack of knowledge of available mental health resources
- Lack of knowledge in how to access available mental health care

Case Example

Post-Deployment Depression, Anxiety, and PTSD Experienced by a Veteran: Harrison, 39, is a decorated military veteran who served in Operation Enduring Freedom (Afghanistan) and Operation Iraqi Freedom (Iraq) as an active military combatant. He is married, with two children, and though he was previously known for his calm, friendly manner, Harrison has seemed detached and withdrawn since returning home from his last deployment. Harrison does not drive anymore, he has difficulty sleeping, and each day he walks to the local bar and has to be taken home each night. Harrison prefers to drink alone. A fellow veteran encouraged him to see a therapist, so Harrison decided to give it a try. During therapy, Harrison opened up emotionally and for the first time since coming home from Iraq, he spoke about the hidden improved explosive device (IED) that killed three soldiers inside the truck he was driving. Harrison explained that he has recurring nightmares about the incident, and that as the driver, he feels responsible for what happened. The therapist helped Harrison address his feelings of guilt by exploring the decisions he made leading up to the incident, the reasons for those decisions, and what he realistically could have done differently. After a psychiatric referral, Harrison is prescribed antidepressant medications to assist his mood and help dull his symptoms. Within a few months, Harrison reported safer drinking habits, healthier sleeping habits, and better family interactions to his therapist. Harrison hopes to start driving to therapy sessions soon.

PTSD Treatment Is Barely Adequate

Terri Tanielian

Terri Tanielian is a senior behavioral scientist specializing in military behavior at the RAND Corporation, which is a research organization that focuses on developing solutions to public policy challenges in order to help make global communities safer, healthier, and more prosperous.

Since October 2001, approximately 1.64 million U.S. troops have deployed to support operations in Afghanistan and Iraq. Many have been exposed for prolonged periods to combat-related stress or traumatic events. Safeguarding the mental health of these servicemembers and veterans is an important part of ensuring the future readiness of our military force and compensating and honoring those who have served our nation. In the wake of recent reports and media attention, public concern about the care of the war wounded is high. In response, several task forces, independent review groups, and a Presidential Commission have examined the care of the war wounded and recommended improvements. Policy changes and funding shifts are already under way.

Key Findings

1. Approximately 18.5 percent of U.S. service members who have returned from Afghanistan and Iraq currently have post-traumatic stress disorder or depression; and 19.5 percent report experiencing a traumatic brain injury during deployment.

"Invisible Wounds Mental Health and Cognitive Care Needs of America's Returning Veterans," by Terri Tanielian, Lisa H. Jaycox, Terry L. Schell, Grant N. Marshall, M. Audrey Burnam, Christine Eibner, Benjamin R. Karney, Lisa S. Meredith, Jeanne S. Ringel and Mary E. Vaiana, RAND Corporation, 2008.

2. Roughly half of those who need treatment for these conditions seek it, but only slightly more than half who receive treatment get minimally adequate care.

3. Improving access to *high-quality care* (i.e., treatment supported by scientific evidence) can be cost-effective and improve recovery rates.

However, the impetus for policy change has outpaced the knowledge needed to inform solutions. Fundamental gaps remain in our understanding of the mental health and cognitive needs of U.S. servicemembers returning from Afghanistan and Iraq, the costs of mental health and cognitive conditions, and the care systems available to deliver treatment.

Understanding Invisible Wounds: the Research Challenge

To begin closing these knowledge gaps, the RAND Corporation conducted a comprehensive study of the mental health and cognitive needs of returning servicemembers and veterans. We focused on three major conditions: post-traumatic stress disorder (PTSD), major depression, and traumatic brain injury (TBI). Unlike physical wounds, these conditions affect mood, thoughts, and behavior and often remain invisible to other servicemembers, family, and society. In addition, symptoms of these conditions, especially PTSD and depression, can have a delayed onset — appearing months after exposure to stress. The effect of traumatic brain injury is still poorly understood, leaving a large gap in understanding how extensive the problem is or how to address it.

The RAND study addressed questions in three areas:

Prevalence: What are the rates of mental health and cognitive conditions that troops face when returning from deployment to Afghanistan and Iraq?

The care system: What programs and services exist to meet the health care needs of returning troops with PTSD, major depression, or TBI? Where are the gaps in programs and services? What steps can be taken to close the gaps?

Costs: What are the societal costs of these conditions? How much would it cost to deliver high-quality care to all who need it?

To answer these questions, a RAND team undertook a series of research tasks. They reviewed existing scientific research on PTSD, depression, and TBI; surveyed a representative sample of current servicemembers and veterans about their current health status, as well as their access to and use of care; and developed an economic model to estimate the costs associated with these conditions. To identify gaps in access to and quality of care, they also assessed the systems of care designed to provide treatment for these conditions and evaluated what is known about the effectiveness of the services being offered. The study was conducted independently from the Department of Defense (DoD) and Department of Veterans Affairs (VA) and is the first of its kind to take a broad, comprehensive view and to consider these problems from a societal perspective.

About One-Third of Returning Servicemembers Report Symptoms of a Mental Health or Cognitive Condition

Rates of PTSD, depression, and TBI

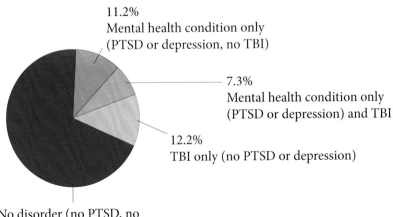

11.2%
Mental health condition only
(PTSD or depression, no TBI)

7.3%
Mental health condition only
(PTSD or depression) and TBI

12.2%
TBI only (no PTSD or depression)

No disorder (no PTSD, no depression) and no TBI 69.3%

- About 300,000 currently suffer from PTSD or major depression
- About 320,000 reported experiencing TBI during deployment

The survey of recently returned servicemembers drew from the population of all of those who have been deployed for Operations Enduring Freedom and Iraqi Freedom, regardless of Service branch, component, or unit type. The survey used random digit dialing to reach a representative sample within the targeted locations. All participants were guaranteed confidentiality; the survey data are not linked to any individual's government records. A total of 1,965 individuals responded. Results showed that:

- 18.5% of all returning servicemembers meet criteria for either PTSD or depression (see Figure 1); 14% of returning servicemembers currently meet criteria for PTSD, and 14% meet criteria for depression (numbers not shown in Figure 1).
- 19.5% reported experiencing a probable TBI during deployment (see Figure 1).
- About 7% meet criteria for a mental health problem and also report a possible TBI.

If these numbers are representative, then of the 1.64 million deployed to date, the study estimates that approximately 300,000 veterans who have returned from Iraq and Afghanistan are currently suffering from PTSD or major depression, and about 320,000 may have experienced TBI during deployment.

Many Services Are Available, but the Care Systems Have Gaps

What programs and services exist to meet the needs of returning troops with these conditions? What are the gaps? What steps can be taken to close the gaps? To address these questions, the RAND team examined the care systems, identified gaps in care and barriers to care, and assessed how best to fill these gaps.

Access gaps

In recent years, the capacity of DoD and the VA to provide health services has increased substantially, particularly in the areas of mental health and TBI. However, gaps in access and quality remain. There is a large gap between the need for mental health services and the use of those services.

This pattern stems from structural factors, such as the availability of providers, as well as from personal, organizational, and cultural factors. For example, military servicemembers report barriers to seeking care that are associated with fears about the negative consequences of using mental health services. Our survey results suggest that most of these concerns center on confidentiality and career issues, and so are particularly relevant for those on active duty. Many felt that seeking mental health care might cause career prospects to suffer or coworkers' trust to decline.

However, the VA also faces challenges in providing access to returning servicemembers, who may face long wait times for appointments, particularly in facilities resourced primarily to meet the demands of older veterans. Better projections of the amount and type of demand among the newer veterans are needed to ensure that the VA has appropriate resources to meet potential demand.

These access gaps translate into a substantial unmet need for care. Our survey found that only 53 percent of returning troops who met criteria for PTSD or major depression sought help from a provider for these conditions in the past year. The gap is even larger for those reporting a probable TBI: 57 percent had not been evaluated by a physician for a brain injury.

Quality gaps

The study identified gaps in the delivery of quality care. Of those who had PTSD or depression and also sought treatment, only slightly over half received a *minimally adequate treatment* (defined according to the duration and type of treatment received). The number who received *high-quality care* (treatment supported by scientific evidence) would be even smaller.

The study also identified gaps in the care systems' ability to promote and monitor quality care. In particular, there is room for improvement in the organizational tools and incentives that support delivery of high-quality mental health care. Without these institutional supports, it is not possible to provide oversight to ensure high-quality care, which includes treatment that is evidence-based and also patient-centered, timely, and efficient. DoD and the VA have begun training in evidence-based practices for providers, but these efforts have not yet been integrated into a larger system redesign that values and provides incentives for quality of care.

The VA has been a leader in promoting quality and may provide a promising model for quality improvement of mental health care within DoD. Significant improvements in the quality of care the VA provides for depression have been documented, but efforts to evaluate the quality of care provided within the VA for PTSD remain under way.

Improving Access to High-Quality Care Can Save Money and Improve Outcomes

Unless treated, PTSD, depression, and TBI can have far-reaching and damaging consequences. Individuals afflicted with these conditions face higher risks for other psychological problems and for attempting suicide. They have higher rates of unhealthy behaviors — such as smoking, overeating, and unsafe sex — and higher rates of physical health problems and mortality. Individuals with these conditions also tend to miss more work or report being less productive. These conditions can impair relationships, disrupt marriages, aggravate the difficulties of parenting, and cause problems in children that may extend the consequences of combat trauma across generations. There is also a possible link between these conditions and homelessness. The damaging consequences from lack of treatment or undertreatment suggest that those afflicted, as well as society at large, stand to gain substantially if more have access to effective care.

These consequences can have a high economic toll; however, most attempts to measure the costs of these conditions focus only on medical costs to the government. Yet, direct costs of treatment are only a fraction of the total costs related to mental health and cognitive conditions. Far higher are the long-term individual and societal costs stemming from lost productivity, reduced quality of life, homelessness, domestic violence, the strain on families, and suicide. Delivering effective care and restoring veterans to full mental health have the potential to reduce these longer-term costs significantly.

Therefore, it is important to consider the direct costs of care in the context of the long-term societal costs of providing inadequate care or no care. The RAND study sought to measure the total costs to society by factoring in treatment costs, losses or gains in productivity, and the costs associated with suicide. In addition, the study calculated the cost effect of getting more people into treatment and improving the quality of care.

Estimates of the cost of PTSD and major depression for two years after deployment range from $5,900 to $25,760 per case. Applying these per-case estimates to the proportion of the entire population of 1.64 million deployed servicemembers who are currently suffering from PTSD or depression, we estimate that the total societal costs of these conditions range from $4.0 to $6.2 billion, depending on whether the costs of lives lost to suicide are included.

The cost of TBI is substantially higher per case, but it varies according to the severity of injury. Estimates of the one-year cost of mild TBI range from $27,260 to $32,760 per case; estimates of moderate to severe TBI costs range between $268,900 and $408,520 per case.

There is a high level of uncertainty surrounding the cost of TBI, because data are lacking; based on our calculations, the total annual cost associated with the diagnosed cases of TBI (2,776 total cases documented through the middle of 2007) ranges between $591 million and $910 million.

While the costs of these conditions are high, we know that effective treatments are available for them, particularly for PTSD and depression. However, these evidence-based treatments are not yet available in all treatment settings. Our model also calculated the costs associated with PTSD and major depression if evidence-based treatments were more widely available (not enough is known to estimate the effect of improving quality of care for TBI, because we lack long-term research on effective treatment and recovery rates).

- If 50 percent of those needing care for PTSD and depression received treatment and all care was evidence-based, this larger investment in treatment would result in cost savings overall.
- If 100 percent of those needing care for PTSD and depression received treatment and all care was evidence-based, there would be even larger cost savings. The cost of depression, PTSD, or co-morbid PTSD and depression could be reduced by as much as $1.7 billion, or $1,063 per returning veteran. These savings come from increases in productivity, as well as from reductions in the expected number of suicides.

Given these estimates, evidence-based treatment for PTSD and major depression would pay for itself within two years. No reliable data are available on the costs related to substance abuse, homelessness, family strain, and other indirect consequences of mental health conditions. If these costs were included, savings resulting from effective treatment would be higher.

These results suggest that investing in evidence-based treatment makes sense both to society and to DoD as an employer. Remission and recovery rates would increase, as would retention, work productivity, and readiness of servicemembers and veterans.

Recommendations and Conclusions

Looking across all the dimensions of our analysis, we offer four main recommendations for improving the understanding and treatment of PTSD, major depression, and TBI among military veterans:

- *Increase and improve the capacity of the mental health care system to deliver evidence-based care.* There is substantial unmet need among returning servicemembers for care of PTSD and major depression. DoD, the VA, and providers in the civilian sector need greater capacity to provide treatment, which will require new programs to recruit and train more providers throughout the U.S. health care system.

- *Change policies to encourage more servicemembers and veterans to seek needed care.* Many who need care are reluctant to seek it. Servicemembers and veterans need ways to obtain confidential services without fear of adverse consequences.

- *Deliver evidence-based care in all settings.* Providers in all settings should be trained and required to deliver evidence-based care. This change will require implementing systems to ensure sustained quality and coordination of care and to aid quality improvement across all settings in which servicemembers and veterans are served.

- *Invest in research to close knowledge gaps and plan effectively.* Medical science would benefit from a deeper understanding of how these conditions evolve over time among veterans as well as of the effect of treatment and rehabilitation on outcomes. The United States needs a national strategy to support an aggressive research agenda across all medical service sectors for this population.

Meeting the health care needs of returning troops who suffer from PTSD, depression, and TBI will be challenging. The prevalence of these conditions is high and may grow as the conflicts in Afghanistan and Iraq continue. The systems of care for meeting these needs have been improved, but critical gaps remain. Without effective treatment, these conditions carry significant long-term costs and negative consequences.

Ultimately, this issue reaches beyond DoD and the VA into the general U.S. health care system and society at large. Many veterans seek care through private employer-sponsored health plans and in the public sector. The broader health care system must adapt to the needs of this population if the United States is to meet its obligations to military veterans now and in the future.

VA Health Program Falls Short in Providing Care

Shefali Luthra

Shefali Luthra is a Kaiser Web reporting fellow. Prior to joining Kaiser Health News, she interned with the Texas Tribune and the Kaiser Family Foundation. Her work has also appeared in the New York Times and the Washington Post. She frequently writes about state and federal health reform.

The military's health program falls significantly short in providing mental health care to active service members, according to a RAND Corp. study published Thursday.

The study focuses on post-traumatic stress disorder and depression, the two most common mental health conditions experienced in the armed services.

It finds some good news: The Military Health Services – which is operated by the U.S. Department of Defense and provides care to active soldiers – is effective at contacting soldiers diagnosed with one of the conditions. In addition, a vast majority of soldiers who get diagnosed with PTSD or depression receive at least one talk therapy session, the study finds. In that regard, it outperforms civilian health services.

But the system faces difficulties ensuring that patients continue with treatment – either by continuing to see a psychotherapist or following up with a doctor after being prescribed medication.

"It's essential to provide excellent care for these service members because of how much we ask of them," said Kimberly Hepner, the study's lead author and a senior behavioral scientist at RAND.

The study examined medical records for close to 40,000 soldiers diagnosed with one of the two conditions between January and

June 2012. It's the largest ever assessment of mental health in the military, according to RAND, a nonpartisan research institute based in California. Of those, about 15,000 had PTSD, and about 30,000 had depression. About 6,000 had both.

After soldiers get their initial mental health visit, the next treatment steps are a different story, the study found. About one in three patients newly diagnosed with PTSD got the appropriate follow-up care after starting treatment – typically, that's at least four visits to a psychotherapist within two months of being diagnosed. For soldiers with depression, less than a quarter of them completed those four visits.

Meanwhile, only about 40 percent of patients who were prescribed medication for one of those conditions followed up with a doctor afterward. Those visits are essential, Hepner said, because the physician can make sure patients take their medication and help them manage side effects. A physician's involvement also ensures that medication doesn't counteract any other prescription drugs the soldiers take.

"Service members received a tremendous amount of medical treatment," she said. "That's why it's even more critical to make sure that it's a successful experience."

Because other studies use different metrics for diagnosing and treating mental health conditions, it's hard to compare these results to those of civilian health systems, Hepner said.

Depending on the experiences soldiers have, military combat can contribute to mental health problems, according to the Department of Veterans Affairs. Meanwhile, research has found suicide attempts seem to be more common in soldiers than in civilians, though it can be difficult to compare. A 2015 study found about 377 out of an estimated 10,000 enlisted soldiers attempted suicide.

The RAND study, which was commissioned by the DOD, is only the first part of an overarching project to assess the quality of mental health care for soldiers. It doesn't yet delve into questions like why these soldier-patients stop their therapy and medication

– considering, for instance, that about 90 percent of those who are diagnosed with PTSD get at least one follow-up visit to therapy, and about 80 percent with depression do.

Potential explanations could include insufficient access to mental health professionals, said Joe Davis, a spokesman for Veterans of Foreign Wars. Many soldiers might also fear judgment from their peers for asking for help.

"It's very easy for senior leaders to say there is no stigma, but far different on the ground at the small-unit level, where everyone relies on their buddy … and vice versa," he said in an email.

Soldiers might also have been unhappy with the mental health care they got, he added, and therefore not return.

The shortage of mental health professionals is one of the biggest barriers to continuous mental health care, said Elspeth Cameron Ritchie, a former military psychiatrist. Since more soldiers have been deployed to Iraq and Afghanistan, the need for doctors has grown, she added.

Beyond questions of stigma and a shortage of providers, there could be an issue of appointments not being available at convenient times, Hepner said. "We ask a lot of service members, and they have a lot of demands on their jobs."

Because soldiers travel a lot, it can be difficult for them to keep up good, continuous access to care, Ritchie said. That difficulty in finding time and flexibility can compound many soldiers' reluctance to keep up with mental health care. Many, she added, worry about others' perception if they are seen regularly visiting a psychiatrist.

"If you need to go to the doctor all the time, people will think, 'Oh what's wrong with that person?'" Ritchie said. "There's a lot of talk about how we should treat this as a broken leg, and there shouldn't be a stigma. But there is a stigma."

The Defense Department's action in commissioning RAND's study is encouraging, Hepner said, because it suggests an active interest in trying to improve mental health care and access to it. DOD could build on efforts to publicly measure how good military, mental health providers are, she said. The department's begun doing that, but Hepner said the public needs more information about quality of care. The RAND findings could have understated the difficulty of obtaining mental health care, Hepner added. RAND focused on patients who had been diagnosed with mental health problems, but it likely missed soldiers who either hadn't seen a doctor at all or who had but hadn't been diagnosed.

Even when they go to the best doctors, soldiers must ask for help, which can be difficult, Davis noted.

For instance, all the soldiers in RAND's study had been identified as needing help. That makes it easier to connect them with care — which could have influenced the high proportion of soldiers who had their initial visit, Hepner said.

"The real risk here is the people we are not addressing," she added.

Suicide Is a Tragic Outcome of Inadequate PTSD Care

Robert Wilbur and James L. Knoll, IV

Robert Wilbur is a freelance writer for popular magazines and newsletters. He conducted research in biological psychiatry for many years. Co-author James L. Knoll, IV, MD, is director, division of forensic psychiatry, at the State University of New York Upstate Medical University in Syracuse.

Samuel Pepys was a member of parliament and a high-ranking figure in the Admiralty, where he was instrumental in strengthening the Royal Navy, but he is best remembered as a diarist. His account of the Great Fire of London, which razed the area where the city — the financial nexus of the United Kingdom - now stands, is perhaps the definitive eyewitness narrative of the tragedy. Fully six months after Pepys saw the Great Fire devour people and buildings, his sleep was broken by nightmares of the horror.

Today we would say that Pepys was probably suffering from post-traumatic stress disorder (PTSD), the mental state that we associate with the broken military dribbling back from 12 years of war in the Middle East.

PTSD denotes a psychiatric illness that follows a physical or psychological trauma, like seeing your buddy's legs blown of by a roadside bomb. But PTSD is older even than warfare; it is probably as old as anxiety itself. However, wars have been a propitious time for studying PTSD, not least because physicians encounter so many more cases of it.

The term PTSD entered the official lexicon of psychiatric diseases in the 1980 edition of the American Psychiatric Association's Diagnostic and Statistical Manual (DSM-III) and

"PTSD: The Soldier's Private War," by Robert Wilbur and James L Knoll IV, Truthout, January 9, 2013. Reprinted by permission. http://www.truthout.org.

underwent revision in the subsequent edition of the manual; today, clinical psychiatrists, many researchers, disability evaluators, the courts and, for better or worse, anyone else who requires a standardized set of criteria, rely on DSM-IV.

Like other diseases, psychiatric illnesses are recognized by their symptoms, and the clusters of symptoms define a syndrome. PTSD has three important symptoms:

1. hyper-arousal — a state of persistent mental and physical excitation that may endure for months or years;
2. avoidance and numbing — psychological defense mechanisms to block out memories of the trauma, or even life situations that resemble the trauma;
3. re-experiencing the trauma in nightmares like Pepys', or experiencing "flashbacks," defined as vivid, waking remembrances of the traumatic event.

In its current incarnation, DSM classifies PTSD as an anxiety disorder, along with free-floating anxiety and panic disorder. One skeptic among many with respect to this classification is co-author James L. Knoll IV MD, associate professor of psychiatry and director of the division of forensic psychiatry at the State University of New York Upstate Medical University in Syracuse. Knoll contends there is strong overlap with other anxiety disorders, but with PTSD, there is very likely a different biological mechanism going on. As a forensic psychiatrist, Knoll is no stranger to PTSD, for he works with crime victims who may have been traumatized for protracted periods of time, if not for life.

Almost every major war in modern times has been accompanied by a different synonym for PTSD, each perhaps with a unique tweak. The first scientifically rigorous investigations of this condition were carried out by Civil War military surgeon J.M. Da Costa. Though the label "Da Costa's Syndrome" is still used in medical histories, Da Costa himself chose the term "irritable heart" because of the severe, frightening pounding of the heart that prevented soldiers from taking to the field. And the treatment for irritable heart? The only sedative-hypnotic of the day: rum.

In the serene Victorian years that followed the Civil War, ladies of means took to their beds with symptoms of palpitations, shortness of breath, tremulousness and perspiration. Their physicians gave them the diagnosis of neurasthenia, a misleading expression which means "nervous exhaustion." These women - and many men of the day - had most if not all of the symptoms of Da Costa's Syndrome. By today's diagnostic criteria, men and women previously designated as suffering from "neurasthenia" would meet the criteria for PTSD.

With the onset of World War I, British military physicians (and their counterparts in the German trenches) soon observed a cluster of symptoms that they attributed to a kind of concussion from the explosion of artillery shells. The condition was dubbed "shell shock," but when these soldiers were examined more closely, 60-80 percent were deemed "neurasthenic" and 10 percent suffered from what was then called "a fugue state" and which we now recognize as numbing.

And so it went from war to war. Da Costa's Syndrome became whatever psychiatric or physiological symptom seemed the most prominent: effort syndrome, neurocirculatory asthenia, combat fatigue, post-Vietnam Syndrome, and finally PTSD. As new drugs became available, physicians tried them, graduating from alcohol to laudanum (a tincture of opium) to chloral hydrate and barbiturates to benzodiazepines and Thorazine-like compounds to antidepressants.

Just as DaCosta's Syndrome, effort syndrome, neurasthenia and PTSD have a common profile on the symptomatic level, so too do they have a common denominator on the physiological level. This was first shown by two British investigators in 1946 (M. Jones and V. Mellersh, Psychosomatics). The scientists were studying the "effort syndrome." When these patients are exercised, it turns out that their blood lactate, a normal product of muscular exertion, is significantly higher than controls without the effort syndrome.

This finding, which still has psychiatrists scratching their heads, was confirmed by several other investigators in the next few years.

There the matter lay until 1967, when two Washington University psychiatrists conducted an ingenious experiment: they infused lactate into an arm vein of normal controls and patients suffering from chronic anxiety. The lactate had no effect on controls, but the patients with anxiety "neurosis" (to use a term that was prevalent at the time) experienced full-blown panic attacks from the lactate infusion; in some instances the reaction was so violent that the infusion had to be stopped prematurely.

So, exercise abnormally raises the level of blood lactate in patients with "effort syndrome," while conversely, infusion of lactate into patients with a history of anxiety provokes panic attacks. Research with lactate continues; of particular interest is that several teams (i.e., Am J Psychiat 1987 Oct;1317-9) have administered lactate infusions to patients with PTSD; the infusions were found to provoke flashbacks of the traumatic event.

The word "panicogenic" was coined for a diverse group of chemicals that trigger panic attacks. Besides lactate, they include carbon dioxide and cholecystokinin. It's not known whether these chemicals are impacting on the physiological substrate of anxiety, or whether their effects are parenthetical. Evidence from the science of pharmacology suggests that they really do mobilize the physiological mechanism of anxiety. The reasoning goes like this: it's not known whether the diverse panicogens all act on the same underlying, natural cause or causes of anxiety. As we'll see, drugs that block anxiety attacks (namely antidepressants) also block the action of panicogens, suggesting that panicogens hit on the underlying cause of anxiety, but this is only an educated guess.

It is well established that most antidepressants block panic attacks, but they do not work like the benzodiazepines (Klonopin, Valium, Xanax, other peer drugs). Antidepressants usually take at least two weeks to kick in, because this is thought to be the time required to boost neurotransmission of serotonin in the brain. On the other hand, benzodiazepines often calm the patient in a couple of hours by inhibiting the central nervous system through their effect on releasing the neurotransmitter GABA (gamma-amino-butyric -acid). Anti-depressants prevent the attacks from "happening." One such antidepressant is the drug imipramine (Tofranil). It has been shown that imipramine blocks the panic attacks artificially induced by panicogens, just as it blocks "natural" panic attacks.

It is especially interesting, therefore, that antidepressants constitute front-line therapy for patients with PTSD. These days, psychiatrists generally use specific serotonin reuptake inhibitors (SSRIs) such as Zoloft, Prozac or Paxil, or a specific serotonin/noradrenaline reuptake inhibitor, notably the drug Effexor. To these, in his clinical practice, co-author Knoll may add low doses of a second generation antipsychotic, of which the most familiar are Abilify, Seroquel or Zyprexa. Antipsychotics are not curative in themselves, but they enhance the effectiveness of antidepressants. A third drug in Knoll's armamentarium is Prazosin. Though marketed as an antihypertensive, practitioners and patients have found Prazosin effective at blocking nightmares. Of particular interest is a study by Michael H. Mithoefer, MD that MDMA (a k a ecstasy) was found to be highly effective for treating PTSD in combination with psychotherapy. And at the University of Arizona, Sue Sisley MD, a psychiatrist and internist, is awaiting delivery of a supply of marijuana from the National Institute on Drug Abuse (NIDA) to begin a trial approved by the Food and Drug Administration (FDA). There has been some interest in propranolol (Inderal) for "erasing" PTSD-type memories, but this is based on anecdotal accounts and small-scale studies. On the other hand, propranolol can cause vivid nightmares - the last thing you'd want in a patient with PTSD.

Besides drugs, psychiatrists are studying other approaches to treating PTSD. Thus, retired Lt. Gen. Stephen N. Xenakis MD is using hyperbaric oxygen therapy. In this procedure, the patient breathes in oxygen at very high pressure. This ties in neatly with what we know about lactate; high levels of oxygen would be predicted to speed up cellular metabolism, burning off lactate in the process.

A second approach for which there are a number of positive claims is transcranial magnetic stimulation (TMS). Briefly, TMS uses an oscillating magnetic field to release neurotransmitters over the course of a month of daily outpatient treatments; it bears no resemblance whatever to shock therapy. We were informed by the manufacturer of the NeuroStar TMS instrument that the military is interested in TMS and has purchased a number of instruments.

For milder expressions of PTSD, some form of psychotherapy might be appropriate. Group therapy enables veterans to share experiences and understand they are not alone, but unless groups are run by an expert, they sometimes turn unruly or authoritarian. Some vets receive individual psychotherapy. Usually this is cognitive-behavioral therapy (CBT), in which the therapist - who generally is not a psychiatrist - challenges the patient's "erroneous" thoughts. Two problems with CBT are, first, there is nothing "erroneous" about roadside bombs and other weapons that kill or mutilate our troops. And second, CBT is a simplistic approach that is not well suited to intelligent, insightful people; in his clinical work, Knoll prefers to use insight-orientated psychotherapy because the "talking cure" is more flexible and sensitive than CBT. Matt Howard of Iraq Veterans Against the War pointed out that CBT is a relatively rapid modality. Whether it is a superior modality is an entirely different matter, for practitioners of CBT require shorter and less sophisticated training than analysts. CBT is also a much shorter course of treatment, which undoubtedly appeals to the cost-cutters in the Department of Defense. On the positive side, CBT is didactic and, indeed, regimented, which means that it lends itself more readily than analysis to research using rating scales and statistical analysis. Nevertheless, the verdict is still not in because no one school of thought is right for all patients.

So, what is to be done when soldiers return from their fourth deployment with PTSD? Vets could legitimately expect a panoply of targeted treatment options. Instead, in April 2009,

Obama's Department of Homeland Security (DHS) launched Operation Vigilant Eagle, which calls for tight surveillance of veterans returning from the Middle East, branding them potential extremists and domestic terrorism threats because they may be "disgruntled, disillusioned or suffering from the psychological effects of war."

Once they reach our shores, veterans have plenty to be disgruntled and disillusioned about. Howard explained to us that, whether it is true or not, military psychiatrists frequently label veterans as suffering from personality disorder or alcoholism. The reason, he explained, was to make it harder for veterans to obtain expensive health care and other benefits after discharge. Howard alleged that when veterans do get care for their PTSD, many are overmedicated when they don't need drugs. This raises the undying debate over drugs versus psychotherapy or a combination of both, but in the age of Bush and Obama, veterans have frequently gotten neither, but instead, the bum's rush.

In a phone interview with Truthout, Aaron Hughes, field organizer at IVAW, said that active-duty servicepersons and veterans are receiving inadequate treatment by the military and the Veterans Administration. Among active-duty soldiers, the suicide rate is 18 *a day* - more of them kill themselves than are killed by enemy combatants. The military goes out of its way to conceal PTSD with diagnoses such as depression and personality disorder, says Hughes. What is more, six months to one year elapse before a PTSD-afflicted soldier is seen by a medical professional, and that medical professional is not a psychiatrist but a physician's assistant who may or may not dispense the correct medication. Some PTSD-afflicted soldiers never even see a PA, according to Hughes.

The VA system can't handle the influx of veterans with PTSD. The reason, says Hughes, is the downsizing of the military, which makes more veterans eligible for care in VA hospitals. Their alternative?

Often, says Hughes, it is suicide.

Organizations to Contact

The editors have compiled the following list of organizations concerned with the issues debated in this book. The descriptions are derived from materials provided by the organizations. All have publications or information available for interested readers. This list was compiled on the date of publication of the present volume; the information provided here may change. Be aware that many organizations take several weeks or longer to respond to inquiries, so allow as much time as possible.

American Psychiatric Association
1000 Wilson Boulevard, Suite 1825
Arlington, Va. 22209-3901
phone: (888) 35-PSYCH or (888) 357-7924
email: apa@psych.org
website: www. psychiatry.org

The American Psychiatric Association works to advocate for the rights and best interests of those using or could be using psychiatric services to treat mental illness. For veterans with PTSD, it offers access to services, and educational resources. The association seeks to serve as the voice of modern psychiatry.

American Psychological Association
750 First Street, NE
Washington, DC 20002-4242
phone: (800) 374-2721
email: public.affairs@apa.org
website: www.apa.org

The American Psychological Association is the leading psychological research and professional organization in the United States. Its membership numbers more than 117,500 researchers, educators, clinicians, consultants, and students. It offers those suffering with PTSD information and access to psychological treatment resources.

Anxiety and Depression Association of America (ADAA)
8701 Georgia Ave., Suite #412
Silver Spring, MD 20910
phone: (240) 485-1001
website: www.adaa.org

The ADAA offers information and services to both consumers and professionals. It has a particular focus on dispelling myths about anxiety and depression. It works to raise awareness of the latest research and treatment options and helping those suffering from anxiety and depression to find the treatment they need.

Depression and Bipolar Support Alliance
55 E. Jackson Blvd., Suite 490
Chicago, IL 60604
phone: (800) 826-3632
website: www.dbsalliance.org

The Depression and Bipolar Support Alliance is a peer-led organization that focuses solely on depression and bipolar disorder. It provides interactive online resources in its efforts to help those with depression and bipolar disorder help themselves with support and inspiration to live their lives to the fullest.

Emory Healthcare Veterans Program
Various locations
phone: (888) 514-5345
website: www.emoryhealthcare.org/centers-programs/veterans-program/index.html

The Emory Healthcare Veterans Programs treats PTSD, traumatic brain injury, and other invisible wounds of war. Its team of experts includes professionals in psychiatry, neurology, neuropsychology, social work, and other areas.

Home Base Veteran and Family Care
1 Constitution Center
Charlestown, MA 02129
phone: (617) 724-5202
website: www.homebase.org

Home Base, founded in 2009, is a partnership between the Red Sox Foundation and Massachusetts General Hospital. It has become a leader in regional and national initiatives with a groundbreaking team of experts to help veterans heal from PTSD and traumatic brain injury. Its clinic is based in Boston.

International Society for Traumatic Stress Studies (ISTSS)
One Parkview Plaza, Suite 800
Oakbrook Terrace, IL 60181
phone: (847) 686-2234
email: info@istss.org
website: www.istss.org

ISTSS is a professional organization that promotes and advances knowledge exchange about traumatic stress, its prevention, and consequences. The organization works to minimize harmful consequences and to advocate for the field of study.

National Center for PTSD
U.S. Department of Veterans Affairs
810 Vermont Avenue, NW
Washington DC 20420
phone: (802) 296-6300
email: ncptsd@va.gov
website: www.ptsd.va.gov/index.asp

The National Center for PTSD is housed with the U.S. Department of Veterans Affairs. Its mission is to foster the care and well-being of returning soldiers and others with PTSD. It attains this through programs of research, education, and training in the underlying science, diagnosis, and treatment of PTSD.

PTSD Foundation of America
P.O. Box 690748
Houston, Texas 77269
phone: (877) 717-PTSD (7873)
email: info@ptsdusa.org
website: ptsdusa.org

The PTSD Foundation of America provides healing support for people impacted by the unseen wounds of war. It is a non-profit organization that offers counseling to both individuals and groups and raises awareness of the needs of the military community. It also serves this community with a Corps of Compassion, the result of networking with government agencies, churches, and other organizations.

Returning Veterans Project
833 SE Main, MB 122
Portland, OR 97214
phone: (503) 954-2259
website: www.returningveterans.org

The Returning Veterans Project helps post-9/11 veterans and service members and their families access free health and wellness services in Oregon and Southern Washington. It recruits, trains, and maintains a volunteer network of more than 300 healthcare providers and equine therapy projects.

Sidran Institute
P.O. Box 436
Brooklandville, MD 21022
phone: (410) 825-8888
email: Contact form on website
website: www.sidran.org/

The Sidran Institute is a non-profit organization dedicated to helping people worldwide understand, recover from, and treat, PTSD and its effects, including addiction, self-harm, and suicidal tendencies. It develops and delivers education programs and resources for support, self-help, and treatment.

Veterans' Families United Foundation
P.O. Box 14355
Oklahoma City, OK 73113
phone: (405) 535-1925
website: veteransfamiliesunited.org

The Veterans' Families United Foundation connects veterans and their families to the resources they need. It was founded in by a mother whose son returned from his tour of duty in Iraq with undiagnosed PTSD. A psychotherapist, she educated herself and realized other families of returning soldiers could benefit from access to service organizations, therapeutic options, and other resources.

Wounded Warrior Project
4899 Belford Road, Suite 300
Jacksonville, FL 32256
phone: (877) TEAM.WWP (832-6997)
website: www.woundedwarriorproject.org

The Wounded Warrior Project is an organization with a mission to honor and empower wounded veterans. To fulfill this mission, it raises awareness and enlists the public's aid, helps injured service members help each other, and offers programs and services to injured service members. It recognizes that each person's path to discovery may be unique.

Bibliography

Books

American Psychiatric Association. *Diagnostic and Statistical Manual of Mental Disorders*, 5th Edition: DSM-5. Washington, DC: American Psychiatric Association, 2013

John D. Conrad. *Among the Walking Wounded: Soldiers, Survival, and PTSD*. Toronto, Canada: Dundum, 2017

Bill Russell Edmonds. *God Is Not Here: A Soldier's Struggle with Torture, Trauma, and the Moral Injustice of War*. New York, NY: Pegasus, 2015

Gordon L. Ewell. *Dung in My Foxhole: A Soldier's Account of the Iraq War and His Postwar Struggles with Injury and PTSD through Poetry*. Trafford, 2011

Erin P. Findley. *Fields of Combat: Understanding PTSD among Veterans of Iraq and Afghanistan*. Ithaca, NY: Cornell University Press, 2011

Nancy Herman. *Afterwar: Healing the Moral Wounds of Our Soldiers*. New York, NY: Oxford University Press, 2015

Charles Hoge. *Once a Warrior, Always a Warrior: Navigating the Transition from Combat to Home, Including Combat Stress, PTSD, and mTBI*. Guilford, CT: Globe Pequot Press, 2010

Bret A. Moore and Arthur E. Jongsma, Jr. *The Veterans and Active Duty Military Psychotherapy Treatment Planner*. Hoboken, NJ: Wiley, 2015

Bret A. Moore and Walter E. Penk, eds. *Treating PTSD in Military Personnel: A Clinical Handbook*. New York, NY: The Guilford Press, 2011

Mark I. Nickerson and Joshua S. Goldstein. *The Wounds Within: A Veteran's Family, a PTSD Therapist, and a National Unprepared*. New York, NY: Skyhorse, 2015

Fiona Reid. *Broken Men: Shell Shock, Treatment and Recovery in Britain 1914-1930*. London, UK and New York, NY: Continuum International Publishing Company, 2010

Arielle Schwartz. *The Complex PTSD Workbook*. Berkeley, CA: Althea Press, 2016

Edward Tick. *Warrior's Return: Restoring the Soul After War.* Boulder, CO: Sounds True, 2014.

Marshéle Carter Waddell and Kelly K. Orr. *Wounded Warrior, Wounded Home: Hope and Healing for Families Living with PTSD and TBI.* Grand Rapids, MI: Revell/Baker Publishing Group, 2013

Leah Wizelman. *When the War Never Ends: The Voices of Military Members with PTSD and Their Families.* Lanham, MD: Rowman & Littlefield, 2011

Jake Wood. *Among You: The Extraordinary True Story of a Soldier Broken by War.* Edinburgh and London, UK: Mainstream Publishing, 2014

Philip Zimbardo, Richard Sword, and Rosemary Sword. *Time Cure: Overcoming PTSD with the New Psychology of Time Perspective Therapy.* San Francisco, CA: Jossey-Bass, 2012.

Periodicals and Internet Sources

Matthieu Aikins. "The U.S. Army's Ambitious Fight Against PTSD." *Popular Science*, March 13, 2013, http://www.popsci.com/technology/article/2013-02/us-armys-ambitious-fight-against-ptsd

Peter Aldhous. "Virtual Environment Provides Trauma Relief for Soldiers." *New Scientist* 214, No. 2866 (May 26, 2012), 17.

American Friends of Tel Aviv University. "Functional MRI Forecasts Which Soldiers Might Be Vulnerable to Suicide." ScienceDaily. September 3 2009. www.sciencedaily.com/releases/2009/09/090902122847.htm

Anna Badkhen. "PTSDland." *Foreign Policy*, September/October 2012.

Fred Balzac. "PTSD and Depression Increase in Veterans of the Iraq and Afghanistan Wars," *Neuropsychiatry Reviews*, November 2008.

Susan R. Barry. "In Harm's Way: Brain Injuries in War." *Massachusetts Review* 52, No. 3/4 (Autumn/Winter 2011), 722-735.

Andrew Bast and Kate Dailey. "The Warrior's Brain." *Newsweek* 156, No. 21 (November 22, 2010), 48-50.

Elizabeth Shimer Bowers. "My Life Was Worth Fighting For." *Prevention* 67, No. 7 (July 2015), 56-58.

Valerie Canady. "Afghan Tragedy Prompts Discussion about PTSD Diagnoses." *Mental Health Weekly* 22, No. 14 (April 2, 2012), 3-5.

Mary E. Card-Mina. "Leadership and Post Traumatic Stress Symptoms." *Military Review*, January/February 2011.

Oded Carmeli. "Brain Training for Troops." *New Scientist* 231, No. 3083 (July 23, 2016), 20.

Joe Collins. "Post Traumatic Stress Disorder Symptoms and Resources," *Veterans Families United*, June 6, 2011, http://veteransfamiliesunited.org/2011/06/06/post-traumatic-stress-disorder-symptoms-and-resources/

Alison Colman. "Recreational Therapy: Helping Soldiers Cope with PTSD." *Parks & Recreation* 50, No. 6 (June 2015), 14-15.

Richard Conniff. "When the Warrior Returns Home," *Men's Health*, October 2010.

John Crawford. "What Science Says about Gender and PTSD." *Army Magazine* 64, No. 5 (May 2014), 70-72.

Tony Dokoupil and Alison Snyder. "Moral Injury." *Newsweek* 160, No. 24 (December 10, 2012), 40-44.

Drugrehab.org. "Addiction and Suicide Amongst Veterans: Finding Hope in the Darkness," http://www.drugrehab.org/addiction-suicide-veterans/

Bob Drury. "The Dogs of War." *Men's Health* 26, No. 8 (October 2011), 168-195.

Dualdiagnosis.org. "Post Traumatic Stress Disorder and Addiction," http://www.dualdiagnosis.org/mental-health-and-addiction/post-traumatic-stress-disorder-and-addiction/

David French. "Casualties of the VA." *National Review* 68, No. 12 (July 11, 2016), 20-21.

Jessica Hamzelou. "The Aftermath." *New Scientist* 231, No. 3091 (September 17, 2016), 38-41.

Tony Horwitz. "The Civil War's Hidden Legacy." *Smithsonian* 45, No. 9 (January 2015), 44-49.

Mervyn Wynne Jones. "Soldier, Veteran, Survivor." *Therapy Today* 24, No. 8 (October 2013), 1-4.

Laura Kasinof. "Women, War, and PTSD." *Washington Monthly* 45, No. 11-12 (November/December 2013), 18-23.

William Martin. "War without End." *Texas Monthly* 42, No. 6 (June 2014), 114-240.

Christian Millman. "Brain Scans May Lead to Better Diagnosis." *Discover* 37, No. 1 (January/February 2016), 28.

National Alliance on Mental Illness. "Depression and Veterans," National Alliance on Mental Illness," 2009, http://www.ouhsc.edu/TVServices/misc/GEC/Sorocco/NAMIFact2009.pdf

Adam Piore. "Big Idea: Help Stressed Vets with SIM Coaches," *Discover*, December 2012.

Vsevolod Rozanov and Vladimir Carli. "Suicide among War Veterans," *International Journal of Environmental Residential Public Health* 9, No. 7 (July 2012): 2504-2519, https://www.ncbi.nlm.nih.gov/pmc/articles/PMC3407917/

Nicholas Schmidle. "In the Crosshairs." *New Yorker* 89, No. 16 (June 3, 2013), 32-45.

Rebecca Segal. "A Call for Research on the Impact of Dogs Deployed in Units to Reduce Posttraumatic Stress." *Military Review* 96, No. 6 (November/December 2016), 91-98.

Dennis Steele. "Soldiers' Minds: No Place for Retreat," *Army Magazine*, May 2010.

Michael Stott. "From Soldier to Civilian." *Therapy Today* 24, No. 8 (October 2013), 1-3.

Laura Tedesco. "The Invisible Wound of War." *Men's Health* 30, No. 3 (April 2015), 87-151.

Mark Thompson. "A Soldier's Tragedy." *Time* 177, No. 9 (March 7, 2011), 46-51.

Moises Velasquez-Manoff. "Before the Trauma." *Scientific American Mind* 26, No. 4 (July/August 2015), 56-63.

Penny Wakefield. "PTSD Doubly Disabling for Female Vets," *Human Rights*, Spring 2008.

Laura Werber et al. "Faith-Based Organizations and Veteran Reintegration," RAND Corporation.

Stephen N. Xenakis and Matthew J. Friedman. "Understanding PTSD." *Wilson Quarterly* 36, No. 1, (Winter 2012), 8-9.

Index

A

acceptance and commitment therapy (ACT), 253
access gaps, 261–262
addiction, 80–81, 151, 166, 236, 281, 285
Affordable Care Act (ACA), 216
Afghanistan, 15–16, 21–23, 30, 34, 40, 69, 100, 102, 109–114, 125, 127, 146, 150–151, 161, 168, 193, 199–200, 205, 210, 212, 221–222, 252, 255, 257–258, 260, 265, 269
AIDS, 154
American Civil War, 14, 76, 134, 142, 168–169, 272–273, 285
American Medical Association, 21
American Psychiatric Association (APA) 17, 66, 69, 70, 92, 103, 115, 126, 129, 151, 169, 271
American Sniper, 46–47
antidepressants, 25, 68, 79–80, 124, 253, 256, 272–275
anxiety, 21, 26, 37, 48, 55, 58, 61, 64–68, 73, 80–81, 91–92, 95, 99, 104–107, 112, 117–118, 120, 122, 127, 135, 147, 149, 152, 167, 170, 172–173, 184, 193, 195, 228–231, 234, 237, 241, 247–248, 250, 252–253, 255, 271–272, 274, 279
art therapy, 232, 235, 242–245, 247
assault, 24, 48, 56, 61, 63, 65, 79, 122, 167, 184, 187, 188, 250
Australian Defense Force (ADF), 172–175
avoidance, 11, 50, 61–62, 99, 119, 144, 170, 173, 179, 228, 238–239, 149, 272

B

benzodiazepines, 79, 273–274
bipolar disorder, 31–82, 89–90, 279
Black Lives Matter, 205
body movement therapy, 234, 236

C

Charlotte, North Carolina, 219–227

cognitive behavioral therapy
(CBT), 96, 104, 106–107,
124–125, 127, 233, 253,
276
cognitive processing therapy
(CPT), 81, 107, 127–246,
253
combat fatigue, 273
combat trauma, 29, 39, 127,
151, 262
co-morbidity, 71, 107, 117,
122, 189, 190, 238, 240
complications, 65–66
Congressional funding, 69
counseling, 16–17, 34, 37, 100,
176, 178, 224–226
creative therapies, 228–242

D

Da Costa's Syndrome, 69, 272,
273
D-cycloserine (DCS), 106
definition, 166–171
dementia, 252
Department of Defense
(DOD), 21–22, 30, 33–35,
40, 42–43, 103, 148, 210,
213–215, 259, 261–262,
264–269, 276
depression, 16, 21–22, 35,
64–68, 74, 78, 81–92,
95–96, 99, 105, 107, 127,
141, 147, 156–157, 168,
172, 189, 195, 202, 222,
229, 232, 236, 238, 241,
244, 248–269, 277, 279,
284, 286
diagnosis, 15–17, 21, 27, 29–
32, 45, 51, 57–60, 65–107,
111, 113–129, 133, 135,
140, 143, 151, 166–172,
179, 182, 184, 217, 253,
273
drama therapy, 230, 234, 243,
244
drug abuse, 16, 56, 65, 68, 112,
143, 151–252, 275
drug treatment, 16, 34, 39, 58,
67–68, 79–80, 83, 105–
106, 178, 251, 253, 268,
273, 275, 277
DSM-III, 14, 27, 46, 71, 72, 78,
92, 94, 115–117, 143–144,
169, 170, 179, 271
DSM-IV, 70–72, 76, 92, 94, 96,
117, 120, 121, 126, 179,
192, 272
DSM-5, 66, 117–118, 120–127,
193–194, 283

E

Euripides, 76, 199–203, 207
exposure therapy, 33, 67, 81,
103–106, 124, 243, 253
expressive writing, 229–231,
233, 239, 240, 243–247
Eye Movement
Desensitization and

Reprocessing (EMDR), 33, 67, 79, 104, 124

F

families, 16, 114, 142, 155, 156, 159, 173, 200, 216, 219–226, 254, 263, 281–285
flashbacks, 14, 20–21, 30, 61–62, 67, 70, 76, 78, 87, 94, 109, 119, 144, 147, 167, 228, 248, 272, 274
Freud, Sigmund, 71, 133, 139, 140, 200

G

Gaupp, Robert, 135
genetics, 71, 74, 79, 157, 169
Gilgamesh, 130
Green Zone 22

H

health care, 16, 35, 43, 69, 75, 82–84, 88–89, 97–98, 100, 108, 209, 212–219, 222, 224, 253, 255, 258, 261, 279, 281
health insurance, 213, 216
Herakles, 74, 199–203, 206–207
hero's welcome, 158–163
history, of PTSD, 71–73

homelessness, 258
horticultural therapy, 234, 236–237
HR2638, 69
Hundred Years' War, 131
Hurt Locker, The, 206
hyper-arousal, 70, 117, 167, 272
hypervigilance, 32, 99, 109, 120
hysteria, 133–136, 176

I

improvised explosive devices (IEDs), 110
International Classification of Mental Diseases (ICD-10). 73, 117, 126
intrusive memories, 61–62, 179, 248
Iraq, 15–16, 19–26, 28–32, 34, 36, 40, 42, 47, 69, 75, 91, 97, 100–114, 125, 127, 150–151, 168, 188, 193, 195, 198–200, 205–206, 210–212, 221–222, 250–252, 255–260, 265, 269, 276
Israel, 150, 153, 162, 163, 165, 195

K

Korean War, 77
Kraepelin, Emil, 138

M

Mayo Clinic, 14, 61
Meagher, Robert Emmet,
    199–202, 206–207
Medicaid, 213
Medicare, 212–213
Mental Health Residential
    Rehabilitation Treatment
    Programs (MH RRTPs),
    253
military sexual trauma (MST),
    212, 250–251
mindfulness therapy, 237–238,
    240–242, 244–247
misdiagnosis, 176–178
multiple deployments, 15, 57,
    59
music therapy, 232–233, 239
Myers, Charles S., 44, 45, 47,
    135, 136

N

National Center for PTSD
    (NCPTSD), 33, 104, 105,
    107, 115, 125
National Guard, 25, 91, 219

National Vietnam Veterans
    Readjustment Survey
    (NVVRS), 93
Native Americans, 153
natural disasters, 65, 82, 116,
    121, 124, 167, 187
nature therapy, 234, 236–237
nightmares, 14, 20–21, 58,
    61–62, 67–68, 70, 78, 91,
    94, 118, 127, 131, 142, 151,
    167–168, 172–173, 228,
    235, 242, 244–245, 248,
    256, 271–272, 275
9/11, 118, 125, 246, 211, 219,
    221

O

over-diagnosis, 15, 17, 29–34,
    46, 48–60, 91–101
oxytocin, 158

P

panic attacks, 107, 147, 274,
    275
Persian Gulf War, 95, 111–113,
    148, 150, 152, 221, 250
phobias, 99, 107, 11-9, 123,
    167
physical assault, 61, 65, 184,
    250
post-deployment health
    assessments (PDHAs), 34

prazosin, 68, 124, 275

prevalence, 15, 21, 29, 40–47, 92, 100, 117, 143, 182–184, 187, 193–194, 221–222, 249–252, 265, 274

prolonged exposure therapy (PE), 103–106, 124, 253

psychosocial rehabilitation and recovery center (PRRC), 253

PTSD Foundation of America, 15

PTSD Symptoms Checklist, 78

public health, 40, 125, 211, 213, 216, 217, 228

Q

quality gaps, 261–262

R

Rambo, 168

RAND Corporation, 258, 259, 260, 263, 267–270

rape, 27, 104, 116–117, 121–122, 124, 147–148, 167, 169, 171, 185, 187, 201, 229, 250

redeployment, 172, 174–175

rehabilitation, 171, 212–213, 253, 265

reintegration, 91, 213, 222, 225, 254

risk factors, 64–65, 161, 175, 181–186, 188–189, 191, 201

S

scientific study, 19–39

self-fulfilling, 91–101

serotonin reuptake inhibitors (SSRIs), 105, 124, 275

Shakespeare, William, 115, 131

shell-shock, 45

skepticism, 31, 56–60, 76, 243, 272

sleep apnea, 57–58, 252

Sophocles, 206

Sparta, 199–201

Stress Inoculation Therapy, 33, 104, 124

suicide, 15, 23–24, 40, 63–64, 83, 86–89, 93, 149–150, 156, 211, 250, 262–264, 268, 271, 277, 284–286

support groups, 84, 89, 153

T

Taxi Driver, 168

technology, 109–114

traumatic brain injury (TBI), 16, 30, 79, 110, 197, 210, 222, 248, 251–253, 257–258

treatment, 16–17, 21–22,
27–28, 33–39, 42–43,
45, 48, 51, 58–59, 61, 63,
66, 68–70, 73, 74, 76,
79–81, 83, 85, 88–92, 94,
96–98, 102–114, 122, 124,
133–137, 140–141, 144,
151–152, 162, 171–178,
183, 190, 213, 228–231,
237–241, 253, 258, 262–
268, 276–277
triggers, 19, 37, 58, 61, 73, 89,
119, 148, 158, 159, 169,
206, 228–229, 233, 237,
274

U

unemployment, 71, 251

V

Veterans Access, Choice, and
Accountability Act, 209
Veterans Affairs (VA), 16,
30, 31, 33–36, 38, 41–43,
58, 69–71, 73–75, 91,
93–95, 97–101, 103, 105,
107–108, 111–114, 153,
164, 166, 195, 209–217,
219, 222, 224, 226, 250,
253–255, 259, 261, 262,
265–277

Veterans of America, 21, 27,
210
Veterans Health
Administration (VHA),
212
Vietnam Veterans Against the
War (VVAW), 46
Vietnam Veterans of America,
27
Vietnam War, 14–15, 45–46,
79, 110–113, 120, 129, 134,
143, 151, 166, 168

W

Walter Reed Army Medical
Center, 30, 112, 213
weapons of mass destruction
(WMDs), 20
World War I, 14, 76–77, 133,
134, 166, 169, 273
World War II, 28, 137, 139,
145, 150, 152, 154, 168,
169